T0347162

TIGERS'
ROAR

TIGERS' ROAR

ASIA'S RECOVERY AND ITS IMPACT

Forewords by
Gloria Macapagal-Arroyo
President, Republic of the Philippines
and
Wei-jao Chen
President, National Taiwan University

JULIAN WEISS
EDITOR

An East Gate Book

Routledge
Taylor & Francis Group

LONDON AND NEW YORK

An East Gate Book

First published 2001 by M.E. Sharpe

Published 2015 by Routledge
2 Park Square, Milton Park, Abingdon, Oxon OX14 4RN
711 Third Avenue, New York, NY, 10017, USA

Routledge is an imprint of the Taylor & Francis Group, an informa business

Library of Congress Cataloging-in-Publication Data

Tigers' roar : Asia's recovery and its impact / edited by Julian Weiss.
   p. cm.
   Includes index.
   ISBN 0-7656-0783-2 (alk. paper)—ISBN 0-7656-0784-0 (pbk. : alk paper)
   1. East Asia. 2. Asia, Southeastern. I. Weiss, Julian.

DS504.5 .T54 2001   2001020480
950—dc21

ISBN 13: 9780765607843 (pbk)
ISBN 13: 9780765607836 (hbk)

Contents

Part VIII: Dragons, Tigers and Would-Be Tigers

Foreword

Gloria Macapagal-Arroyo
President, Republic of the Philippines

This is a rich collection of some forty papers, most of which have been written especially for this book by Asian and American experts. It covers nearly every issue related to the important subject of East Asia's economic recovery.

For anyone who wants to grasp the whole subject in its many dimensions, this book should be required reading. There is certainly enough here to satisfy the needs of the journalist, the academician, the government official, and the concerned member of civil society.

As the leader of a country aspiring to be a full participant in the regional economic recovery, my thoughts on the subject tend to range somewhat narrowly and along practical lines. What, I ask myself, is required of my country to achieve a sustainable economic recovery? First, and most critical I would say is developing an institutionalized intolerance of official corruption.

There are conflicting views in the region about what precipitated the panicky flight of capital at the onset of the Asian financial crisis. But it seems clear enough that the decision not to return flown capital fully is due to the lingering perception that some businesses in the region cannot be depended on because of the existence of corruption, the lack of transparency, and the absence of a level playing field.

Investors' new intolerance, acquired during the Asian economic crisis, has evidently been communicated to the general populations of the region, who have begun to perceive the connection between official corruption and their economic misery. It has taken the form more recently of popular anger directed against corruption, particularly corruption in high places. As the world knows, people power in the Philippines has just succeeded in unseating a president for corruption.

We first used this power fifteen years ago, when we succeeded in ousting a dictator. Since then, no would-be dictator has dared rear his ugly head. It will be the same, we hope, with the more recent exercise of people power. No president should ever again dare be tainted with corruption

In any case, my administration intends to take full advantage of the mighty impetus provided by this demonstration of popular power and pressure—which continues to be exercised—to pursue as priorities the institutionalization of intolerance for corruption and the establishment of transparency and a level playing field.

Still looking at the situation in my own country, I would say that another critical requirement is participation in the new world economy.

No country's recovery can really be sustainable unless the country takes steps to ensure the international competitiveness of its economy. We have already taken some of these steps. For example, in previous administrations, market and structural reforms were carried out continuously for more than a decade.

My administration will of course maintain these reforms and carry on from where the previous administrations have left off. But in a world where the productivity and competitiveness of economies increasingly depend on the application of information technology (IT), it is essential to expand in this area too.

Specifically, the Philippines needs to capture a niche in the information technology sector of the global economy, since this sector is increasingly powering the growth of that economy. And we need to begin to apply this technology to the rest of the economy, wherever possible and appropriate.

This is why another goal of my administration is to promote and support the development of the information and communication technology sector in the Philippines. At present this means establishing the policy and legal framework for the IT sector, attracting more investment for the building of infrastructure and expanding the human resource development opportunities currently available.

We are not starting from scratch. According to some surveys, the Philippines already ranks very high in terms of the quantity and quality of its IT workers. The Philippines enjoys other compatibilities in the new sector—in addition to fulfilling other broader requirements for achieving success in developing information technology. I am referring to proficiency in English, which is indispensable (for now at least) and the freedom that exists in a society that has sufficiently adopted a democratic and market orientation.

These are the thoughts on my administration's priorities that the publication of this book has engendered. A third critical requirement comes to mind. My country's economic recovery cannot really be attained, or sustained, unless the region as a whole succeeds in recovering, too. But I shall leave to you, Gentle Reader, the pleasure of finding out for yourself what the book has to say on the larger economies of the region and other important topics.

May 2001
Malacanan Palace
Manila

Foreword

Wei-jao Chen
President, National Taiwan University

During the last three decades of the twentieth century, the most impressive development process occurred in Asia, especially East Asia. The rapid development in the so-called "Four Tigers" is generally regarded as a near-miracle, a phenomenon hailed by researchers worldwide. The financial crisis in 1997–98 had a major impact and worries about the region's future grew. Some asked whether miraculous development in the past was a mirage or a bubble.

Yet, East Asian countries survived and recovered sooner than generally expected. In recent years, the accumulated foreign exchange reserves in Japan, Taiwan, (Mainland) China, and Hong Kong have been among the top leaders in the world list, and the output value of information products in Japan, Taiwan, and Korea rank second, third and fourth in the world.

Many factors contributed to the rapid development in East Asia. But, from the perspective of one who has been engaged for years in medical care and higher education, I believe there are several key points. First is the popularity of education; parents place a high value on it. Even though they suffered from extreme poverty and hardships they insist on giving their children the best education they can afford. The older generations always sacrifice themselves for the happiness of the younger generations.

Second is governmental policy-making. Despite the fact that their political leaders were not the best, they made the right decisions at the right time, building a solid foundation for development. In Taiwan, the credit goes to those few who decided to develop information technologies, or ITs, and to establish major industrial parks.

Third is the peoples' diligence. People in these countries traditionally take industry and thrift as virtue, laziness and idleness as shame. The virtue of industry and thrift remains a legacy throughout the generations, despite being eroded by materialistic comforts brought by economic development.

Nonetheless, East Asia is encountering problems. In terms of political development, some countries are more advanced toward democratization than others. There are the problems that result from an incompetent system's attempt to function efficiently, from governments ruled by men —and not laws—and from controversial relationships between government and commerce.

The unsteady situation across the Taiwan Strait, where China and Taiwan face each other, is undeniably the most urgent question today. In terms of cultural development, some countries need to tolerate multicultural approaches; multicultural impact is crucial to the development of a knowledge-based economic society. Yet, Japan emphasizes a pure homogenized race, and in Indonesia, Chinese immigrants are expelled. Other countries suffer from the destruction of their ecology and must balance conflicts between economic development and environmental protection.

This book, *Tigers' Roar: Asia's Recovery and Its Impact*, is the outcome of the collaborative efforts of a group of scholars, experts, and business leaders who specialize in many fields of study related to East and Southeast Asia. Their insightful analyses and research on the transformations, topical issues, and future prospects of East Asia would certainly add value to the field of Asian studies. Their collective document is useful to scholars, students, businessmen, government officials and decision-makers who must learn more about the region.

March 2001

Introduction

It is Year 2 BB—*b*efore the advent of *b*andwidth enhancements which are likely to, in Internet-style, revolutionize business and society. A deceptive calm ripples across the Pacific, the vast sea connecting the world's high-tech and economic and military superpowers. In East Asia, where tectonic plates of geopolitical stability remain precariously balanced, a power shift has already begun. In times past East Asia and the West challenged each other on the see-saws of commercial, financial, and technological prowess. The gauntlet has again been dropped; the competition is under way.

Will the next few years mark the beginning of the long-awaited "Asian Century?" If so, what are the implications of its advent? This book may answer part of the question. The chapter authors identify major challenges facing East and Southeast Asia, a vast region containing the fabled Four Tigers (Taiwan, Korea, Hong Kong, Singapore), Japan, China, and their Southeast Asian neighbors (Thailand, Indonesia, Malaysia, Vietnam, and the Philippines). It is home to 1.9 billion people, and its collective GDP—even after thirty months of severe financial dislocation and protracted economic recession—is above US$7 trillion.

Flying—and Grounded—Geese

Conceptualizing this book transported me back to a different era, when as a correspondent writing business feature articles I reveled in conjecture over the heralded "Flying Geese" theory. It was the early 1980s, and Asia's ascent was profound: seemingly unstoppable "Japan, Inc." was invading high-tech's commanding heights while a Tiger juggernaut was capturing global markets. Most believed a leader—Japan—would safely escort other geese upward through the skies of value-added economic growth. Events leading up to, and including, the protracted economic and financial crisis, "the Asian contagion," dispelled that theory.

Then, as today, one striking feature was the region's dynamism. As noon-time waves lap Oahu's (Hawaiian) shores, southeastern China's industrial heartland awakes to a new day. A half-continent away, Yokohama's loading docks bristle with crates of "Made in Japan" computer games destined for consumers around the globe. At the same time, rubber tappers in Selangor (Malaysia) walk barefoot, performing a decades-old ritual. The sun rises over Singapore's Forex exchanges, as—light years apart—thousands of new arrivals mill about Shanghai rail stations, seeking their share of China's new affluence. At a high-tech research park in Tainan (Taiwan) a brand new chip fabrication plant stands silhouetted against the landscape. Meanwhile, the mid-day sun beats down upon Filipino terraced farming plantations in Mindanao. Hong Kong's stock analysts prepare for the day's market gyrations while counterparts in Europe and North America await their decisions.

This is the face of East Asia—increasingly more assertive than ever, re-thinking its relationship to the world, re-defining itself. These pieces on the world's geopolitical and economic chessboard are not static, they are in flux.

Powerhouse Asia

Without strong domestic markets and the ability to spawn consumer demands, the region is captive to an export-led growth that is no longer capable of sustaining economic development. This will change. Once full recovery occurs, this region will (again) grow faster than the rest of the world, creating commercial opportunities *for* the West *in* Asia while simultaneously increasing competitive challenges *to* the West *from* Asia. In contagion-racked countries now undergoing fragile recovery, five- or six-percent GDP increases tallied yearly will, by 2005, yield a combined output of US$8.5 trillion.

The center of global "gravity" has already shifted to Asia. Korea, Hong Kong, and Taiwan are formidable players on the global economic stage, posting US$1.5 trillion of the world's US$5.4 trillion in trade. Their neighbors possess the resources (more than twenty-five percent of world supplies of petrol, natural gas, natural rubber, tin, and other commodities), technology base (Taiwan is now the world's semiconductor manufacturing kingpin), and the population (nearly one-third of the world's total) that make the region an undisputed linchpin of the international system.

Although economic and commercial opportunities abound, the region contains the world's most volatile tinderboxes: the Taiwan Strait and the Korean Peninsula. Both are within a short plane ride from the high-tech citadels of Seoul, Japan's Kyushu Island, and the "Greater China" manufacturing megalopolis comprising Hong Kong, Canton, and Guangdong. Other security-related challenges abound: the volatile Central Asian (former Soviet) republics are in close proximity; and Indonesia must confront the specter of social chaos, political uncertainty, financial collapse, and, possibly, fragmentation. Passing through the Indonesian archipelago's Strait of Malacca is some forty-five percent of the world's shipping, including 1,200 mammoth oil tankers (and hence Asia's petrol lifeline).

The Search for Answers

No single volume can address all the pertinent issues of this region or cover each country's prospects and challenges in detail. Yet key factors affecting the area can be identified without myopia and void of ideological constraints. East and Southeast Asia contain many "moving targets." No one person could write this book, as I explained to Dr. David Lampton in the summer of 2000, when I returned from my thirty-sixth trip to the region. Dr. Lampton—Director of China Studies at the Washington-based Nixon Center and at the time my professor at Johns Hopkins University School for Advanced International Studies—agreed. So did M.E. Sharpe's senior Asian editor and "guru," Doug Merwin. Thus began a voyage of discovery.

In these forty-four chapters, forty-five authors comment on the forces and factors shaping East and Southeast Asia. Many of the authors disagree with each other—and certainly with me! Such debate is healthy.

For dialogue is needed to assess the region's rise. Despite economists' and Asia-watchers' vision of a flock of geese darting through serene skies, Asia's ascent will be neither orderly nor tranquil. Her policy-makers and inhabitants will be confronted by potential problems in many areas, among them energy, demographics, environmental degradation, urbanization, security, competitiveness, and internal power struggles. "Tigers" and Tiger-wannabees must cope with other factors as well. China's rise and her quest to emerge as hegemon, Japan's uncertain destiny, ways in which societies reconcile the impact of advanced and transplanted technologies—these all mandate new strategies. Asia is a vast social laboratory whose experimentation is ongoing, and whose test results are uncertain.

America's Asian Odyssey

A new generation of Americans seeks to discover Asia. Previous contact with that *other* side of the Pacific was shaped by the quest for commerce. Early introductions to the Far East were voyages of both tragedy and hope. Philadelphian John Waln, cited as the first American Sinologist, noted in the 1820s that absence of a legal system prevented expansion of trans-Pacific trade, and that kowtowing to the Chinese was essential to curry favor with them. In his 472–page opus, *China: Comprehending a View of the Origins*, *History*, *Antiquity*, *and Empire*, Waln also cautioned that China imitated Western innovations and then reproduced them at lower prices. He observed that foreigners falsely accused the still-isolated, then-humbled former superpower of widespread infanticide.

Today, there is no single China, but several Chinas co-existing simultaneously: dark shadows of corruption; bright rays of change; nascent markets, and "connection capitalism" . . . all side by side.

Our impressions can no longer be guided by romanticists, nor by hardened Asiaphobes. American institutions will be put to their hardest test as they cope with new realities surfacing across the region. This editor's editorial: Everyone talks about "Asia policy," but America's diplomacy lacks a holistic approach. This must change while we have the resources—and still command respect. For all our clumsiness, America's ideals—respect for the common man and for the democratic enterprise—are held in high regard by a young generation of leaders emerging across East and Southeast Asia. But from Kyoto to Kaohsiung to Kuala Lumpur, Asians felt diplomatically abandoned during the economic contagion of the late 1990s. Worse, we tend to lecture instead of listening.

The Region: A Snapshot . . .

. . . or several snapshots. The cluster of prescient chapters contained in this book highlights major issues whose outcome will determine history's course. Permit your intrepid scribe and humble editor to summarize other issues.

On July 1, 1997, forecasters speculated about which nation would emerge as "the next Tiger," how soon the Tumen River Basin (joining Manchuria and Siberia) and the Bentara Growth Triangle (in Southeast Asia) would emerge as the next "hot" economic development frontiers, and how many countries would post ten-percent or higher GDP growth rates. While 10,000 journalists honeycombed Hong Kong looking for a story (the changes imposed by the handover to Beijing) that had already—albeit in a subtle manner—occurred, the big story was barely noticed: next door, Thailand initiated a sharp currency devaluation, triggering a contagion whose aftershocks are felt four years later.

Another issue: what of English's commanding heights in the fields of today's great movements: culture, business, and technology? When "intelligent" translators become widespread, millions of Mandarin speakers can let those English dictionaries collect dust. Forget flying geese of yesteryear; leapfrogging is in vogue. Power, wealth, and stability are being re-defined. The old and very recent paradigms are no longer relevant. And yes, water could emerge as the "oil" of the twenty-first century.

The following are worth watching: the interface between new high-tech gadgetry and business; efforts to train workers in the latest applications of information technology; defections from agreed-to APEC (Asia-Pacific Economic Cooperation group) free-trade deadlines; and whether East and Southeast Asia's export engines are less dependent on American markets. Who are the winners in the WTO era? By what criteria do—or can—we pick them? Even in the midst of a ten-year protracted slump, Japan's net external assets are $1.2 trillion; during the same decade America's net external liabilities soared thirty-fold (reaching $1.5 trillion). Are we "trading places" again? Asia's liquidity crisis, the development of bond markets, and the pace of financial restructuring remain critical in determining the strength of Tiger and would-be Tiger recoveries, and global over-capacity in key industries, Asian contract manufacturing prowess, and Vietnam's long-awaited rise will all play a part in the region's business drama. Will the first decade of this century find another transistor, or automobile, or computer, to propel another of mankind's great industrial revolutions?

Science and R&D are not winner-take-all contests: China's space program will extend the concept of multi-polar power centers into the stratosphere. This is an age where we probe the ultimately large (galaxies) and dissect the infinitesimally small (atoms). Our concepts of mega-scale defense can be thwarted by microbes. Related to science and the knowledge-based economy, or KBE, one wonders: Will would-be Silicon Valleys collapse, or will a California earthquake submerge much of the currently reigning Valley?

During the past century, more than 180 Americans received Nobel prizes in the sciences—thirty-eight times as many as were earned by counterparts in Japan. What contests shape the next great *tekko riku* (high-tech) battles? How will *jishu gaizao* (technology renovation) impact the global contest?

Reading the tea leaves, one finds the region-wide "stew" peppered with undefineable ingredients. Leadership struggles within East and Southeast Asia are inevitable soon, a full changing of the guard is likely across the region. Culture and perception are determinants of the largely benign East-West struggle already underway. Both factors may cause the West to rethink its assumption. The doubling of Chinese websites in 1999 and a forty percent increase in Internet users this year has not ushered in many hoped-for reforms nor improved dialogue with foreigners.

How people think, react to events, and perceive their destinies are powerful determinants of world affairs. What about the intelligentsia and tomorrow's leaders? The region's demographic riddles are never-ending: with more than twenty percent of its population aged over sixty-five in less than two decades, stresses and strains on Japan's infrastructure will increase. How will this Northeast Asian archipelago cope? And her neighbors, too, must adjust labor strategies, pension-planning, and social policies because of the graying phenomena.

Even in the pre-contagion era, when events in the region were fairly predictable, things were never dull. By studying this part of the world, one agrees to jump on an intellectual and philosophical roller coaster, sometimes traveling in slow gear but often at warp speed. The track is endless, and one is certain to get a seat with a terrific view. And don't worry about waiting in line; the ride has barely begun.

For the inspiration to write this book I wish to thank teachers, philosophers, and scribes—past and present—who guided me along the path of discovery. Acknowledgments include veteran "Asia hands" John Goyer, US-ASEAN Business Council; Dr. Robert Sutter, formerly at the National Intelligence Council and now at Georgetown University; and Ed Castro at the Philippines Embassy (in Washington).

Julian Weiss

Part I

A Region in Transition

ASEAN, East Asia and the Pacific Rim: Thoughts on the New Regionalism

Simon S.C. Tay

A New East Asia

There is a rising sense of East Asian identity. In a November 1999 summit, Association of Southeast Asian Nations (ASEAN) leaders and their counterparts from the non-ASEAN "Three" (China, Japan, and South Korea) sent a strong signal. Other meetings—notably the foreign ministers' first ever meeting in July 2000, after the ASEAN ministerial meeting—are instructive.

Functional cooperation is starting in finance. A system by which ASEAN countries exchange information and comment on each other's policies is being expanded to include the Three. In March 2000, ASEAN and Three finance ministers agreed on stand-by arrangements for currency swaps in the event of sudden raids on currencies by foreign investors. Some suggest grander measures. The idea of an Asian Monetary Fund (AMF), first proposed by Japan in 1997 and summarily dismissed

Paper prepared for the Asian Leaders 2000 Conference, Beijing, April 2000, organized by the Asia-Australia Institute.

by the United States and others, is being reconsidered. Others propose a common currency or a version of the European Union (EU) model.

These ideas signal a change. In the past decade, the Asia-Pacific Economic Cooperation (APEC) forum was the preferred framework. APEC embraced the United States, Canada, Chile, Australia, New Zealand and others to build a community spanning the Pacific Rim. In matters of security, the ASEAN Regional Forum included Russia, Europe and India. And East Asia was never seen as a separate group except when Malaysian prime minister Dr. Mahathir Mohammed proposed an East Asian Economic Grouping (EAEG). This, like the AMF, is challenged by fellow Asians as well as by the United States. ASEAN united Southeast Asia at the sub-regional level, but little cooperation existed among countries in Northeast Asia.

It is against this context that a "new" regionalism—acknowledging that East Asia is broader than ASEAN, yet narrower than the entire Asia-Pacific—is emerging. The "ASEAN plus Three" formula appeals to many policy-makers.

Drivers of Regionalism

Why has this sense of regionalism arisen? Asia has no strong and enduring history of unity and accepted commonality, either in polity, culture, language or religion. The antecedents of East Asian regionalism have been brief and contested: in the fifteenth century, when the Ming empire of China ruled the waves and extracted an acceptance of suzerainty from kingdoms in East and Southeast Asia; and during the wartime Japanese "co-prosperity sphere." Neither set a happy precedent.

Why, then, East Asia now? Several factors are at play. The now-ending economic crisis is one; new crises should be expected. The need for forms of cooperation have grown. Cooperation to manage existing integration explains, in part, the new regionalism—and regionalism is thus a process for dealing with globalization, and as such constitutes a forward-looking perception that should be welcomed.

The monetary crisis spurred frustration among APEC, the Asian Regional Forum (ARF) and the IMF, and added to the perception that the United States—in its present unipolar moment—largely ignores the region. America failed to lead international institutions like APEC and the WTO in a quest for economic remedies. Questions over the United States were also felt in regional security issues. Notwithstanding the importance of American security engagement as a foundation for region-wide peace, Asians seem ambivalent. We swing between fearing the United States will either ignore us or—on the other hand—intervene unilaterally according to the whims of the American populace. East Asians desire a sustained and consultative American engagement, but domestic American politics hinder this process.

Then there is ASEM, the Asia-Europe Meetings held since the 1990s. ASEM's goal was not to build a community for all but to have an inter-civilizational dialogue between two regions. In this sense, ASEM is built upon the supposition that East Asia has an identity, although an institution or recurring process are still lacking.

Some Cautionary Notes

Some believe that East Asia must imitate Europe. There is talk, for instance, of a common currency, an East Asian free-trade area and an Asian monetary fund. These ideas, and even perhaps a grand vision of union, might be possible over the longer-term. But we should recognize East Asia's limits: The first is the American presence. Japan and South Korea in Northeast Asia and Thailand and the Philippines in Southeast Asia have defense alliances with the United States. In addition, U.S.-based multinational corporations are major investors in these countries.

American roots in the region stem from the Cold War era, when East Asia was beset by poverty and instability. Some (especially in China) see in this the play of U.S. neo-imperialism. But others consider Washington a relatively benign power. Without American engagement, the region loses security balance; there is no collective framework for peace-keeping and other measures. Incidents in East Timor expose weaknesses in ad-hoc solutions. Resentment over Australia's intervention—and Prime Minister Howard's unfortunate comment that his country would serve as an American deputy—were telling. East Asia is concerned over U.S. hegemony and with Washington's tendency to shift between ignorance and unilaterally-guided intervention. The United States remains a vital non-regional actor. If it strongly opposes the nascent institutional identity of the region, such identity will fail. If Washington is comfortable with the idea—or even supportive—there is no guarantee of success, but chances increase significantly.

The second limiting factor is that of China-Japan relations. These relations are troubled by suspicion, notwithstanding high levels of Japa-

nese investment in the PRC. The politics of apology/amnesia with respect to World War II trouble Japan's ties with Korea and with ASEAN.
Yet ASEAN maintains a pragmatic emphasis on trade, investment, and
other aspects of the relationship. This is a sharp change from the 1970s,
when the Japanese premier's visit to the region was marked by street
protests. To a far lesser extent, South Korea under President Kim Dae
Jung has taken steps towards reconciliation.

China-Japan relations are adversely impacted by American involvement. Japan is dependent on the bilateral alliance with the United States,
and when China-U.S. relations are strained, the Chinese view Japan as
America's junior partner. Conversely, when Washington-Beijing links
are improving, Japan shows concern that its special place vis-à-vis the
United States is threatened. Also, crises have erupted with regard to
Taiwan-related strains on Beijing-Tokyo relations.

History, present circumstances, and future prospects point to a need
for reconciliation between China and Japan as a foundation for East
Asia. Japan must come to terms with its past, building a future that includes its neighbors as partners. And Japan's role is further complicated
by a decade-long recession and lackluster attempts at domestic financial reform. The jury is still out on her efforts—and on the strategy of
massive public spending to boost GDP. One strand—exemplified by
Tokyo's governor Ishihara—is a narrow nationalism. Such a stance would
likely lessen chances for reconciliation between Japan and her neighbors. A second strand among non-bureaucratic elites—seen in Taichi
Sakaiya's writings—calls for radical reform and "internationalization."
Until internal debates take place, Japan's role as a regional leader is in
doubt. Similarly, leadership in an Asian Monetary Fund is debatable.
Therefore, Japan cannot be the main actor in East Asia, and it has been
suggested that smaller-sized and medium-sized countries such as South
Korea and those of ASEAN have a greater role to play than their power
would dictate.

What East Asia Might Be, and What It Should Not Be

The driving forces and limits of the nascent sense of East Asia suggest
regionalism should have the following characteristics:

   1. Open and Flexible Caucus, Not an Exclusive Group or Bloc:
Given the existence of both larger and smaller institutions (Asia-Pacific

and international, ASEAN), there is little need for another organization. The new East Asian regionalism might serve best as a caucus to discuss mutually acceptable positions. These could be raised before larger, already established, institutions.

2. Functionality, Not a Politically Fixed Nature:
There is a need for management and cooperation in the face of both integration and globalization. Economic and financial cooperation has been emphasized; "ASEAN Plus Three" is possible. This formula would exclude some important economic players, such as Hong Kong, Taiwan, and Australia, in favor of much smaller economies.

3. Issue-Led Leadership, Not Great Powers:
In traditional regionalism models, central leadership is critical. Without a historical reconciliation between China and Japan, however, centralization is not possible. East Asia lacks any single figure who is acceptable to all sides and who is able to handle the task of leadership. Medium-sized countries might therefore lead the region. Limited forms of leadership—with different countries handling different issues—are also possible. Such leadership would arise from initiatives taken by individual states. On investment and development assistance, for example, Japan's stature might be acceptable, whereas Singapore might hold the central position on free-trade initiatives. Thailand and Malaysia could be entrusted with regional peace-keeping. Leader countries would shift according both to the abilities of individual countries and to the views reflected in region-wide caucuses. Japan might represent the group's views in the G-8; China might play a similar role in the UN Security Council.

ASEAN's chairmanship of the ARF could be shared with its Northeast Asian neighbors, at least in function if not in form. East Asia would continue the ASEM process with a surer sense of itself as a region.

4. Coalitions of the Willing:
The above principles suggest East Asian regionalism should not be a fixed bloc with permanent membership and permanent leaders. A framework for "coalitions of the willing" can arise on specific issues. Such coalitions may dissolve or evolve to new issues, and they would work with existing regional and sub-regional institutions such as APEC, ARF, and ASEAN. The idea of coalitions might even extend beyond East Asia to include Australia or parts of Europe. The proposed ASEAN Free Trade

Area link to New Zealand and Australia was an early example of flexible regionalism. Such coalitions could play a vital role in the development of larger institutions. If the Japan-Singapore trade agreement comes to pass, it will be the first Northeast-Southeast Asia economic link.

If East Asia's new regionalism draws from these principles, it would not displace existing institutions, including ASEAN. Instead, a framework for different initiatives and coalitions would surface, stimulating existing processes and institutions. East Asian representation in the IMF and other bodies is an alternative goal. If these principles are used, a considerable departure from the European experience will have been effected, largely because of adverse existing realities and a determined wish to launch initiatives despite them.

Some Concluding Comments: What Next?

East Asia's new regionalism demands both a vision and bold steps. This is in contrast to incremental steps, taken in APEC and ARF, whose pace slowed—or failed—during the economic and financial crisis. East Asia may not be ready for more than incremental initiatives in cooperation based upon recognized needs. Nevertheless, these initiatives could lead to more grandiose steps, much as collaboration in the coal and steel industries was a first phase in Europe's supra-nationalist experiments. In order to succeed, other developments—including a China-Japan reconciliation—would also have to occur.

In the context of this background and likely scenarios, what can be done? In light of this question, I offer the following comments and suggestions:

Financial Cooperation

Financial cooperation should proceed within the framework of the (1999) Manila Declaration. ASEAN Plus Three is a firm basis for this, but other relevant players—Hong Kong, Taiwan and Australia—should be included.

Free Trade

With the stalling of the WTO and APEC, regional, sub-regional, and bilateral efforts assume a new importance. Efforts by Singapore and New Zealand for a free trade agreement were announced at the 1999

APEC Summit and concluded within the year. The Japan-Singapore economic pact mentioned above is another worthy initiative, as is Singapore's move to offer the ASEAN Free Trade Area (AFTA) privileges to non-AFTA members.

Economic Cooperation

Many aspects of East Asian economies are complementary. Nevertheless, a number of sectors—especially between China and the newer ASEAN members—are competitive. Rationalization and regional industrial policies are challenges; vested interests will resist removal of trade protections they enjoy. Yet, progress may nevertheless be possible.

An area that may have special potential is the "new" economy, the "e-economy," which may have fewer vested interests resisting harmonization and cooperation than do traditional economies. Similarly, initiatives that use or drive the new economy may be fruitful areas of cooperation. The linking of security exchanges might be one step.

The Environment

ASEAN has made attempts to address environmental issues directly at senior government levels. However, there is no forum in East Asia—or in the Asia-Pacific—to take similar action. Such a forum should be created to establish links between environmental issues and economic prospects, to raise environmental awareness, and to ensure better coordination among environmental (and possibly other) agencies. In this way, a broader East Asian process can assist (not displace) local initiatives.

There are also parallels between Indonesia's haze pollution and environmental problems in Northeast Asia. The incidents of acid rain and yellow dust storms are worthy of attention, and greater collaboration—through joint research, information exchange, etc.—may assist affected countries at both ends of East Asia.

Piracy

There is a common regional and international interest in keeping the seas of the region safe for commercial vessels. This is especially so with respect to the Strait of Malacca, a vital international shipping lane. Piracy in the Strait is increasing; this implies such potential hazards as criminal activity, increased accidents, etc. Regional cooperation among Singapore, Malaysia and Indonesia would be useful. There is a role for financial assistance from Japan, but patrols should first be accepted by other states.

In general, East Asia regionalism may be evidenced in areas of recognized interdependence and need. It is useful to distinguish between differing transnational issues. There are economic, psychic, moral, and physical spillovers, including the movement of refugees, human rights abuses, neglect of labor rights protection, and so on. Increased cooperation is more likely when spillovers are economic and physical because in such cases both the interdependence and the need to manage it are more apparent (moral and psychic interdependence is inherently less obvious). Trends are perceptible but there is no certainty. Negotiations have increased and cooperation has begun in some areas. But talks can turn cold while cooperation can cease, or be limited with no further progress.

In the immediate future, East Asian regionalism has one over-riding need: to explain itself to the United States and to others, distinguishing it from the earlier (and rejected) EAEG. It should also be explained that Washington is not being deliberately excluded and that security issues will be neither placed at the top of the agenda nor dealt with cautiously. Non-Asians will realize that APEC and ARF are now well established, a fact giving justification for East Asia's move toward regionalism.

Such a construction of East Asia may fall far short of the grand vision some advocate. But it will be easier for now to create dialogues and functional bi- or multilateral initiatives that might serve in future as a foundation for more extensive cooperation.

East Asia's Transnational Challenges: The Dark Side of Globalization

Paul J. Smith

Introduction

On June 20, 2000, British customs inspectors conducted a routine check of a vegetable truck that had entered the United Kingdom at the port city of Dover. As they investigated more closely, they were horrified to discover the bodies of sixty Chinese nationals—men and women—who had been sealed inside a refrigerator trailer. Only two of the Chinese were still alive, due to the fact that they were lying close to the rear doors. The others endured a grueling and torturous death as they banged on the sides of the truck or attempted to claw their way through the back door. Eventually they would be subdued by oppressive heat and a dwindling oxygen supply. When investigators finally discovered the Chinese, they found the bodies lying on the truck's floor, alongside boxes of tomatoes and piles of clothing. Officials later charged the Dutch driver of the truck with fifty-eight counts of manslaughter.

The views expressed in this document are those of the author and do not reflect the official policy or position of the Asia Pacific Center for Security Studies, the U.S. Pacific Command, the Department of Defense, or the U.S. Government.

Following extensive investigations, British officials realized that they were witnessing one small component of a multi-billion-dollar human-smuggling operation that transports thousands of East Asians to low-wage jobs around the world. Indeed, Western European governments have recently become alarmed at the growing trend of human-smuggling from East Asia, particularly the People's Republic of China. From another perspective, however, British officials were also confronting the long tentacles of East Asian-based criminal syndicates that operate throughout the world. In addition to trafficking in human beings, these organizations smuggle narcotics and other commodities, engage in maritime piracy and murder, organize prostitution rings, and commit numerous other crimes.

The Dover smuggling incident is just one indicator of the rise in transnational crime that is becoming endemic in many parts of East Asia and that, arguably, has worsened in the wake of the economic crisis that began in 1997. Increased political instability and economic disenfranchisement in many East Asian countries have fueled an unprecedented increase in lawlessness and organized criminal activity. Many governments in the region, facing reduced funding for law enforcement or marine patrol activities, realize that they are virtually powerless against transnational criminal organizations that are often well-financed and not constrained by national jurisdictional boundaries. Moreover, this political weakness is transforming certain parts of the region—particularly Southeast Asia—into fertile ground for one of most destructive and dangerous transnational threats: international terrorism. International terrorist organizations are eager to expand their operations into East Asia, where terrorism is not yet a daily concern. The recent activities of the Philippines-based Abu Sayyaf Group (ASG)—with its alleged links to international Islamic terrorist organizations—may be a portent of the future.

In the aggregate, transnational security threats pose a direct and protracted danger to East Asia's continued economic growth and prosperity. They also threaten political development, particularly in countries with nascent democratic institutions. If allowed to flourish, these threats may ultimately sow instability throughout the region and ultimately threaten the viability of governments and regional institutions.

Transnational Security Threats: the Dark Side of Globalization

Transnational security threats can be defined as nonmilitary threats that cross borders and either threaten the political and social integrity of a nation or the health of that nation's inhabitants.[1] In East Asia, they often are driven by nonstate actors that do not hesitate to use violence against private individuals and government officials. Common transnational threats in East Asia include such activities as narcotics trafficking, terrorism, or human smuggling. Because of their international scope, transnational security threats constitute the dark and violent side of globalization. Liberalization of trade and increased migration, hallmarks of an increasingly global economy, bring numerous economic and social benefits to Asian countries. But this same liberalization makes it easier for terrorists and criminals to cross national borders and establish international networks. Similarly, the communications revolution brings information and entertainment to millions of people, but it also cultivates a desire within thousands of individuals who, in hopes of finding greater opportunity abroad, eagerly pay money to human smugglers for a chance to live in the "promised land."

In East Asia, transnational security threats are particularly common in countries plagued by political weakness or poor governance. Criminal groups often search out or gravitate toward those areas in which government power or influence is limited or nonexistent. Jurisdictional disputes between countries also provide criminal groups with an opportunity to thrive. Maritime pirates, for instance, often hide out in disputed seas or islands where host nations (often claimants) are often reluctant to deploy law enforcement or military forces.

One particular issue of governance, corruption, plays a major role in promoting transnational crime and terrorism. Official corruption is a thread that weaves many transnational criminal and terrorist threats together and, unfortunately, is a common problem throughout East Asia. In Thailand, law enforcement is reportedly "negotiable" and particularly friendly toward those possessing large amounts of cash. In China, some local officials (in southern provinces) are allegedly involved in maritime piracy. Allegations of official North Korean involvement in narcotics trafficking have catapulted the issue of official corruption to an entirely new level. The North Korean government apparently views narcotics trafficking as just another means of raising state funds.[2]

Transnational crime and terrorism are also facilitated by the proliferation of small arms and advanced weaponry throughout the region. The end of the Cold War led to a global arms glut, thus making arms plentiful and inexpensive throughout the world. Additionally, new technological devices and techniques, once restricted to governments, are now available on the open market. Criminals and terrorists can now easily access satellite imagery data, global positioning satellite (GSP) technology, the Internet, and other high-tech systems.

As transnational security challenges grow in the region, they are causing tensions among neighboring states. Thailand, for example, is frustrated by the continued influx of narcotics from neighboring Myanmar (Burma) and has contemplated cross-border military strikes. Some states are concerned that China is not doing enough to combat maritime piracy and, in fact, may be contributing to the problem by protecting corrupt officials who might actually be involved in such crimes. If transnational security challenges continue to worsen, tensions among Asian states, and also within East Asian organizations such as the Association of Southeast Asian Nations (ASEAN), are likely to grow. This chapter will argue that four particular transnational threats—narcotics trafficking, illegal migration, terrorism, and maritime piracy—constitute the greatest threats to regional stability.

East Asia's Narcotics Scourge

In 1996, Vietnam was shaken by allegations of high-level official involvement in heroin trafficking from neighboring Laos. Subsequent investigations, prompted by last minute confessions from a Laotian drug smuggler facing a firing squad, confirmed the allegations and revealed that one of Vietnam's rising stars among police officers, Vu Xuan Truong, was at the center of the scandal.[3] Twenty-one other policemen, some border guards, and various other officials were also implicated in the scheme. The group had allegedly trafficked more than 400 kilograms of heroin and about 500 kilograms of raw opium from Laos into Vietnam.[4] Eight of the accused—including Vu—were sentenced to death, six received life sentences, and the remainder received a variety of heavy jail terms. The scandal revealed the extent to which illegal narcotics had infiltrated Vietnam. Three years later, Vietnam confronted another major heroin trafficking scheme in the country's central province of Nghe An, which borders Laos.

Many Vietnamese leaders are understandably dismayed by the recent cases of narcotics-related scandals. Some of them point their fingers at the country's policies of liberalization and opening up to the outside world. But another view is that Vietnam is confronting the same scourge that is challenging most other governments in the region. Indeed, trafficking in illegal narcotics is a growing and insidious transnational threat that touches virtually every country in the Asia-Pacific region. Porous international borders allow organized crime groups to use multiple countries to smuggle illegal drugs to destinations within the region and to other markets such as Western Europe or the United States.

Myanmar is the world's second largest producer of illicit opium and heroin (exceeded only by Afghanistan), much of which is transported across porous borders shared with Thailand and China. Heroin smuggled into Thailand is often transshipped to markets in Asia, Europe, and the United States. Similarly, Chinese officials are concerned that their porous borders with Myanmar are transforming their nation into a drug transit corridor connecting Myanmar to markets in Asia and the West. Chinese seizures of both opium and heroin have increased dramatically since 1995.

Methamphetamines are a more recent narcotics threat affecting much of the region. At a recent antinarcotics conference, Southeast Asian leaders declared the influx of the drugs a major threat to the population of the region. These drugs are pouring out of Myanmar into Thailand and other Southeast Asian countries in increasing quantities. In Singapore, where the drug is only beginning to make its debut, police seized about 10,000 methamphetamine tablets during one six-month period in 2000. In contrast, Thai authorities seized over 6.5 million tablets in one month alone during the same year. Thai military officials also estimate that about 600 million amphetamine pills flowed into the country from Myanmar during 1999.[5]

Traditionally Southeast Asian nations did not act as consumers of the narcotics that came out of the Golden Triangle Region (encompassing northern Thailand, Laos, and Myanmar). But that trend is changing. Asian officials are increasingly alarmed by the growing presence and use of these drugs, especially among their youth. Methamphetamine consumption is skyrocketing and thus imposes significant social and health costs on affected societies. Among youths in Thailand, methamphetamines are increasingly becoming the drug of choice. Heroin, too, is becoming popular among local populations. Vietnam, which traditionally played a role as a transshipment country, now has more than 150,000 heroin addicts whose habit is attributed to drugs that were intended for shipment to the West. Similar trends can be seen in Thailand and China.

Illegal Migration and Human Smuggling

In early 1998, Indonesia suffered some of the worst economic effects of the financial crisis that swept through much of East Asia beginning a year earlier. Facing soaring levels of unemployment, thousands of Indonesians decided to try their luck by migrating to neighboring Malaysia in hopes of finding employment or other opportunities. Many of them succeeded, but Malaysia, despite having access to inexpensive and eager labor, was anything but ecstatic. In fact, the Malaysian government, which was busy putting its own economic house in order, responded to the Indonesian migrant influx by deploying naval and coast guard ships, as well as air force patrol aircraft, in an attempt to stem the outflow. The Malaysian government rather undiplomatically described the response as "Operation Nyah" (translated as "Operation Go Away"). In the first few months of 1998, Malaysian authorities arrested over 19,000 Indonesian migrants. Most were eventually deported back to Indonesia.

The Malaysian backlash against mass migration from Indonesia in 1998 reveals a festering economic and political issue that virtually all East Asian countries confront: rising illegal migration due to dramatic disparities in wealth and economic development. Unemployment, poverty, and population pressures in the region's poorer nations are spurring thousands to seek opportunities in more prosperous neighboring countries. Compounding the challenge is the fact that many East Asian countries do not view themselves as "immigration countries" and consider the influx of job-seeking migrants to be a cultural and political threat. Some countries also blame illegal migrants for importing crime and infectious diseases into their societies.

Many Asian countries unofficially tolerate a reasonable amount of illegal migration, at least to the extent that it satisfies the demands of local industries that have trouble recruiting local workers. But when economic growth slows, or when a wave of antiforeign sentiment surges, governments often react by launching major "sweeps" intended to gather and deport illegal workers. Most countries in the region are not interested in promoting large-scale permanent immigration; consequently, illegal migration will most likely grow in scale and probably generate significant tensions between host and source nations.

One of the growing by-products of rising immigration pressures is the trafficking of people, for labor as well as the global sex trade. Tens of thousands of Asians are smuggled within the region and to far-flung destinations such as North America, Europe, and the Middle East.

Perhaps the most capable human-smuggling networks are those of ethnic Chinese origin. Chinese smuggling syndicates, known as snakeheads, have demonstrated remarkable skill in moving human cargo throughout the world. At least 100,000 Chinese nationals, according to many estimates, are smuggled out of China annually; many are headed for Japan, Western Europe, and North America.

Migrants are often abused or killed during transportation and even after they have reached their destination. The growing practice of transporting illegal immigrants in cargo ships and sealed container trucks is resulting in increased mortality, as was seen in the recent tragedy in Dover, England. In the United States, so-called safe houses are used by smugglers to kidnap, torture, or rape vulnerable migrants. In many cases, smugglers extort additional funds from the migrants (beyond the typical $30,000 to $40,000 transportation fees), and the "safe houses"—with their array of abuses—serve as key instruments in getting families back in China to pay up.

Human smuggling is likely to grow in Asia, due to the vast economic disparities that exist within the region. Migrants in Fujian province in China understand that they can earn substantially higher wages by taking a trip—often facilitated by a smuggler—across the Taiwan Strait. Young women in the Philippines are offered waitress jobs in Tokyo, and only after being smuggled into Japan do they realize that they have been drawn into the sex trade. As long as the demand for migration exists, there will be smugglers to offer their services.

Growing Terrorism in East Asia

On April 23, 2000, armed men representing the Philippine separatist Abu Sayyaf Group (ASG) raided the Malaysian diving resort of Sipadan and seized more than twenty-one tourists from Malaysia, Germany, South Africa, Lebanon, Finland, and the Philippines. The men, with their hostages in tow, sped off in the same two speedboats in which they had arrived and crossed back into Philippine territorial waters. Once established in their bases, they entered into negotiations with the Philippine government to arrange an exchange for the hostages. They made a variety of demands including the creation of a separate state and the restoration of fishing rights for local fishermen. Within a few weeks, the ASG began demanding $1 million for each hostage.

In subsequent weeks, the group seized additional hostages (including foreign journalists covering the story) and periodically released others. Fearing an attack by the Philippine military, the ASG stated that hostage releases would occur on a staggered basis. Eventually, the kidnappers obtained at least some of the ransom money they had desired. By early August 2000, the group had reportedly taken in over \$5.5 million in ransom money. In a bizarre twist, the government of Libya offered to pay \$25 million in exchange for most of the hostages.

The kidnapping by the ASG might be dismissed as a brazen transnational crime perpetrated by a small group of insurgents eager to raise money. Yet closer examination reveals that the ASG constitutes a threat not only to the Philippines, but to other countries in the region. The ASG is the smallest and most radical of the Islamic groups fighting for an independent Islamic state in the southern Philippines. In 1991, the group separated from the Moro National Liberation Front and has since pursued a strategy of sporadic bombings, assassinations, kidnappings, and extortion as part of its struggle. It has also expanded its attacks to Philippine urban areas, including Manila. But what disturbs most terrorism experts are the purported links between the ASG and extremist Islamic groups based in the Middle East and South Asia.[6]

One such linkage involves Osama Bin Laden, the alleged mastermind of the U.S. embassy bombings in Kenya and Tanzania. The Saudi Arabian millionaire has reportedly funneled financial support and deployed trainers to the ASG as well as the Moro Islamic Liberation Front (MILF).[7] In 1995, Philippine authorities discovered a connection between Bin Laden and the ASG when they raided a flat in Manila rented by Ramzi Ahmed Yousef, the mastermind of the 1993 World Trade Center bombing. Evidence revealed that Yousef had traveled to the Philippines as a representative of Bin Laden in order to orchestrate a series of high-profile terrorist attacks including the assassination of the Pope and the simultaneous destruction of multiple U.S. airliners.[8] Such transnational linkages are considered the future of terrorism in Southeast Asia. Many non-Asian terrorist groups view Southeast Asia, where religious and ethnic tensions are rising, as fertile territory in which to spread their activities.

East Asia is also home to the world's most virulent outbreak of chemical- and biological-weapons terrorism, perpetrated by the Japanese cult Aum Shinrikyo. The group follows a religious philosophy that includes tenets of Buddhism, Hinduism, Christianity, and predictions of the sixteenth-century astrologer-prophet Nostradamus. Over a period of years it managed to build up a chemical- and biological-weapons arsenal that rivaled that of many small nations.[9] In March 1995, the group, by releasing sarin nerve gas in the Tokyo subway system, killed eleven people and injured more than 5,000. Subsequent investigations revealed that the group had attempted numerous other chemical- and biological-weapons attacks, including an unsuccessful attempt to kill thousands of Tokyo residents by releasing anthrax spores from a tall building.[10] Despite a vigilant and determined crackdown by the Japanese government, Aum Shinrikyo continues to operate in Japan; however, it now calls itself *Aleph* and has credible and sustained strength, with 1,119 members. Whether the group has the inclination or the capability to launch a similar attack remains to be seen.

Maritime Piracy

On November 16, 1998, a Hong Kong–owned cargo ship, the *Cheung Son*, traveling from Shanghai to Malaysia, lost contact with its owners as it passed through the Taiwan Strait. Despite repeated attempts to contact the ship, the owners could not get the crew to respond. What the owners did not know—and discovered only later—was that the ship had been attacked by a gang of maritime pirates who were able to board by posing as antismuggling police. Once they were aboard the ship, the pirates ordered the twenty-three-member crew to lie on the ground where they were bound, gagged, and blindfolded. The pirates then executed the crew with machine guns and other weapons. They then methodically weighted the bodies and tossed them overboard. Many of the bodies later turned up in fishermen's nets.

The attack on the *Cheung Son* was one of the most violent maritime attacks in East Asia in recent years. Although Chinese authorities eventually caught most of the perpetrators—many were later caught celebrating in a karaoke bar in the southern Chinese city of Shenzhen—they could not allay fears about growing dangers in the sea-lanes surrounding China. As China pursues economic modernization, it is also witnessing a flourishing of violent criminal gangs. The more sophisticated syndicates view maritime piracy as simply another means of earning illicit profits.

Despite rising lawlessness around China, the greatest threat of maritime piracy is unquestionably in Southeast Asia, especially the waters around Indonesia and the Philippines. Nearly two-thirds of maritime piracy attacks in 1999 occurred in Asia, and about 113 of 285 reported cases in the region took place in Indonesia's ports and territorial waters.[11] Southeast Asia is home to the Strait of Malacca, one of the busiest shipping routes in the world; moreover, the strait has been characterized as one of the world's shipping "choke points."[12] It is not surprising, therefore, that the growing threat of maritime piracy is viewed by global shipping and insurance companies with increasing alarm.

Rising maritime piracy in the region has largely correlated with the region's economic and political problems resulting from the 1997 economic crisis. In Indonesia, political instability and economic malaise are linked to rising pirate activity, perhaps due to reduced funding for law enforcement or naval patrols. Unemployment has skyrocketed in many parts of the region, and this has spurred some people—including legitimate sailors—to turn to piracy. Moreover, the pirates themselves have become more sophisticated. Today, pirates are often members of international criminal syndicates, some of which have been known to track shipping routes and schedules on the Internet before attacking the ship. Gangs may also obtain sensitive inside information about a ship's cargo, its destination, and the size of its crew.[13]

Another reason maritime piracy is thriving in Southeast Asia is the lack of a sustained, regional approach to the issue. Apart from operating in areas that have weak law enforcement, pirates also take advantage of areas where states have competing territorial claims. In some cases, pirates commit a crime in one state then seek refuge in another. Mutual suspicion among states can also undermine a regional approach. Japan has proposed deploying its coast guard in joint patrols to help fight piracy, but that suggestion has received a cool response from China, which is not keen to see an enhanced Japanese military presence in the region.

Unless a regional approach to combating piracy can be found, the practice is likely to worsen. What is more disturbing is the increased likelihood of violence—as in cases like the *Cheung Son*. In 1998, over 51 crew members were killed (and 31 wounded) in various pirate attacks in the region. During the first quarter of 2000, pirates boarded over 39 vessels and took 23 crewmembers hostage, leaving more than 21 sailors missing.[14] Shipping routes through Southeast Asia will become even more dangerous unless the issue is taken seriously.

Conclusion

The East Asian economic crisis that began in 1997 has generated a number of unfortunate consequences; political instability, increased economic insecurity, ethnic and religious discord, and international tensions. Perhaps the most dangerous legacy of the crisis, however, is the growth of transnational crime and terrorism. Weakened governance and the lack of genuine regional cooperation provide fertile territory for such threats. Ironically, as criminal or terrorist organizations gain a solid footing in a particular region, they also foster instability and weakened governance, thus contributing to a vicious and destructive cycle.

Transnational security threats harm societies in at least two basic ways. First, there is the harm to humans as individuals. For example, tens of thousands of East Asians are—and will be—the victims of human smuggling, drug addiction, maritime piracy, murder, or other manifestations of transnational violence. Additionally, these threats harm societies by sowing discord among nation-states. In extreme scenarios, tensions over transnational threats might provoke interstate conflict.

If East Asian countries are going to address these threats effectively, they must cooperate in the most intimate way possible: by sharing tactical intelligence, building mutual trust, and putting aside political rivalries in order to address a wider concern. Although genuine cooperative efforts may not result in the total eradication of transnational security threats, they may at least control and manage them. The alternative is simply too bleak. Transnational challenges, if allowed to fester and grow, will undermine countries and societies at their core and ultimately foster instability and chaos throughout the entire region.

Notes

1. Paul J. Smith, "Transnational Security Threats and State Survival: A Role for the Military?" *Parameters*, Autumn 2000, p. 78.

2. Douglas Farah, "The North Korean Connection; U.S. Says Cash-Strapped Pyongyang Sponsors Heroin Production," *The Washington Post*, March 26, 1999, p. A21.

3. "Vietnam Investment: Reluctance to Privatise," *EIU ViewsWire*, May 19, 1997.

4. "Court Appeal in Vietnam's Biggest Drugs Case to Open Tuesday," *Agence France Presse*, June 23, 1997.

5. "Thailand Gets U.S., China Support in Anti-Drugs War," *The Straits Times* (Singapore), October 7, 2000, p. 30; "Malaysia Not Threatened by Methamphetamine Drug 'Yaba,' Says Chor," *Bernama, The Malaysian National News Agency*, October 30, 2000.

6. *Patterns of Global Terrorism, 1999.* United States Department of State publication 10687, released April 2000. www.state.gov/www/global/terrorism/1999 report/appb.html

7. "Philippine Newspaper says Bin Laden Continues to Support Rebel Group," *Deutsche Presse-Agentur*, February 13, 1999

8. Peter Chalk, "Terrorism—Bin Laden's Asian Network," *Jane's Intelligence Review* vol. 5, no. 12 (December 1, 1998), p. 6.

9. Peter Chalk, "Terrorism in the Asia-Pacific," Paper presented to the August 2000 Conference, "Transnational Security Threats in Asia," Honolulu, Asia-Pacific Center for Security Studies.

10. "Sowing Death: A Special Report—How Japan Germ Terror Alerted World," *The New York Times*, May 26, 1998, p. A1.

11. Bertil Lintner, "The Perils of Rising Piracy," *Jane's Defence Weekly* vol. 34, no. 20 (November 15, 2000), pp. 16–17.

12. Jake Lloyd-Smith, "Armed Siege on the High Seas," *South China Morning Post*, November 10, 2000, p. 22.

13. Jack Hitt, "Bandits in the Global Shipping Lanes," *The New York Times*, August 20, 2000, p. 37.

14. "Asia Industry: Countries Join Forces to Fight Rise in Maritime Piracy," *EIU ViewsWire*, May 22, 2000.

ASEAN Economic Integration: The Challenges Ahead

Rodolfo C. Severino, Jr.

The Association of Southeast Asian Nations (ASEAN) was founded with three interconnected and ambitious objectives in mind: regional peace, stability, and prosperity. Economic cooperation was to be a key to achieving these goals. At the time of ASEAN's creation, the Indochina (Vietnam) War was raging and the Cold War threatened to wipe out Southeast Asia's hopes for a better life. In addition there were disputes among Southeast Asian nations.

In these unpromising circumstances, the countries of Southeast Asia set their minds, their labors, and their resources toward developing their economies. It became increasingly clear that national development programs would be strengthened by openness and cooperation, not only with the rest of the world, but more importantly within the region. Economic cooperation would give each member of the new association a stake in the economic well-being of the others, thereby assisting regional peace. This was the logic supporting the European Community and the European Common Market: firmly locking economies together would bind the core nations closely—and war would be unthinkable. Peace among nations and economic progress would bring about stability, making further development possible.

ASEAN designed cooperative programs in industry, minerals and energy, in finance and banking, in transport and communications, and in food, agriculture, and forestry. Two programs, ASEAN Industrial Projects and ASEAN Industrial Joint Ventures, were created and preferential trading arrangements were implemented.

AFTA Is Born

After many years, ASEAN leaders realized that these tentative (and modest) measures for regional economic cooperation—nobody dared talk of "economic integration" then—were not enough. Looking to the future, they knew these steps were not enough to foster economic efficiency and attract needed investments. At their fourth summit in Singapore in 1992, they therefore moved to a new stage, making the leap from cooperation to integration by resolving to transform the region into an ASEAN Free Trade Area (AFTA). In fifteen years, tariffs on goods traded within ASEAN, with some exceptions, would be either eliminated or reduced to a maximum of five percent. A legally binding schedule of tariff reductions and fixed timetables were included in this plan. The objective was to create an integrated regional trade market that would attract investments more effectively than the smaller national domestic markets. The dramatic plan would stimulate commerce and growth, and raise—for ASEAN members—stakes in one another's purchasing power and economic progress.

In four years, from 1993 to 1997, the value of intra-ASEAN trade almost doubled, from less than US$44 billion to more than $85 billion, from less than twenty-one to almost twenty-five percent of total trade. The recent financial crisis took its toll: trade dropped to $71 billion in 1998, increasing a year later. This dramatic rise in intra-ASEAN trade cannot be attributed entirely to AFTA. Yet AFTA's significance is noted: the world's largest companies have displayed extraordinary interest in its progress, and ASEAN leaders, meeting in Bangkok in December 1995, advanced AFTA's completion date to 2003. A few months later, ASEAN adopted the ASEAN Industrial Cooperation scheme (AICO), according to which products of companies operating in two or more ASEAN countries enjoy full AFTA treatment immediately. Thus the 1997–98 economic and financial crisis did not cause either ASEAN countries to retreat into isolation or ASEAN or AFTA to fall into disarray.

AFTA Speeds Up

What ASEAN needed during the period of economic contraction was to regain that confidence and foster foreign investment. The logical step was to deepen, expand and accelerate regional economic integration. In 1998, at their summit in Hanoi, ASEAN leaders again advanced AFTA's completion date, this time to 2002 for the six original AFTA signatories, with the other signatories having a few more years to adjust to regional free trade.

The beginning of 2002 is but months away. This year fully ninety percent of tariff lines will drop significantly, and by 2010 all tariffs among the original six members will be abolished. ASEAN is committed to removing non-tariff barriers, and average tariff rates for goods traded within AFTA are under four percent. The financial crisis brought hardship to specific industries in individual countries; ASEAN is ready to make allowances for relief of these industries. A rules-based system will—in accordance with international convention and practice—govern such contingencies.

Dismantling trade barriers is not enough, however. Trade must be made easier, and ASEAN has worked to harmonize tariff nomenclatures, streamline customs procedures, and make product standards mutually compatible. Services—a larger part of ASEAN economies—are now subject to sector-by-sector liberalization negotiations.

The ASEAN members seek to attract more foreign capital by integrating themselves as a market for goods and services and allowing investments to move freely within the region. The ASEAN Investment Area agreement is helping this process. The few exclusions will be phased out, and other impediments to investments are being removed. ASEAN now promotes itself as a single investment area to multinationals based in Japan, the United States, and Europe.

ASEAN economies are bound closely together through infrastructure linkages. Consolidated expansion of the already extensive road network on mainland Southeast Asia—one covering 33,480 kilometers—is afoot. An agreement to facilitate treatment of goods in transit and agreements on multi-modal transport and interstate transport are also under negotiation. The feasibility study for a railway from Singapore to Kunming in southern China was presented to ASEAN leaders in November 2000. This project and others along the vast Mekong Basin will stimulate economic opportunities there, facilitating the integration of old and new

ASEAN members. Some of the projected mainland power grid interconnections are operating. In addition, a trans-ASEAN gas pipeline network
should, as it moves to completion, ensure regional energy security. Other
projects include telecommunications interconnectivity and the standard-
ization of telecommunications equipment. One challenge is to package
such mega-projects in a way that attracts investors.

Into the Information Age

ASEAN is using information and communications technology (ICT) to
strengthen regional economic integration. The (at press time) proposed
e-ASEAN Framework Agreement will harness both the facilities and
the policy environment required to encourage greater use of ICT. The
framework covers skills development, the use of ICT in the delivery of
public services, and the liberalization of trade in those goods and services related to such new and current high-tech equipment.

The economic and financial "contagion" demonstrated, if further proof
was needed, how integrated ASEAN economies already were. Markets
should therefore be more deeply—and rapidly—integrated. Meaningful
cooperation in financial matters should be pursued much more intensively. ASEAN finance ministers set up a surveillance mechanism
through which the member country governments can monitor macroeconomic developments, thus encouraging those governments—through
a peer review process—to strengthen economic fundamentals and accelerate necessary reforms. Association leaders decided to enlarge the
currency swap arrangement through which ASEAN countries could help
one another in case of balance-of-payments difficulties.

Analyses within ASEAN highlight the fact that market integration
and financial cooperation alone cannot shore up investor confidence
and enhance competitiveness. Attention must be paid to the domestic
investment climate in each of the ten ASEAN members. This goes beyond AFTA, market integration, and economic and financial cooperation. Yet such initiatives are needed to face future challenges.

Each of the ten governments must put in place necessary laws and
policies. The rule of law has to be fortified. The competitive field must
be leveled. Transparency must be fostered, and the integrity of governmental and corporate institutions and processes must be upheld. People's
skills must be upgraded to ensure competitiveness. Security and order
must prevail—and be perceived to do so.

The Next Step

This broad stage may require ASEAN countries to concern themselves with governance issues without, of course, interfering in one another's internal affairs. This is not without precedent in ASEAN: tariff policy and other trade restrictions are a matter of sovereign right. Yet AFTA obligates ASEAN members to make commitments to each other in bringing down—through domestic legislation—regional trade barriers. The counties are doing so with respect to obstacles to intra-regional investments and are about to tackle services in a similar manner. Finance ministers frequently conduct peer reviews by looking into one another's national economic policies and reform measures. Other ministers and officials discuss national policies and practices that have an impact on atmospheric pollution levels. Moreover, ASEAN governments should be able to discuss, in a frank but friendly and discreet manner, all elements guiding investment climate (governance, the rule of law, transparency, corruption, etc.). After all, the image of disorder in one country affects perceptions of region-wide stability. Impressions of an inhospitable investment climate in one country deeply influence the regional climate.

ASEAN ministers have begun to conduct such dialogues with increasing frequency and intensity, responding to the challenges of regional economic integration. For them, this is a matter of regional solidarity. And that is what ASEAN is all about.

ASEAN, Asia, and the Rise of Regional Identity

Adam Schwarz

The new millennium has ushered in a stronger sense of regional identity across East Asia, and ASEAN, the ten-member Association of Southeast Asian Nations, is playing a key role in bringing it into focus. The ASEAN Plus Three grouping, with the Three consisting of China, Japan, and South Korea, has given East Asia its most promising regional forum in the fifty years since most Southeast Asian countries were founded. It provides the very early stages of an institutional manifestation of an East Asian community.

The progress so far is modest, and has produced more rhetoric than action. There is no NAFTA in the offing for East Asia, much less a European Union type of community. But these and other ambitious ideas are now at least on the table. For ASEAN, its continued existence comes as a surprise to many commentators. It is true that the organization has hit hard times since the advent of the Asian financial crisis. But reports of ASEAN's death are premature. It still has a role to play, both in Southeast Asia and in the region more broadly.

Thanks in part to the gatherings made possible by ASEAN, there are today regular discussions of Asian currency unions, Asian parliaments, Asian Monetary Funds, Asian anti-piracy patrols, and Asian military pacts, among other topics. Already, there exist some modest currency-swap arrangements and free-trade initiatives within the region. A number of other smaller, more achievable measures are also being discussed.

To be sure, there remains a wide gulf between a rising sense of regional identity and the capacity to convert this identity into a functioning set of institutions and initiatives. The obstacles to Asian regionalism are many and complex, and will be discussed in more detail below. But it is important not to lose sight of the rising desire to see some form of regionalism take shape.

ASEAN, despite the many predictions of its demise and many accounts of its irrelevance, remains both institutionally viable and in the forefront of this demand for a heightened regional identity. In terms of measurable output, ASEAN's progress is often painfully slow. But it remains relevant for many Southeast Asians simply by representing a supranational desire for community in Southeast Asia. And it is eagerly seeking an even greater degree of relevance by providing a neutral field for the larger powers of Northeast Asia to meet and overcome past animosities, the same animosities that have kept Asia divided for most of the twentieth century.

When and whether ASEAN will achieve that greater sense of relevance is unclear. The main ASEAN members have undergone a very difficult period since 1997 and their recovery is far from assured. This chapter will begin with a summary of ASEAN's ups and downs since 1997. It will continue with an attempt to identify the impetus for a stronger regional identity and the obstacles to achieving it. It will conclude with a few implications for policymakers.

ASEAN's Decline and Nascent Recovery

The financial crisis that swept across Asia beginning in mid-1997 did more than bankrupt companies and send currencies into a tailspin. It also severely dented ASEAN's confidence. As a grouping, ASEAN found itself ignored or impotent in the search for solutions, whether for treating forest fires in Indonesia, stopping the destruction of East Timor, or responding collectively to the financial crisis. The strength of ASEAN economies, and the confidence this generated internally, turned out to have been exaggerated.

In addition, the crisis forced the biggest ASEAN members—Indonesia, Thailand, Malaysia and the Philippines—to focus almost exclusively on domestic affairs and consequently pay less attention to regional matters. The crisis came unfortunately close on the heels of a major organizational expansion. Between 1995 and 1998, Vietnam, Laos, Cambodia, and Myanmar were admitted to ASEAN. The new members added geographic and demographic heft but also diluted the sense of unity among the original six members and further slowed down the group's already cumbersome decision-making apparatus. Not surprisingly, some momentum was lost in furthering the group's free-trade initiative, the ASEAN Free Trade Area (AFTA), once the less economically developed new members were admitted.

Finally, Indonesia's difficult and ongoing transition from a deeply entrenched authoritarian system to a fledgling democracy has also damaged ASEAN's resolve. As ASEAN's biggest member by far, Indonesia has long been considered the grouping's anchor state and de facto leader. When President Suharto fell in May 1998, the Indonesian anchor slipped, and ASEAN has yet to fully recover. Moreover, Indonesia's emergent democracy has highlighted the widespread political differences within ASEAN.

But for a variety of reasons, ASEAN is beginning to pull out of its crisis-induced funk, although, certainly, it has a long way to go. One reason is that some ASEAN members, such as Malaysia and Thailand, are beginning to see some gradual economic recovery. ASEAN has begun to work on mechanisms that would allow the group to react more quickly to problems within its borders. One idea borrows from the European troika: if approved, a committee formed by the three countries that host the annual ASEAN meetings in the current year, the year before, and the year ahead would be able to act as an ASEAN management team.

Part of the recovery has psychological roots. Following the financial crisis, ASEAN's political clout on the world stage receded along with its economic growth. ASEAN leaders, after an initial period of denial (which is not completely finished), are now trying to seek new ways to make the organization more relevant. In the current economic climate, it has been frustratingly slow to get any traction behind these efforts. But some are bearing fruit.

AFTA is mostly on track to reach its goal of five percent or lower tariffs on intra-ASEAN trade by 2003 for the original six members and a few years later for the newer members. At the September 2000 ASEAN economic ministers' meeting in Chiang Mai, a good deal of coverage was given to Malaysia's demand to be given a tariff-reducing extension in the case of automobiles. The demand, which was granted, was undoubtedly a setback, at least in a public-relations sense. But the reality is that at least ninety percent of the traded goods of the original six ASEAN members already meet the AFTA goal of five percent or lower tariffs. Automobile parts, a more important traded good than automobiles, were not affected by the Malaysian demand.

ASEAN leaders have grown less concerned in recent years about the emergence of a two-tier ASEAN, the first tier comprising the original six members and the second, the newest four. In the late 1990s, ASEAN was in danger of letting its most economically backward members set the pace precisely because the organization's leaders were uncomfortable with the notion of a two-tier ASEAN. Today, the more economically advanced members are again setting the pace of change, even if this comes at the cost of a widening divide within the organization. There is a realization that ASEAN has no time left to delay; if its leading members do not forge ahead on economic integration and free-trade initiatives, the organization will be left behind. Singapore's decision to move ahead with its own free-trade agreement with Japan is one such example.

Indonesia remains a drag on ASEAN's progress. The archipelago faces a massive political and economic rebuilding task, with few resources left over for regional or international role-playing. But here again ASEAN is attempting to adjust. Leaders from Malaysia, Singapore, Philippines, and Thailand, while taking pains not to slight Indonesia, have taken the lead on other issues on a case-by-case basis.

An Asian Identity Emerges

In 1990, Malaysian Prime Minister Mahathir Mohamad unveiled his vision for an East Asian community, which he dubbed the East Asia Economic Group (EAEG). Although it won plaudits from academics and second-tier officials, it was widely ignored by most of the rest of Asia. At the very end of the 1990s, the ASEAN Plus Three grouping had come into being with loud support across East Asia—and its membership was the same as the EAEG. What accounted for the change?

A first reason is the demonstration effect of other regional groupings such as the European Union and the North American Free Trade Area. Across the region, Asians are increasingly asking why Asia does not have its own organizations. A related concern flows from the financial crisis and the effect it had on Asian attitudes towards the main international financial organizations. Many Asians felt the West and Western-dominated institutions like the International Monetary Fund and World Bank dictated unfavorable terms to crisis-stricken Asian nations. There is a growing sentiment across the region that Asians need more say at the top ranks of the major world councils, including the leading United Nations organizations. And one way to effectively obtain that representation is for Asia to articulate its demands in a more unified manner, which in turn requires effective regional organizations.

Relative to 1990, China is today less wary of ASEAN's intentions, and the China-ASEAN relationship is much less suspicion-filled. China's tremendous strides in economic development over the past decade have turned a good deal of ASEAN suspicion into ASEAN envy. China's decision not to devalue its currency during the financial crisis also generated considerable goodwill from ASEAN nations.

Overall, China's bilateral relations are much stronger today with Myanmar, Malaysia, Thailand, Indonesia, and even Vietnam than they were ten years ago. Although Beijing still prefers working mainly through bilateral fora, it has grown more comfortable operating in regional settings. For its part, ASEAN is today more comfortable with China than it was in 1990; it largely takes China at its word when China denies any territorial ambitions. ASEAN's main priority is to draw China out into the global trading system. Unlike Washington, ASEAN is worried mainly about Chinese autarky, not Chinese hegemony. Moreover, for many ASEAN strategists, China remains a useful hedge against the return of a threatening nationalism in Japan, which remains the region's dominant economic power.

As for Japan, it worries it has lost ground to China in Southeast Asia, despite the former's generous aid during and after the financial crisis. Japan has kept alive the idea of an Asian Monetary Fund, which is popular in ASEAN circles, and has been highly supportive of an ASEAN currency-swap arrangement designed to counteract future currency runs. Japan views ASEAN Plus Three as a way to broaden its relationships with Southeast Asia away from an almost exclusive focus on economic issues.

Asia, generally speaking, has less confidence in the strength of the U.S. commitment to the region today compared with 1990. The ending of the Cold War tended to weaken U.S. ties with allies in the region, while new concerns raised by the United States such as trade, human rights, labor, and democracy tended to fray relations with many countries in the region. There is also a growing sense in Asia that U.S. leadership of the global free-trade movement is waning, that its commitment to the Asia Pacific Economic Cooperation forum is growing cooler, and that its faith in organizations such as the World Trade Organization is declining. Taking all this together, many Asians draw the conclusion that Asia needs its own organizations to protect Asian interests.

Caveats Aplenty

As noted earlier, there remains a lot of space between the wish for a united Asia capable of acting as a bloc and the creation of the institutions necessary to bring this about. Asia is still largely in the wishing phase. Many obstacles remain to be overcome before the regional ambitions being discussed today can be realized.

For one, it is worth bearing in mind that Asia is not a region in the way the United States is, or even in the way Europe is. There are still many differences among Asian nations, politically, economically, culturally, and historically. Relations between Southeast Asia and Australia/New Zealand are a case in point. The leading Southeast Asian nations of Indonesia, Malaysia, and the Philippines are not yet willing to see ASEAN's free trade area become formally aligned with the set of economic arrangements that lower tariffs between Australia and New Zealand. Similarly, the Asian members of the Asia-Europe Meetings (ASEM) forum have rejected membership requests by Australia and New Zealand. Within ASEAN, minor political and territorial squabbles remain an obstacle to more unified action.

Crucially, relations between Asia's two biggest powers, China and Japan, remain uneasy. It is precisely this relationship that ASEAN hopes to strengthen through auspices such as the ASEAN Plus Three grouping. Everybody recognizes that pan-Asian organizational ambitions will remain stillborn until China and Japan mutually agree that Asia is big enough for both of them.

More broadly, the uncertainty of China's political future poses another threat to Asian regionalism. All agree that China is destined to be a great power; many doubts remain as to how China will use its power. Will it respect current borders and obey global trading rules? The jury is still out. Optimists were cheered, to give one example, by China's accession to the WTO. But pessimists remain alarmed, to give other examples, by China's refusal to declare that it will not occupy additional reefs in the disputed South China Sea and by its resistance to joint antipiracy patrols in regional waters.

Finally, Asia remains a region of economies deeply dependent on export markets in Europe and the United States. Asian leaders will need to tread carefully to avoid giving in to protectionism and exclusive trading blocks. If they did give in, Asia would be the chief loser. In addition, poorer nations such as Indonesia will continue to be dependent on the goodwill of international donor organizations for many years to come; it can ill afford policies that may put it into conflict with them.

In sum, many obstacles lie ahead on the road to a more vibrant Asian regionalism. But this does not mean the desire for such an outcome is not an increasingly important political variable in Asian politics. It is, and it is almost certain to continue as one.

The West should not look upon this trend as a threat. Asian regionalism does not have to come at the expense of good relations with the West or at the expense of existing extraregional organizations such as APEC, ASEM, and the ASEAN Regional Forum. But the West should expect Asians to continue the search for common East Asian voices and positions to bring to these organizations. And it should not come as a surprise if ASEAN plays a key role in formulating and articulating those voices and positions. ASEAN, despite its many shortcomings, is almost uniquely qualified to play the cohering, honest-broker role that East Asia sorely needs.

Australia's Asian Identity

Gerard Henderson

Don't worry. It was all a false alarm. Despite the warnings of Samuel P. Huntington and Owen Harries, Australia remains very much a Western nation, albeit a physically isolated one.

In his influential article "The Clash of Civilizations?" (*Foreign Affairs*, Summer 1993), Huntington quoted *National Interest* editor Owen Harries as authority for the proposition that Australia was about to junk the Western alliance. In Huntington's words, Australia's "current leaders" (circa 1993) were "in effect proposing that it defect from the West, redefine itself as an Asian country and cultivate close ties with its neighbours."

By 1996 Huntington re-worked his *Foreign Affairs* essay into a full-length book. *The Clash of Civilizations and the Remaking of World Order* (Simon & Schuster, 1996) contains a dogmatic tone, with Huntington declaring: "In the early 1990s . . . Australia's political leaders decided, in effect, that Australia should defect from the West, redefine itself as an Asian society, and cultivate close ties with its geographical neighbours." The author suggests that, in the long term, Australia may be held responsible for the decline and fall of the Western world: "At the beginning of the twenty-second century, historians might look back on the Keating-Evans choice as a major marker in the decline of the West."

In the March 1996 election, John Howard defeated Paul Keating and a politically conservative Coalition replaced the Labor Party in Canberra.

By this time, according to Huntington, Australia had already defected from the West.

It's perhaps understandable why he appears to have blindly followed Owen Harries' interpretation of contemporary Australian history. Welsh-born Harries lived in Australia during the 1950s, 1960s, and 1970s and was appointed Australian ambassador to UNESCO in 1981. Presumably, Huntington believed that Harries was well informed on Australian foreign policy. *National Interest* gives little coverage to Australia. But in its Spring 1998 issue, Harries published an article by Eric Jones (a professorial fellow at the Melbourne Business School) entitled "Australia and the Asian Crisis." He ran the line that what he termed the "Asian affiliation of trade" had become "gospel" to Australian companies— and this line enjoyed bipartisan support at the political level.

Jones also asserted that in the early 1990s Paul Keating "decided to make his government the vehicle for a crusade to 'Asianise' the country" and alleged that Labor wished to "transfer" Australia's "cultural allegiance from West to East." Professor James also wrote: "Australia is the nearest Western country to that great bonfire of the vanities, the Asian crisis; the fear is that it may also be the most combustible."

Defining Australia

The problem with prophecies is that most of them turn out to be false. The Australian economy is very strong, having survived the Asian economic downturn without general distress. Moreover, those who watched the 2000 Olympics on television would have noticed that Sydney is a developed, tolerant, multicultural city. The fact is that no senior Australian politician, either social democratic or conservative, has ever suggested that Australia should be "Asianised" (whatever that might mean) or that Australia should defect from the West. Neither Samuel P. Huntington nor Eric Jones cited one original source to support the allegation that the Keating Labor government decided that Australia should become Asianised and/or defect from the West.

Indeed both overlooked contemporary statements made by Paul Keating during his term as prime minister. In 1993 Keating said: "Claims that the government is attempting to turn Australia into an "Asian country" are based on a misunderstanding. . . . [I]t is at the core of my view of Australia and of the government's approach to relations with our neighborhood . . . [that] Australia is not and can never be an "Asian nation" any more than we can—or want to be—European or North American or

African. We can only be Australian and can only relate to our friends and neighbours *as* Australian."

That was it. In the lead up to the March 1996 election, John Howard did not query Australia's involvement in the Asia-Pacific region during the prime ministerships of Bob Hawke or Paul Keating. In an address entitled "The Coalition's Asia Focus," delivered in October 1995, Howard said he "never disputed the importance placed by the current [Keating] government on our regional ties."

Rather he rejected the "attempts" by the Keating government "to depict themselves as those great Australian statesmen who 'discovered' Asia." John Howard then listed details of the Coalition's interaction with the Asian region over the previous half century. However, soon after his election to office, John Howard began to insist that under Labor rule the country focused too much on the Asia Pacific. Addressing the Foreign Policy Association in New York in June 1997, the prime minister referred to "the impression that was sometimes given in the past that Australia had to pursue an Asia-only policy and downgrade the weight it gave to associations with Europe and the United States."

Like all political leaders, John Howard delights in making political points at his opponents' expense. The allegation that, under the Keating government, Australia has an "Asia only" foreign policy should be viewed as a comment primarily intended for domestic political consumption. In fact, Australia enjoyed excellent relations with the United States and Western Europe during the Labor administration (1993 to 1996). The same can be said for Malcolm Fraser's conservative government in the second half of the 1970s and the early 1980s, in which John Howard served as senior minister.

There was a continuum of foreign policy during the twenty-year period from 1977 through the late 1990s. In the Howard government's Foreign and Trade Policy White Paper titled *In the National Interest* (August 1997) it is pointed out that "Australia's most important strategic and economic interests lie in a region—the Asia Pacific—of great cultural and historical diversity." Not surprisingly, the White Paper acknowledges Australia's historical and cultural links "to Europe and the United States" along with shared "important economic and strategic interests" with Australia's traditional allies.

Aussies on the Regional—and the World—Stage

It is a matter of record that Australia played its part in virtually all the international conflicts of the twentieth century—in cooperation with traditional allies Britain and/or the United States. The list includes World War I, World War II, the Korean War, the Malayan Emergency, Konfrontasi (Indonesia's confrontation in the early 1960s of Malaysia), Vietnam, and the Gulf War. Over the past quarter century the Australian Defence Force (ADF) has been deployed to the Sinai, Fiji, Namibia, Somalia, Rwanda, Western Samoa, Papua New Guinea, Cambodia, Indonesia (drought relief in Irian Jaya), and East Timor in various observer/drought-relief/peacekeeping/peace-enforcing roles. Some commitments were more popular than others. But all enjoyed majority support at the time.

Why? Australia has been involved militarily in support of traditional allies because—rightly or wrongly—it agreed with each particular cause. But there is another reason. Australia is a small, multicultural, Western style democracy at the base of the Asia Pacific. It is in Australia's national interest to ensure that trade and people can readily move to and from our shores. In other words, more than many nations, Australia has a vested interest in international security. The reasons relate directly to population size and isolation.

Australia is a large nation geographically and possesses a middle-sized economy—the fourteenth largest in the world. However, with nineteen million people (twenty-three million if you add New Zealand to make up Australasia) Australia is relatively small. Many Australians have some Irish background—including John Howard (of Protestant stock) and Paul Keating (of Catholic background). Ireland's population is 3.5 million—five million if Northern Ireland is included to make up the island of Ireland. The Netherlands is close to Australia's size—at about seventeen million, and many Dutch have settled successfully in Australia. However, both Ireland and the Netherlands are part of the 375 million–strong, and growing, European Union. And the Netherlands is a NATO member. Canada has a population of some thirty million. Like Australia, it is an immigrant nation. But Canada is part of 300 million–strong North America and a member of the 400 million–strong NAFTA (North America Free Trade Agreement), which includes Mexico and seems destined to move even further south. Canada is also part of NATO.

Unlike Ireland, the Netherlands, and Canada, Australia has no obvious similar "fit." APEC (the Asia Pacific Economic Corporation forum) is important—but it will never have a similar role to that of the EU or NAFTA. Moreover, Australia is not part of the developing Asian economic grouping ASEAN Plus Three—namely, the ten ASEAN countries plus the three key nations of Northeast Asia (China, Japan, and

South Korea). This group meets biennially with the EU to make up ASEM (Asia-Europe Meetings). Malaysia is strongly opposed to Australia either becoming part of ASEM or joining the ASEAN Plus Three group. In a speech to the National Press Club in Canberra in August 2000, Dr. Ashton Calvert (secretary of the Australian Department of Foreign Affairs and Trade) acknowledged that "Australia's participation in newly emerging forums in East Asia is made more complicated than it otherwise might be by the preference of some participants to restrict membership of forums like ASEAN Plus Three strictly to East Asian countries, at least for the foreseeable future."

In his speech, Dr. Calvert pointed out that "close engagement with Asia is an abiding priority in Australian policy." This makes sense, especially in view of the fact that there is no realistic possibility that Australia can join NAFTA or the EU. The problem for Australia turns on the fact that, at the moment, engagement with Asia is restricted to participation in the ASEAN Regional Forum, in addition to bilateral relations.

Australia has the CER (Closer Economic Relations Agreement) with New Zealand. And that is as far as formal links go. This explains Australia's significant role in establishing the Cairns Group of primary producing exporters and in the creation of APEC—along with its strong on-going support for the World Trade Organization. As the White Paper points out: "For a trading nation such as Australia, the alternative to active participation in the global economy and the affairs of its region is irrelevance and decline."

Diversity and Cultural Affinity

Australia's cultural links with Asia are greater than ever—due primarily to the ever growing number of Australians of Asian background, to increasing high levels of trade with the Asia Pacific, and to Australia's attraction as a tourist destination. According to the research of demographer Charles Price, the "ethnic strength" of Australians of Asian background is currently around seven percent and is likely to double over the next quarter of a century. The "ethnic strength" measurement records ethnic backgrounds in a society in which there is much ethnic intermixture.

The inflow of Asians over the three decades since the abandonment of the White Australia Policy has added to Australian's multicultural diversity. But it is quite misleading to suggest that there is any causal relationship between Asian immigration to Australia and any (alleged) decision by an Australian government to transfer Australian "cultural allegiance" from West to East.

Australian governments, conservative and social democratic alike, have always understood that Australia's traditional alliances are central to the nation's long-term security. That's why Australia has played its part in international conflict in the twentieth century. And that's why Australia, unlike New Zealand, has remained part of the ANZUS Alliance. Without question, Australia benefits from its alliance with the United States—with respect to security, technology access, and intelligence sharing. However, the United States also gains from its connections with Australia. Australia continues to make its contribution to intelligence—including hosting the U.S.-Australia Joint Facilities at Pine Gap. In addition, it provides an important, safe, and pleasant anchor for the U.S. Navy and the men and women who sail with it. In short, Australia is a valuable ally in an alliance which has mutual benefits.

Certainly Australia has a difficult relationship with Malaysia—which is likely to remain strained while Dr. Mahathir Mohamad remains prime minister. John Howard expected that the relationship would improve under his government. This has not happened. Also, Australia's role in East Timor has upset significant sections of the Indonesian leadership group. In other words, Australia's relationship with two of the key ASEAN members is strained. This places diplomatic stresses on Australia at a time of instability in parts of the Asia Pacific.

It may well be that tensions will diminish on the Korean Peninsula and in the Taiwan Strait in the short to medium term. If not, increased tension between North Korea and South Korea and/or China and Taiwan would have strategic and economic implications for Australia. As well, there could be obligations resulting from the Australia-U.S. alliance. Then there is the ring of instability in the area to Australia's north, most particularly secessionist movements within Indonesia—including West Papua—along with instability in New Guinea, Fiji, and the Solomon Islands.

In June 2000 John Howard issued a public discussion paper entitled *Defence Review 2000*. It recognized that "at present no country has any intent to use armed force against Australia" and stated that Australia's "most immediate strategic interests are in the arc of islands stretching from Indonesia to the islands of the Southwest Pacific." The discussion paper focused on the ADF's forthcoming "block obsolescence" when much of the ADF's key war-fighting platforms—aircraft, ships, and Army vehicles alike—will have to be replaced "in the period 2007 to 2015." This at a time when the defense technology gap which Australia has enjoyed in the region is being overtaken.

Australia's defense problems can be overcome. But more short-term work needs to be done in the Asian region. Repairing Canberra's relations with Kuala Lumpur and Jakarta will take time. However, Australia could play a role in revitalizing APEC—which gives the impression of having run out of steam in recent years. For a physically isolated nation like Australia, such a policy would make much sense. Contrary to the assertions of Samuel P. Huntington, Australia has not junked the West. Rather, Australia's priorities are to enhance its involvement in the Asia Pacific.

Asia Thinks International: One Country's Approach

Tan Chi Chiu

Singapore's response to the Asian financial crisis led many to recognize that internationalization is part of a strategy of resilience. Internationalizing the mindset of our own people makes Singapore adaptable in the global market, increases knowledge about Singapore as a unique society, and builds people-to-people goodwill. Furthermore, improving Singapore's image is helpful and makes us more attractive to investment and foreign talent. Harnessing Singaporeans' contributions to the home country—from wherever they live—has enormous potential.

Increased prosperity has bred a certain complacency among Singaporeans, especially the younger generation. They did not undergo the trials experienced by the pre-independence generation. Many young Singaporeans are content to work and live within the confines of Singapore's shores, with overseas forays only for education and vacation. Plugging fully into the global market has been a challenge, as the younger generation balk at living in unfamiliar cultures away from extended family support. Despite modern communications and mass media, Singaporeans' understanding and appreciation of foreign cultures—as well as their ability to function efficiently in them—needs improvement.

Formal education can go only so far. One can envisage a new generation of Singaporeans who are technologically competent but unable or unwilling to function outside of their native country. Training youth to become "world-ready" is important, and initiatives to remove youth from "comfort zones" and into foreign environments are increasing. Overseas community service expeditions are one example.

Nongovernment organizations such as the Singapore Red Cross Society, World Vision, and Touch Community Services have expanded their youth expedition projects. Government-sponsored organizations such as the National Youth Council (NYC), National Youth Achievement Awards (NYAA) Council, and Singapore International Foundation (SIF), were established to promote overseas experiences. Youth expeditions were given a massive boost when, in early 2000, the government provided more than US$1 million, allowing SIF to create the Youth Expedition Project (YEP). This is a support structure for youth groups desiring to mount overseas community service expeditions. The YEP provides project development guidance, partial funding, training, and active follow-up. YEP developed a unique system, Expeditionary Service Learning (EXSEL), which equips trainers with the skills to be effective in the field.

In the process, Singapore youth learn about themselves, about leadership, teamwork and adaptability, cultural sensitivity and socio-economic developments overseas. The YEP is growing and some 3,000–5,000 youth will take part each year by mid-decade. This puts youth expeditions on the level of a societal movement, and for many young men and women, an overseas community work stint is a rite of passage.

Other important initiatives include sending young people to international conferences, seminars and workshops. They are exposed to issues ranging from concepts of democracy to preservation of the environment. The NYAA seeks to develop youths' personal capabilities. Networks formed between Singaporeans and youth of other nations builds international understanding, educating them to feel part of a global community, while it prepares them to accept foreign talent arriving in Singapore.

In addition, our country built an active humanitarian relief and development assistance profile. Despite its small size and limited resources, Singapore has shown its sincerity to other nations through helping in relief work when disasters occur. Examples include offers of aid on the occasions of earthquakes in Bali (Indonesia), the Philippines, Turkey, and Taiwan, floods in China, Bangladesh, and Vietnam, food shortages in Indonesia and even war in the Gulf. Many humanitarian efforts were large-scale efforts conducted by the Singapore Armed Forces, but increasingly, civil groups are going forth, especially in cases where the government has not committed official aid.

In developmental assistance, SIF has taken the lead in managing development programs and volunteer training for Singaporeans. Emphasizing accountability, partnership, and sustainability, the Foundation's Singapore Volunteer Overseas Programme mounted projects in ASEAN, elsewhere in Asia and in Africa. SIF also equips civil organizations in equipping Singaporeans for disaster relief missions.

Sending Singaporeans overseas as informal ambassadors is not enough. On the nongovernmental level, efforts to promote Singapore's image—as politically stable but also as a desirable location for foreign talent—have accelerated. It is in our interest to become better known and better understood. Numerous visiting programs for journalists, businessmen, senior administrators, and politicians have been put together and hosted by organizations such as the Economic Development Board (EDB) and SIF. African and Japanese bureaucrats, government committees from Vietnam, congressional staffers, and American Congressmen, among others, have accepted SIF's invitation to visit Singapore and to learn about our governance, culture, lifestyle, and civil institutions. Not only do such visitors leave with a better understanding of Singapore, but any negative notions and misconceptions are clarified.

Finally, Singapore's only real resource is its people. Despite educational efforts to produce imaginative, competent, adaptable, and knowledge-based workers, the talent pool in Singapore remains small. Talented Singaporeans are mobile, and a large community already lives and works abroad. Many students studying overseas are tempted to stay abroad to work for foreign firms.

Singapore realizes it must take a wider view of what it is to be Singaporean. It is no longer sufficient to consider as Singaporean only those living within the island's shores. It is imperative to embrace a worldwide community of Singaporeans and keep their links to the homeland alive so they will contribute directly to Singapore's economy and support Singapore's interests. Singaporeans are actively "head-hunted" to return home. Singapore student counselors and others are active in more than seventy-five Singapore clubs and business associations the world over; SIF works with them. The aim is to strengthen Singaporean identity through social and cultural interaction, conferences and dialogues. The second generation of emigrants is invited to Singapore for a summer camp to discover cultural roots. In this way, contributions of Singaporeans everywhere can be harnessed.

People and relationship factors are important in the aftermath of the "Asian contagion." They provide essential ballast as Singapore seeks to establish its place in the global economy. Despite being a small, vulnerable nation, Singapore maintains a sound reputation, international links, and goodwill that will keep it securely anchored as periodic waves of uncertainty sweep the world.

Globalization in Asia

Ricardo Saludo

At the start of the third millennium, the prospect seems irresistible that globalization will take hold and transform Asia in the decades ahead. This is despite still-formidable conservative forces opposing the political, economic, social, and technological tsunamis wrenching the region open and driving revolutionary change.

How this prospect may become paradigmatic is the subject of this chapter: What major trends are bringing the ways of the world to Asia, and how will the region respond? This continental drama will undoubtedly be a disruptive, often chaotic and sometimes violent struggle, as more than three billion people seek to understand, tame and ultimately harness the forces of globalization. And in this clash of past, present and potential futures, the year 2001 could go down in history as the turning point when the region decisively opened its gates to the world.

Certain seminal developments look set to elevate this year to the status of historic strides in globalization's march. Foremost is China's entry into the World Trade Organization (WTO), which is expected in 2001, after fourteen years of negotiations with leading world trading powers, and the nation's even more intense internal struggle to commit itself to new social and economic reforms. These reforms are far more dramatic—and fraught with danger—than anything attempted since the late paramount leader Deng Xiaoping launched his Open Door policy in December 1978.

Past liberalization efforts have in large part allowed new businesses to flourish, but without greatly threatening the state-owned enterprises (SOEs) dominating the economy and providing most jobs. However, the latest reforms initiated by Premier Zhu Rongji in 1998—and given added impetus by the agreed market concessions for WTO entry, aim to force Chinese companies, including SOEs, to boost efficiency and compete against foreign rivals. Those that cannot are supposed to be taken over or go bust. Meanwhile, government banks have to reduce policy-oriented loans—a key source of state-enterprise funding—in favor of commercial ones. To cut costs, SOEs are jettisoning social services long provided to employees and surrounding areas, including whole cities. All this threatens to stir up unrest and undermine the Communist Party's grip on power, which is why many are concerned that Beijing might backtrack. But if China is able to stay the course with respect to this most difficult element of liberalization, then the future of reform and the "open door" will probably be assured.

A similar make-or-break moment faces reform in countries hit by the 1997–98 Asian Economic Crisis, as well as in Japan, which has been in a slump for a decade. Incipient recovery in these nations could remove the impetus for change. Consider ruling parties and politicians: Japan's Liberal Democratic Party, Hong Kong Chief Executive Tung Chee-hwa, the Barisan Nasional coalition in Malaysia, and President Abdurrahman Wahid of Indonesia. All are unable or unwilling to speed up reform or are actually blocking or reversing it. If the region slips back into the bad old ways, a new crisis may erupt, one that will almost surely be worse than the previous one. While such a disaster could spur reform, it could just as well force countries to erect defensive barriers against disruptive global trade and money flows.

The good news is that more and more Asians are encountering, embracing, even espousing global ideas, ideals, and information. Besides trade, travel and overseas education, the expansion of international media and the Internet across the region has been the main force behind the influx of foreign news, know-how, entertainment, and culture.

In the 2000s, global media and the Internet are further stretching their reach in Asia, fueled by economic recovery, the quest for new markets and the desire by governments, businesses, communities, and people to plug into the world's pool of information and technology.

Thus, India is providing farmers with Internet access so they can, among other functions, check grain prices to bargain better with middlemen. South

Korea aims to put a web-linked computer in every classroom and household; Singapore is getting close to that goal. Global media and Internet giants are eager to be among the first to bring cable, satellite, and Internet access to Asia's homes and offices—largely unwired now but expected to match America in the number of Internet users in five to seven years, especially if web-linked cellular phones take off. The upshot: it will get harder and harder to restrict access to global information and culture. As more of the world reaches the region's eyes and ears from this year on, it will increasingly influence how Asians live, think and feel.

What are the most powerful trends that will drive globalization in the region? Asia's economic miracle (and it *was* a miracle, not because it couldn't be explained, but because it was phenomenally fast) was the most powerful force for change in the region during the last half-century.

In the 2000s, economic trends will also rank as the premier force for globalization. Foreign trade will continue burgeoning, since growth in crisis countries will rely primarily on exports. This is due to constraints on domestic demand for some years to come due to diminished credit and domestic investment amid the bad-debt overhang, which amounts to as much as forty percent of annual economic output. Thus, with exports crucial to major economies, Asia will have to keep trade flowing.

More than the influx of foreign products, however, it is overseas business methods and technology which are the main impact of foreign trade and investment. The need to compete with imports, raise capital from abroad and, in foreign-controlled companies, please overseas bosses and shareholders will force Asian enterprises to adopt best-practice procedures, know-how, and equipment. For instance, Chinese SOEs listing in New York and Hong Kong are having to use international accounting standards demanded by regulators and investors.

In the wake of the crisis, overseas companies have taken over dozens of Asian banks and enterprises, bringing their management into these businesses. The restructured acquisitions in turn put pressure on other firms in their sectors to improve competitiveness, often by also adopting techniques and strategies from abroad. Thus, businesses adopting world-class techniques and technology will be rewarded not just with more sales, but also with cheaper capital—enabling them to squeeze or buy out unreformed rivals.

Needless to say, there is and will continue to be strong resistance to globalization in business, from non-competitive enterprises as well as workers either threatened with retrenchment or unable to adopt world-class methods and disciplines. Such resistance can be formidable, especially where there are limited social safety nets to cushion the pain of restructuring. Indeed, even an autocracy like China has to temper its reform drive, pulling back when restiveness among SOE bosses and workers threatens to boil over. A further drag on reform is the sheer lack of managers, accountants, technicians, and other experts with the training and attitude to implement global standards.

Could such obstacles block or reverse globalization in business? Not forever. For the time being, some Asian countries can thumb their noses at the world, especially those with high savings rates, like Japan and Malaysia, which are able to generate most of their capital needs. But Asian savers are now seeking better returns, buying foreign stocks if necessary. In the coming years, for instance, the Japanese will be looking for more lucrative ways of investing some US$1 trillion kept for many years in the postal savings system. Domestic firms will need to look as good as the best enterprises in the world if they want a piece of that pie.

Democracy's march across Asia is another strong globalizing, and globalization, trend. For one thing, freedom lets in overseas media shut out or restricted by past authoritarian regimes. More important, democracy increases public pressure to reduce corruption and cronyism, promote the rule of law, protect human rights and expand citizens' participation in government. That often means adapting laws, structures and processes from countries, mostly in the West, with much longer experience in democracy. In addition, increased political activity often leads to links between local groups and foreign ones with similar aims, like workers' rights, gender equality or environmental conservation. Amnesty International and Friends of the Earth have many Asian chapters.

So will Asian democracies follow the Western norm? There will be substantial differences. Political systems, especially democratic ones, mirror the societies that give rise to them. Asia's social conditions will shape its democracies, and two overriding characteristics will make Asian democracy different from the Western variety. One is widespread poverty, which afflicts a billion Asians—one in three. The other is the great proportion of people living in the countryside in most of the region, including the three most populous nations, China, India, and Indonesia. Poor, far-flung populations have limited access to information, are easy prey to domination by local bosses, and feel distant from the centers of national power.

One result: Asian democracy is marked by a division between the reform and issue-oriented politics of affluent, educated, modernizing city folk and the feudal ways of a largely poor, tradition-bound peasantry. The latter have yet to cast off the politics of patronage under which they submit to petty chieftains for a job, a road, a dole, something. Hence, for several years to come, democratic politics in Asia outside highly urbanized Japan, South Korea, Hong Kong, and Singapore will be a struggle between a reform-minded urban middle class and the long-entrenched elite still able to milk the rural masses for votes.

Who will win this contest? It may well be decided by non-political factors. The spread of information technology could raise political awareness in the countryside. Economic liberalization could lessen the peasants' dependence on local officials, though if the costs of reform are inordinately imposed on the poor, they will oppose it.

This battle for democracy, along with the drive for economic reform, is part of a broader struggle over what has been confusingly called "Asian values." I say "confusingly" because the term *Asian values* has narrowly focused on Confucian ethics, and because Asian values have somehow been assumed to be immutable. Asians from Arabia to Japan do share common values, but Confucianism is just one manifestation of them. Also seen in Middle Eastern, Indian, and Southeast Asian cultures, the region's basic mores can be summed up in three words: fate, face, and family.

Fate refers to the world view that sees a higher entity—God, society, nation, clan, even one's corporation—on which the person depends and which he or she must serve. It is notable that all the four largest faiths—Buddhism, Christianity, Hinduism, and Islam—originated in Asia. Face is the great importance Asians attach to how other people regard them, the face society gives them. And the demands of both fate and face are in large part satisfied by striving for the good name and well-being of one's family through generations. These values contrast with Western rationalism and individualism, which puts what a person wants and thinks above all.

Globalization is challenging fate, face, family and what Asians would consider upright. The drive for profitability and shareholder value, even to the point of retrenching loyal employees, goes against the paternalistic Asian enterprise, which embodies the fate value. Singapore leader Lee Kuan Yew has said that Western-style freedoms violate the Asian tenet of putting society above the individual. But autocracy also goes against the same rule if a despot's self-interest is served at the community's expense. Clearly, there is need for Asian-style democracy and business policy that puts the common good above all. On the level of personal ethics, the hedonism in much foreign entertainment media undermines devotion to God or other spiritual ideals, as well as the family's central role.

In the face of globalization, what will the region do? One thing is certain: economies that depend on foreign trade and investment for growth must stay open to the world. Hence, their enterprises will need to adopt the most competitive methods and technology—or die. But democracy will enable opponents of globalization to mount intense protests. These would attract widespread support if governments and businesses fail to alleviate the adverse impact of liberalization on the masses. Given the already strained public finances of crisis-hit countries after shoring up their banking systems, social safety nets will almost surely be inadequate. So, many governments will probably have to slow down and occasionally reverse reform in the coming years to keep unrest manageable.

Staunching the influx of foreign mores and media will be equally difficult for nations aiming to have the latest know-how and technology. Hence, there will be increasing conflicts between Asians who live by traditional ways and beliefs, and those who embrace global culture. In particular, womens, gay, and lesbian groups will increasingly fight for their lifestyles, with support from abroad. The youth, too, will be more assertive, with the help of industries targeting products at them. Many traditionalists, meanwhile, will intensify religious fervor, from Hindu rightists in India and Christian so-called charismatics in the Philippines, to militant Islamists in South and Southeast Asia. Many devotees will turn to violence in their opposition to foreign culture, as in Indonesia.

How can Asia and the world better manage globalization to maximize its benefits and minimize its pains and conflicts? Three words: respect, compromise, and compassion. A sure way to increase discord is for interfacing cultures to regard each other with contempt—as colonizers did the native communities they "discovered." Today, people should know better and treat other ways, beliefs, and traditions with respect, which is the first step toward dialogue and understanding. Compromise then becomes possible, where cultures learn to give one another enough space to flourish in harmony. Japan is likely to face the biggest test of its spirit of respect and compromise toward other cultures; for economic reasons, it will probably have to allow huge armies of foreign workers into the country, after centuries of ethnic homogeneity.

Inevitably, and despite efforts to accommodate different cultures and communities, there will be losers in the globalization process. Companies will go bust; tiny cultures will die out; outdated ways and ideas will disappear. Compassion for groups that suffer pain and decline, and substantial efforts to address their woes, are crucial to reducing opposition to globalization and smoothing its advance. Otherwise, people who see no relief or gains for themselves in globalization may be tempted to strike at it. There will also need to be greater attention to reducing and repairing the ecological damage wrought by progress.

In addition, compassion demands understanding of the difficulties and delays that accompany reform efforts in many countries. Giants like China, India, and Indonesia, in particular, burdened with decades if not centuries of entrenched habits and traditions, will never be able to change fast enough. But the pace of reform is not the most important thing; rather, it is the overall forward direction. And if Asia has learned anything from its three-decade economic miracle and its three-year crisis, it is the value of endless exchanges with the world—for trade, technology, learning, interaction, and cooperation. Ultimately, this is the reason Asia will accept, if not embrace, globalization.

Part II

Changes in Business

The Rise and Pause of Multinational Corporations in Asia

Franklin L. Lavin

When thinking about multinational corporations (MNCs) in Asia, consider the following snapshots . . .

- A senior executive from a U.S. fast-food franchise explains that from a business point-of-view, the company was better off when some of their Indonesian stores were burnt down: "We weren't making any money from those stores in a particular Southeast Asian country and there was no graceful way we could close them down."
- A multinational corporation selling industrial goods to a large state-owned company in a different country chafes at a requirement that they use a local middleman to sell their goods: "This is not an opportunity for corruption. This is mandated corruption."
- One of the largest glass manufacturers in the world quits the China glass market, writing off a multi-million dollar investment because their local joint-venture partner went into competition against them.
- Japan is the second largest economy in the world but has created virtually no global brands in fifty years. Some experts point to cumbersome capital markets in Japan as to why there are no Japanese start-ups such as FedEx or Apple Computer.

- A Dutch pharmaceutical company has a US$100,000 order unpaid from a state-owned company in China. "We can't sue. And we can't stop selling to this client," complains the general manager.
- A large beverage producer looks at Vietnam: "We sell about a can of soda a day per person in the United States and two a year per person in Vietnam. Talk about potential."

Despite all of the hardships, complaints, and setbacks, still they come. What are the MNCs trying to do in Asia? How should they behave? Who benefits from their presence? And as we examine these questions, we must bear in mind that although the European, the Japanese, and other MNCs have a broad presence in Asia, it is the U.S. MNCs that have the largest profile.

MNCs have operated in Asia for about as long as the West has been active in the region, for many of the original explorers and traders operated through some of the most famous MNCs in history—the Dutch East Indies Company and the British East Indies Company. But the MNCs that we see today in the region bare little resemblance to these seventeenth-century forebears.

The pattern for the modern MNC began to emerge in the post–World War II prosperity. In this model, Asia's attraction was that large-scale companies could save by shifting production to Asia and taking advantage of lower labor costs. This was the pattern of MNC activity in the region in the 1950s and 1960s, with most MNCs investing in Japan, which was then recovering from the war.

But as many of the countries of East Asia began to move toward middle-income status in the 1970s and 1980s, the MNCs became increasingly serious about marketing to the East Asian consumer. No longer was the region simply a source of cheap labor, but it was a market as well.

This pattern of Asia serving as both a production platform and a destination for completed goods repeated itself through the 1980s and 1990s. On the production end, companies began to locate in Asia the higher value-added aspects of their work, such as assembly, logistics, management, and finance. Asia's increasing affluence led manufacturers to customize products specifically for the Asian markets, eventually localizing research and development and even producing original products exclusively for the Asian markets.

Some products lent themselves more than others to this evolution. Many household products such as laundry detergent simply had to be packaged with local language instructions. Manufacturers also recognized that local consumers were typically less affluent and frequently would be satisfied with middle-range brands. Subsequently, they saw that local consumers usually had less storage space and less disposable income and that they tended to shop more frequently, so smaller packages (even single-use packages) were appealing.

By the 1990s this type of customization was quite sophisticated, with Disney releasing its movie *Mulan* in three separate Chinese-language versions, one each for the Hong Kong, the Taiwan, and the Mainland markets, each using the voices of local stars and celebrities to give the product better reach.

So as Asia grew in prosperity, talent, and purchasing power, the MNCs responded in kind, serving both as an engine for growth and as the beneficiary of growth. Or, to use the nomenclature of business schools, the Asian economies were part of the global supply chain and the global demand chain for the MNCs.

This model, with various permutations, was the dominant one for much of the post-war era. During this period, the 1980s stood out as the shining decade, enjoying the calm of the post–Vietnam War period, the opening of China and the economic take-offs of Korea and Taiwan.

The case could be made that the end of the 1980s was a sort of end of history. The debate was over. The Western model of market economics, combined with a democratic political system, was triumphant. No other model offered the equivalent basket of material prosperity combined with political freedom.

The only question for MNCs was: How fast? The rest of the world would slowly but surely rise to OECD levels of income, and purchasing patterns would converge to Western levels as well. Given that market development would take time, that mistakes would be made, and that investments would be required, how much money did the parent company want to invest in these markets?

And the MNCs knew that as the global supply and demand chains fully matured, decisions would have to be made as to what goods should be produced in China, sourced from Korea, assembled in Malaysia, financed through Hong Kong, and shipped through Singapore. It was a bit difficult to see just where in the end we all were going, but the direction was unmistakable. Asia was going to get bigger, better, faster, and wealthier. And one's competition was looking at the same picture as oneself.

As a result, companies tended to err on the side of optimism. Better get into China *now*—or Vietnam, or Indonesia—and establish market position. Thus by the early to mid-1990s there was an investment bubble as well as a somewhat infectious Asian-optimism.

Then the bubble burst. Not only was there the catastrophic currency collapse and the resultant economic turmoil afflicting Asia in 1997–98, but other developments occurred. There were at least four factors that conspired to challenge the model favored in previous decades: the opening of the rest of the world (ROW), the surge in the U.S. economy, the technology shift, and local political inefficiencies.

The Opening of the ROW

The newest challenge MNCs face when considering Asia is the one of geographical competition. Eastern Europe, India, Latin America, South Africa, and Russia have all gone through political transformations or evolutions over the past decade. MNCs now have many new markets from which to choose. So the type of argument normally heard relative to an investment in China or Indonesia—there are so many millions of us so you had better come here—loses a bit of its strength when the company can also look at Brazil, India, Russia, and dozens of other countries. This change is heightened by NAFTA and other trade initiatives that push American MNCs toward Mexico and other Latin America countries.

Companies have limited budgets for expansion, and East Asia now has to compete with many other countries. Smart business practices demand that the MNCs allocate investment and attention in a somewhat even-handed fashion. The MNCs will now exhibit greater selectivity as they consider Asian projects, with a particularly careful eye on return. Also of note is the fact that the proliferation of emerging markets means Asia will not continue to command the same type of respect from the head office as it has in the past.

U.S. Economic Boom

The second challenge MNCs face when looking at Asia is that of opportunity costs. Here is a simple test: Assume two companies, each identical in size, products, management strength, and so on. The first company invests in China to develop its market there. The second company foregoes China and instead uses its money simply to repurchase its own stock. Which company would be better off today? In other words, would a company's China operations perform better or worse than the company's overall average performance?

For virtually every American multinational, the answer would be to stay out of China and buy back the stock. Use the additional profits to go into Asia in the twenty-first century. Better yet, buy up a competitor who went into Asia in 1990 and as a result has a lagging stock price.

Not a fair question, one might counter. China is one of the most difficult markets in the world. It takes a while to develop, so one cannot expect all countries to perform the same way. This is a fair point, but just a polite way of noting that an investment in China flunks the test.

If the objective is not high returns but some sort of strategic advantage, then companies should try to accomplish their strategic goals as cheaply as possible. This means a minimalist foot-in-the-door entrance strategy in which the MNC simply tries to keep options open with minimal expenses—another polite way of saying China flunks the test.

Others will say they have no choice; chief among these will be network service providers, companies such as airlines and banks, whose clients demand that they be in each market. In other words, a bank or an airline might have unimpressive profits—or even losses—in China, but if it forgoes that market, it might put at risk some profitable U.S. business.

The relentless growth in the U.S. economy underscores the weaknesses of the Asian economies. In the fourth quarter of 1999, U.S. GDP grew at about seven percent. This means that the over nine trillion–dollar U.S. economy grows by an entire China about every fourteen months, by a Thailand every month. Why spend a year or two planning a entrance strategy into China when a company can capture essentially the same revenue by staying in the United States?

The answer, of course, is that at some point the China market will be wealthy enough to justify the effort. Which is a polite way of saying it is not at that point today. Only when the current U.S. economic expansion begins to cool a bit will the Asia market regain some of its former attraction.

Technology Shift

The third challenge MNCs face when considering Asia is the increasingly important role of the technology sector. The central shift in the United States from labor- and capital-intensive production to technology-intensive production makes Asia all the more unimportant. It turns out that the Silicon

Valley of Asia is . . . Silicon Valley. Technology innovation works better if it is concentrated in one R&D location. It is simply easier, faster, and cheaper to put a tech facility in the U.S. than anyplace else in the world. Yes, there will be innovation in Singapore, Hong Kong, Taiwan, Cyberjaya, and Mumbai, but all of these are fated to be secondary locations.

The technology shift works against Asia more broadly as the importance of the developed markets increases. Sales of soft drinks and toothpaste might largely correlate with per-capita GDP, but sales of software and computers will be substantially overweighted to the developed countries.

In an economic sense, the performance of poorer nations should be measured in absolute terms: Do kids in India have enough to eat? Do students in Indonesia have access to schools? Do families in the Philippines have access to clean water?

But in a technological sense, the performance of poorer countries must be measured *relative* to the developed nations. What percent of the students have access to a computer, as compared to the United States? What percent of the businesses use resource-planning software as compared to the United States? Complex inventory-planning software is helpful only with the existence of complex inventory. High-end switching equipment only matters if you have high-end communication needs. The increasing importance of technology suggests that some Asian countries are barely staying even in their position regarding the United States, even as they move to middle-income status economically.

Political Inefficiencies

Although the trend toward economic rationalization and political openness continues, the process is slow and uneven, and it sometimes slips backwards. After the fall of the Berlin Wall, state-directed economic planning appeared intellectually dead. But politically, the planning model remains very much alive and has enduring appeal to government elites, appeal that matches the model's enduring record of failure.

Asia has indeed witnessed political openness and reform, most notably in Korea and Taiwan, both of which countries moved twenty years ago from authoritarian martial law to multiparty elections and open media. But other places have not moved much at all. And in most markets the pace of reform has not kept pace with the expectations of U.S. MNCs. The challenge of building an open society is one that will move only slowly toward resolution, and this gap is one that MNCs will find increasingly burdensome in a business environment where information flow is a requisite for success.

Conclusion

After the glory days of the 1980s and the collapse of the Asian bubble in the 1990s, what does the future hold for MNCs?

First, there is a strong and growing consensus that MNCs are part of the solution, not part of the problem. MNCs create better paying jobs than local firms. They help integrate the economy into broader trade and production flows. They transfer technology and train middle management. Yes, some might be guilty at times of ill-advised corporate practices on environmental and labor issues. But in general the MNCs are as likely as the local corporations to play by the rules, probably even more so.

In fact, the voices that disagree the loudest with the assertion that MNCs are beneficent come almost entirely from the alienated left in the industrialized democracies. The poorest countries in the world today are those that have no MNC presence. The world's most rapidly growing economies, such as those of Singapore and Hong Kong, are those that have successfully attracted MNCs.

For Asia, the MNCs provide incentives for countries to run a good shop: by mitigating corruption; promoting political stability, openness, and accountability; and minimizing barriers to flows of goods, labor, and finance. For the MNCs, overseas expansion can mean better performance and better returns to shareholders.

A mature, sober relationship is based on these fundamentals.

Countries such as Vietnam that remain indifferent to these characteristics will find the world passing them by. Economies that take these points seriously, as Taiwan does, will increasingly be rewarded and will emerge as technology hubs, with better standards of living and more competitive economies.

We will see a high degree of customization and segmentation. An MNC that has fifteen different strategic business units might operate eleven of them in Hong Kong but only four of them in China. And it might place its back-office processing for all of them in India. As local business environments improve or deteriorate, businesses will adjust more closely among the countries in which they operate. So an Asian government will increase economic inefficiencies at its peril.

It is no coincidence that the polities that have been the most tolerant and welcoming of MNCs—Taiwan, Singapore, and Hong Kong—have been those that have flourished. The ones that have been the most ambivalent—India, Indonesia, and Vietnam—have not done as well.

It would be unfair to conclude that the MNCs necessarily caused this uneven prosperity: it also reflects that governments that are open, tolerant, and given to rational economic policies will be those that welcome MNCs. Thus MNC presence in part contributes to the prosperity and in part is simply a coincident indicator. But whether one views MNCs as important elements of economic progress in Asia, or more as the canary in the coal mine, whose continued well-being assures us that the environment is conducive to progress, MNCs are a key part of the Asian economic story.

Productivity Growth and the Prospects for Asian Global Dominance

A. Gary Shilling

Productivity growth has always been the key to an economy's strength and is reflected in the global bottom-line opinion poll, the currency's value.

In the 1700s, worldwide trading was the hot new technology and the Dutch were the best at it. The guilder was the most desirable currency, but it faded in favor of the sterling late in the century as the Industrial Revolution got underway in England. As the first major country to industrialize, Great Britain enjoyed preeminent productivity growth for a century, but like the Dutch earlier, the British got too comfortable with success and let their leadership slip away to two upstarts, America and Germany, in the late 1800s. With Germany devastated by two disastrous wars, the United States led productivity growth in the twentieth century, and the dollar's strength reflected that growth.

Asian Takeover?

America did not look like the top dog in the 1980s and much of the 1990s, however, as imports nearly wiped out U.S. manufacturing, and the fruits of economic restructuring were yet to be harvested. In the 1980s, Japan dazzled the world with her mushrooming production and exports. Armed with huge export earnings and legendary domestic saving, the Japanese bought so many U.S. trophies such as Pebble Beach, Rockefeller Center, and Iowa farm land that many Americans thought they would soon be put out of business by the Japanese or working for them.

Japan faded in the early 1990s, but the four original Asian Tigers—Taiwan, South Korea, Singapore, and Hong Kong—and the new Tigers—Malaysia, Indonesia, the Philippines, and Thailand as well as China—became the focus of global attention. Their low costs, strong work ethic, and family values attracted a flood of foreign investment money.

The productivity growth in all of these Asian lands looked impressive. Productivity, however, is not like pornography as described by former Supreme Court Justice Potter Stewart: It is hard to define, but you know it when you see it. Correctly defined, productivity is "physical output per unit of inputs," but management, capital, and other important inputs are so hard to quantify that most observers settle for "output per hour worked," with labor inputs only. It is also true that you do not always know genuine productivity—or the lack of it—when you see it. In the case of Asia, few, except Paul Krugman of the Massachusetts Institute of Technology, realized at the time that Asians were simply putting more people, more machines, and more capital to work without creating the technological innovation that is the true measure of meaningful productivity growth. This became clear when Asian economies came unglued.

Asia's growth in the 1980s and 1990s was led by exports, much of which went directly or indirectly to the United States, as has been the case since the revival of Japan's economy after World War II. Japan's postwar success with this strategy culminated in the late 1980s bubble economy, which saw cheap bank loans and the huge pool of consumer saving (chart 1) dissipated in real estate and stock market speculation that was destined for collapse.

Early in 1988, when the bubble economy was still expanding, I wrote a book that compared the 1980s economy in Japan with the Roaring Twenties in the United States. In that book I predicted that the 1990s in Japan would resemble the 1930s depression in America, but suggested, for two reasons, that it might take even more time for Japan to revive than America had required. First, World War II spending ultimately pulled the United States out of its economic and financial morass, and there was nothing on the horizon to similarly revive Japan within ten years.

Chart 1

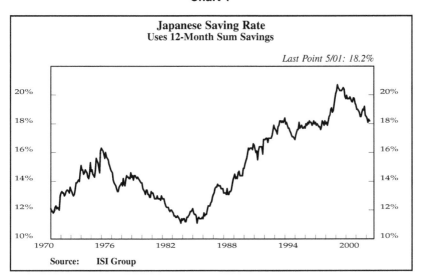

Japanese Saving Rate
Uses 12-Month Sum Savings

Last Point 5/01: 18.2%

Source: ISI Group

Second, I saw the Japanese as being much slower to make decisions, thus delaying dealing with financial and other problems.

A Decade Later

Sadly, this forecast proved true. Unresolved troubles have kept Japanese consumer spending depressed as has the decline in retail prices, which encourages waiting for still-lower prices before buying. Many years after the fact, failed department store chains and insurance companies have been allowed to go out of business—and now only because of public protests over the expenditure of more bail-out money. Gigantic fiscal stimulus has made Japan the world's biggest government debtor, but most of the money has been squandered on projects like paving rural river beds.

Banks are writing off their bad real estate and other loans very slowly, in part because of continually weak stock prices (chart 2). Due to earlier links to corporate customers via share holdings, Japanese banks have about 150 percent of their core capital in stocks, three times the international bank norm. Selling those long-held equities at a profit offsets loan losses, but soft Japanese stock prices have eliminated most of those paper gains. Nevertheless, something has to give as banks must now price their stocks and other assets at market value, not cost.

Chart 2

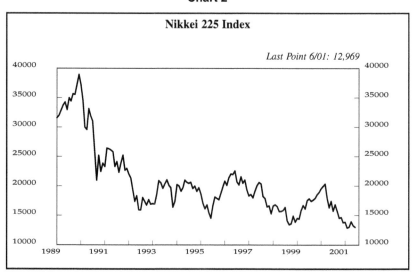

Nikkei 225 Index

Last Point 6/01: 12,969

The ongoing deflationary depression has two important implications outside Japan. First, with consumer spending continuing to be depressed and with government debt at levels that discourage further big fiscal stimuli, Japan is resorting to growth the old-fashioned way, at least the old-fashioned way for Japan exports. In this regard, Japan's economic planners want a weaker yen to make her goods cheaper abroad. Second, Japan has provided almost no help via imports to revive the rest of Asia.

Resource Misallocation

As noted earlier, investors rushed to the new and old Asian Tigers after Japan's sun set in the early 1990s. They were, however, so enamored with growth prospects that they demanded almost no accountability, business plans, or explanation as to how their money would be spent, as discussed in my recent book, *Deflation* (1999). So, in countries like Indonesia, Malaysia, Thailand, and the Philippines, where power was extremely concentrated and crony capitalism prevailed, much of this money went into excess-capacity showcase buildings, and uneconomic projects, in addition to the usual graft and corruption. Much the same occurred in South

Korea, where *chaebols* sported debt-equity ratios about ten times the U.S. norm. In Hong Kong, real estate speculation thrived as Tiger-boom-inspired demand met supply that was limited by government policy.

Falling Tiger currencies in 1996 and early 1997 foretold trouble, but few understood the vast misallocation of resources until Thailand stopped supporting the baht on July 2, 1997, initiating a domino-like collapse of neighboring financial markets and economies. Some recovery in a number of those countries occurred in 1999 and 2000, but largely due to the soaring U.S. economy and the resulting demand for Asian exports. Note, for example, that the Chinese economy grew 8 percent annually in the third quarter of 2000, but exports leaped by one-third.

Serious Reform?

More important, Asian recovery has cut short many seriously needed business and financial reforms. Indonesia remains a political and economic basket case. The *chaebols* have successfully resisted many of the South Korean government's attempts to reduce their industrial reach and huge debt levels. Thai banks are still in considerable trouble, and no significant restructuring is taking place. The Philippines is immersed in corruption that reaches even to the former president.

This resistance to change is not very surprising. After all, most of those countries are semi-dictatorships, or at least have huge concentrations of power. If the people on top really wanted reforms, they would have introduced them years ago. Obviously, they do not, so now that the IMF's austerity approach is discredited and global lenders have reduced their oversight, it is back to business as usual. A wonderful example of the ground rules in Asian finance was the recent public pledge by large Chinese securities brokerage houses, in an attempt to rebuild confidence, not to steal their customers' capital. Previously, the norm was the reverse.

The Acid Test

Despite substantial setbacks in Japan since the early 1990s and in the rest of Asia more recently, many still believe that their problems are history and that an Asian-dominated century lies ahead. They see Asia eclipsing the United States because of its strong work ethic, family values, perceived moral standards, and high rate of saving. Their faith, however, may be severely tested by the next American recession.

As noted earlier, most Asian exports end up in the United States one way or other. The American merchandise trade deficit of over $450 billion (chart 3) means that the United States is buying over $450 billion of the world's surplus goods—goods that in the ongoing world of surpluses have virtually no other market. Notice that Japan and most Asian lands enjoy large export surpluses—huge in relation to their economies' sizes. Obviously, these economies will be in big trouble if U.S. imports fall off, but this is what is happening as a result of the ongoing American recession.

In business downturns, consumers facing unemployment and weak incomes cut down on all spending, especially on imports. This is particularly true now since the recession is intertwined with a major bear market in U.S. stocks. Stock appreciation in recent years has been so consistently robust that consumers have relied on it in lieu of saving out of wages and other current income to finance education for their children, future retirement, and other commitments. Consequently, the individual saving rate has been driven to below zero (chart 4).

The disappearance of much of that stock appreciation in the bear market will, of course, evoke wrenching reappraisals and considerable consumer retrenchment; and that retrenchment will probably continue beyond the recession and reverse the twenty-year decline in the saving rate. Stock-appreciation gains in recent years have masked many reasons for Americans to save. Debt levels are astronomically high in relation to income. The postwar babies need to save for retirement and can do so now that their children have left home and have taken their college tuitions and other expenses with them. Doubts about ever receiving Social Security benefits, especially among young Americans, should spur saving. Income shares continue to move into the high-income hands of the traditional big savers. And home equity has been largely exhausted by many Americans through loans and, therefore, is no longer available for emergencies and retirement income.

A long-term climb in the U.S. individual saving rate will be significant for the United States—and for the rest of the world— as it curtails American consumer-spending growth. Bear in mind that U.S. consumers buy more than twenty percent of all the goods and services produced in the world.

The Enigma—China

Japan may be the whale in Asia—for now, a beached whale—but China is the 500–pound gorilla, an animal with health problems that could

Chart 3

Merchandise Trade Balance			
	Trade Balance Latest 12 Months ($ billion)		Trade Balance Latest 12 Months ($ billion)
Australia	−1.4	China	19.9
Austria	−5.6	Hong Kong	−11.9
Belgium	12.1	India	−5.4
Britain	−44.0	Indonesia	25.7
Canada	48.2	Malaysia	15.7
Denmark	6.7	Philippines	6.1
France	−0.2	Singapore	7.7
Germany	57.4	South Korea	14.3
Italy	3.3	Taiwan	12.2
Japan	95.6	Thailand	2.8
Netherlands	17.3		
Spain	−38.2	Turkey	−24.6
Sweden	12.9	Czech Republic	−3.4
Switzerland	0.1	Hungary	−2.4
		Poland	−10.2
United States	−455.5	Russia	59.7
Euro-11	−6.8		
		Egypt	−10.4
Argentina	1.7	Israel	−7.4
Brazil	−1.6	South Africa	3.8
Chile	1.7		
Colombia	1.6		
Mexico	−9.5		
Venezuela	17.2		

Source: *The Economist* (July 28, 2001)

exacerbate the Asian difficulties initiated by U.S. consumer retrenchment. In China's coastal areas 200 million people are productively em-
ployed, one billion in the hinterland would like to be, and 100 million
more are squatting in coastal cities looking for work. State-controlled
banks are technically broke because of bad loans to inefficient government businesses that employ about 100 million. It is difficult to restruc-
ture those businesses or banks and write off the loans, however, since
that would cause 30 million to join the ranks of the unemployed.

China now depends on government spending and exports for growth
as consumer spending remains moribund and mired in deflation, much
like that in Japan. Obviously, a U.S. consumer retrenchment will erode
China's huge net exports to America, which rival Japan's. So, too, will
her entry into the World Trade Organization. Adhering to WTO rules

Chart 4

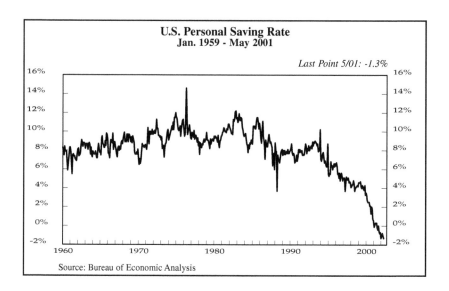

U.S. Personal Saving Rate
Jan. 1959 - May 2001

Last Point 5/01: -1.3%

Source: Bureau of Economic Analysis

will not change Chinese exports appreciably. She already can export to the United States and other major markets relatively freely. She will, however, be required to be much more open to imports that will compete with local, inefficient production in many cases.

To be sure, China can and probably will find all sorts of health and safety reasons to exclude many imports, much as Japan has been doing for years. Furthermore, China will probably find ways to prevent foreign ownership of local production, as required by WTO rules. Foreign capital and expertise would help modernize the country and ultimately promote growth, but the power of government officials who would lose out and the continued suspicion of foreigners, which goes back to the nineteenth-century Opium Wars and the Boxer Rebellion of 1900, will probably rule the day.

On balance, WTO entry will probably add to China's problems of unemployment, inefficient and noncompetitive state-owned production, and a retrenching American consumer. Her reaction might well be to float the now-fixed yuan and use WTO entry as a face-saving occasion. Given China's basic difficulties, the yuan would probably move down after the initial euphoria of WTO entry fades. Note that devaluation is no stranger

Chart 5

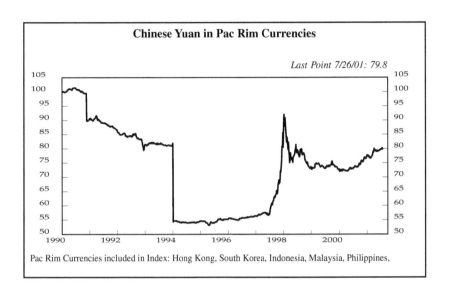

Chinese Yuan in Pac Rim Currencies

Last Point 7/26/01: 79.8

Pac Rim Currencies included in Index: Hong Kong, South Korea, Indonesia, Malaysia, Philippines,

to China, which has cut the yuan's value five times in the past fifteen years, including the seventy percent devaluation in 1994, which perhaps instigated the 1997–98 collapse in other Asian currencies (chart 5).

More Asian Devaluation

A cheaper yuan would, on balance, erode the currency advance of China's Asian competitors since 1997 (chart 5), and these lands would probably retaliate with yet another round of competitive devaluations. At a minimum, Hong Kong's long-standing link to the U.S. dollar would shatter. Furthermore, Asian currency devaluations might well spread to Latin America and elsewhere, much as they did in 1997–98—perhaps even more so, if the U.S. consumer is no longer a willing buyer of the world's excess output and, consequently, developing countries are extra hungry for export buyers. Already, many Asian currencies are falling in response to weakening exports to the United States

The Chinese, of course, are not stupid and realize that yuan devaluation could initiate a round of competitive currency cuts, leaving them back where they started. They also know that a weak yuan increases the local-currency cost of their dollar-denominated debts. They can see that in Indonesia, where the weak rupiah has made life very difficult for firms, which, like auto maker Astra, have sizable foreign-currency debts. Still, yuan devaluation seems likely. Nations that start wars know their opponents will retaliate and may even win. Yet, wars are started all of the time. Rational behavior is not always—not even often—the norm.

The Perils Of Export-Led Growth

Export-led growth has tremendous advantages. It earns the foreign exchange needed to import the equipment and technology that help a country move up the scale of production sophistication. From a basis of textiles, ceramics, and toys, Japan and other Asian lands that followed her example in the postwar era progressed to shipbuilding and manufacturing of autos, consumer electronics, and semiconductors. Still, as long as Asian countries rely on exports for growth, their economic power and independence will be limited.

To begin, since they are all export-led, they cannot grow by simply buying each other's exports. Countries outside Asia are required as net buyers of their products, and, as discussed earlier, America is by far the biggest. The impending shift of American consumers from two decades of borrowing and spending to a saving spree will reveal the negative side of Asian export growth.

Furthermore, the less sophisticated of Asian-Tiger exports to the United States will be increasingly hampered by the growing American trend toward sourcing from low-cost New World countries. NAFTA has turned Mexico into a major exporter to the United States of everything from motor vehicles to telemarketing. Free-trade agreements will probably be extended to Chile and other South American countries, giving their U.S.-bound exports the competitive edge over those from Asia.

Not only will this trend squeeze Asian tigers, but it will make them more and more dependent on Japan as an investor and as a market for their exports. Neither form of dependence is very exciting. Japan does not seem to have the will to extricate herself from her deflationary depression of the past ten years. Recall that the increase in her consumer sales tax, introduced in 1997 with disastrous consequences, is still in effect despite almost nonstop weakness in consumer spending.

Farm Teams

In terms of investments, Japan treats the Asian Tigers as farm teams. As the yen rose sixty-five percent against the dollar from 1984 to 1995, Asian-

Tiger currencies fell with the dollar. So, Japanese producers who could no longer compete in global markets moved production facilities to those low-cost developing countries. Still, this was a reaction to the strong yen, and is unlikely to be repeated unless Japan changes so radically that she becomes a technological leader with the associated perennially strong currency. In addition, that earlier experience showed that Japan was eager to produce in cheaper Asian countries but had no desire to transfer technology that would allow them to advance and compete with Japan.

Finally, except for Hong Kong and Singapore, Asian exports are predominantly old-economy goods, and these goods are becoming less important as developed countries become more service oriented and as the goods they demand contain more intellectual property and are less commodity-intensive. Asian Tigers, for example, are gearing up to become major vehicle producers and exporters, but the problems with Daewoo and Hyundai foretell the resulting problems of global excess auto capacity. The dependence of Asia Tigers on old-tech production is also shown by their heavy reliance on imported petroleum and the huge production-cost increases resulting from the 1999–2000 oil-price spike. In contrast, the United States, Europe, and Japan use about half the oil per dollar of output they used thirty years ago.

Concentration on the production of commodities for export makes many of the Asian Tigers very sensitive to costs since the low-cost producer gets the customer's order. There is always another country with even lower costs that is eager to industrialize and export. Witness how the production of commodity hand tools moved from Japan to South Korea and most recently to China and India.

To be sure, nearly two-thirds of the exports from Singapore and the Philippines and one-third to one-half from South Korea, Taiwan, and Malaysia fall in the new tech area—electronics. Nevertheless, most of these goods are low tech, even commodities. In Taiwan, for example, companies that produce semiconductors on a contract basis for foreign firms are known as "foundries" because they are stamping out DRAMs and other commodity chips.

The Importance of a Middle Class

To reduce dependence on exports, Asia needs to put much more emphasis on domestic consumer spending. This, in turn, will require a much bigger and more powerful middle class that will demand bigger slices of the pie. At present, in many Asian countries it is relatively easy to emphasize exports and capital spending to produce more exports since those at the top have almost all of the political and economic power and the rest of the populations has little.

Furthermore, the Asian middle class will need to become very strong to overcome the ingrained export mentality. South Korea is developing a middle class that is striving for a bigger share of the economy, but with only limited success so far. Japan, of course, has a vast middle class. Still, the "export or die" mentality is so strong that consumers still suffer from non-tariff barriers to imports that promote such high living costs that the average Japanese has the same income as an American, but only two-thirds the purchasing power.

Aging Populations

Asian Tigers have very young populations, but Japan and China have the opposite, and aging populations will subdue the economic strength of these two dominant Asian countries in the decades ahead. All developed countries have aging-population problems, but Japan's is the most acute, in part because of her zero immigration policy. In 1990, Japan had 5.8 people of working age for every one of retirement age, but that ratio will fall to 3.0 by the year 2030 (chart 6). In contrast, the ratio in the U.S. will fall from 5.3 in 1990 to 4.9 in 2030. Compared with other developing countries Japan will be devoting more of her economic strength to taking care of nonworking citizens in future years.

China, with far fewer resources, will have an even more difficult time. Her one-child-per-couple policy—aimed at limiting population growth—and rising life expectancy mean that in the next thirty years the number of China's retirees will increase threefold to a quarter of the total population, while the pool of working-age people shrinks. The Chinese pension system is a poorly managed pay-as-you-go scheme, and its liabilities, which will only grow, currently equal half the country's annual economic output.

The American Obstacle

One final roadblock to Asia's growth in economic power in the decades ahead is U.S. leadership in today's new-tech areas. America dominates them all—semiconductors, computers, telecommunications, the Internet, and biotech. Is it possible for Asia or any other area to overcome this commanding lead?

Historically, leadership has changed only with the next generation of

Chart 6

| The Ratio of Working-Age to Retirement-Age Populations | | | | | | |
Year	Canada	France	Germany	Italy	Japan	U.K.	U.S.
1960	7.7	5.3	6.3	7.5	10.5	5.6	6.5
1990	5.9	4.7	4.5	4.7	5.8	4.3	5.3
2010	4.7	4.1	2.8	3.9	3.4	4.5	5.3
2030	3.5	3.3	3.0	3.4	3.0	3.9	4.9
2040	2.6	2.6	2.1	2.4	2.6	3.0	3.1

Source: The Federal Reserve Bank of St. Louis; Organization for Economic Cooperation and Development

new tech, and those bursts do not occur frequently. In the United States the canals and river boats were the hot new tech of the early 1800s, but the next wave did not occur until the American Industrial Revolution and railroads dominated the last thirty years of the nineteenth century. Auto manufacturing and electrification of homes and factories became dominant next, but not until the 1920s. Then there was a gap of almost seventy years before the current new-tech industries became big enough to drive the economy.

Will Asia Dominate?

Despite all of these problems, which will impede its growth in coming years, Asia can still dominate this century if it achieves the technological innovation and resulting productivity growth that have always been the key to economic leadership. Look back at the earlier leader, Holland, a tiny country whose only natural advantages were its geographical position at the mouth of the Rhine River and its fields where tulips grow well. Another leader, England, a small island with few natural resources except coal, dominated the world for a century. In the United States, the New England region grew economically strong through early industrialization but now is known principally for picturesque towns and beautiful fall foliage.

Still, I wonder whether Asian culture, with its emphasis on group decision making, family values, and Confucian philosophy, is compatible with the independent, entrepreneurial attitude that seems necessary for technological advancement.

To be sure, Asia has enjoyed technological leadership in the past, especially in China, which was the world's most advanced country a thousand years ago. The Chinese invented paper around A.D. 105. Government service exams were established in 154 B.C. As for her other technological innovations, the compass came about A.D. 1100, gunpowder around A.D. 1000, block printing about the same time, and silk by A.D. 1300. None of these was known in Europe until much later. Chinese porcelain of unrivaled quality was discovered by Europeans in 1709, and peaches, apricots, citrus fruits, chrysanthemums, goldfish, wallpaper, the folding umbrella, and the crossbow all came from China.

With this huge technological lead over the rest of the world, why did the Industrial Revolution start in the West, and China then sink to third-world status? In part this happened because Chinese thinkers spent their time developing techniques for controlling people's minds while the West concentrated on controlling matter. Furthermore, the earlier huge success of China and her high living standards made her highly resistant to change.

The Success of the Songs

More specifically, during the Song dynasty (960–1279), great technological, cultural, and economic levels were achieved. Food supplies—thanks to the importation of a fast-growing Vietnamese species of rice and better cultivation techniques—were so ample that no further agricultural improvements were thought necessary. Society and the economy became static, and the large civil service, which absorbed many of the best minds, rigidly promoted the status quo.

This attitude persisted centuries later. During the Ming dynasty (1368–1644), Chinese sailors traveled the China Seas and the Indian Ocean and ventured as far as the east coast of Africa. But their travels stopped suddenly in 1433, in part because of resistance from the government bureaucracy that favored the revival of a strict agrarian-centered society. They decided that the Chinese had achieved the world's best civilization, so foreign influences were neither needed nor welcome. In fact, the Chinese had never respected other governments as equals and regarded all foreign envoys merely as bearers of tribute. Little did those bureaucrats know that their negative attitude toward progress would leave them so far behind when the Industrial Revolution occurred that European powers would easily take over and split up China in the mid-nineteenth century to obtain markets for their factories' output and raw materials to produce them.

In any event, it is not past glories but productivity growth, inspired by technological leadership, that propels global economic leadership. Overcoming short-run problems and then achieving that leadership remains the challenge for Asia in the twenty-first century.

Riding the Wave: Japanese Corporations in the Twenty-first Century

Takashi Chiba

Should present difficulties cause the Japanese business model—once heralded and revered across the world—to change? Is the eleven-year protracted recession a sign that corporate institutions must undergo a needed transformation? Are Tokyo-and Osaka- based corporations likely to respond to changes such as globalization?

To answer these questions, I must first recall my student days at Hitotsubashi University in Tokyo. In one class, Professor Zenya Takashima observed that there is a difference between natural science and social science. In the former, theory can effectively be tested, and in the latter this is not so. The historical background and cultural legacy of different groups are deeply rooted and play a role in a group's (or a country's) perceptions of business. They determine hierarchies and relationships.

However, in the social sciences, theories cannot be tested. We only see their results.

Decades later, I see how corporate structure and economic performance are linked to culture and history. Social organization and national outlook are shaped by unique circumstances. Japan—insular, island-based, homogeneous, resource-poor—has a unique national vision, business ethic, and social contract (between companies, society, and individuals).

All this has led to the country's conservative approach, creating structures of business organizations accordingly. The same factors existed
during the Meiji Restoration and have continued to the present. They
determined the rise of, and the continued success behind, "Japan, Inc."
during the postwar era. Western-based corporations felt nervous, paying much attention to the "Made in Japan" management then threatening Western domination of world markets.

The nation emerged as the world's export titan, with companies such
as Hitachi capturing the mantle of high tech's commanding heights. Then
came the burst of Japan's "bubble" economy in 1989–90, followed by
the East and Southeast Asian economic and financial crisis. Now many
observers, most of them Western, proclaim Japanese management must
change significantly in order for recovery to occur.

Such pronouncements are based on the West's prevailing view that
there is a universal standard, an ideal corporate structure for all people
in different countries, and in all situations.

The one constant factor in this newly changed economic equation is
that a distinct set of conditions—all rooted in culture and history—has
guided the structure of business. And those unique conditions are in-
stilled in the country's psyche. Changing them will inevitably result in
unnecessary sacrifices in the social order.

The three components central to economic growth—human resources,
capital, and technological resources—are vital. Yet Japan gave priority to
human resources. Hence, the goal of stability in employment emerged as a
cornerstone in the human resources strategy. So-called "lifetime employment" provided a stability in keeping with the Japanese vision of society.
Education has long been an essential tool to bolster human resources. Maximum efficiency of the workforce, improvements in mass production techniques, and strides in production engineering (as opposed to the West's
emphasis on basic research) all guided the historic post-war recovery. Japan
borrowed quality control but went a few steps beyond, fostering small-group
quality circles and encouraging worker participation.

These approaches were derived from the cultural outlook and conditions in a resource-poor, isolated, agricultural archipelago. Japan became hardware-oriented, as is logical. Government targeting of foreign
markets and industrial sectors replaced the role of corporations in strategic planning. Expanded government influence had an enormous impact
on Japan's corporate structure before the bubble era ended in 1989–90.
A "convoy system" of companies and industrial sectors was created,

with a flotilla of different ships protecting each other on the seas of global commerce. The boundary conditions remained unchanged for some four decades. Resulting economic expansion was a by-product of culturally mandated corporate structure and managerial strategies.

Other characteristics of the business model were shaped by historical and cultural factors. And because rapid economic expansion made capital scarce, banks provided indirect financing to a greater degree than seen in other developed countries. Thus emerged the "main bank" system, with close links between companies and their banking partners, featuring interlocking bank-business ownership of individual company stock. In time, banks exerted great control over all operations of the leading-edge Japanese corporations, and a "closed circuit" system developed. Public disclosures, common in the West, were not required to the same extent in Japan under these circumstances.

At the same time, contractors and suppliers—large and small alike—were vertically integrated into networks or conglomerates called *keiretsu* systems, securing stable supplies of materials and components for large-quantity, high-quality mass production.

Trading companies *(sogo shosha)* created to handle export-import commerce in manufactures and raw materials were a unique Japanese creation to overcome a scarcity of natural resources. These *sogo shosha* flourished worldwide. Their forward-looking strategies made them middlemen from Mecca to Malaysia, from Taipei to Tampa. It is worth noting that when America tried to launch its own version of trading companies in the early 1980s, the experiment failed: the underlying concept of an integrated trading company was alien to American business culture.

Volume and marketshare, not profitability, were company goals. Future expansion, not short-term performance, characterized the business ideal. Low stock dividends for shareholders were generally accepted because there was an understanding that long-term gains would accrue by way of accumulated reserves and investment.

Social stability and stable economic growth in the context of export-driven GDP increases worked well for society. Four decades of unparalleled success resulted. From a poor per capita income of 47,000 yen (US$470) in 1950, Japan achieved a 3,503,000 yen per capita income ($35,003) by 1990.

In effect, this was a *developing* country system that prevailed even after Japan's status reached that of a highly developed, Information-Age economy. But the system remained completely compatible with the nation's socio-cultural roots.

A shake-up in the global currency and monetary situation came with the Plaza accords (which mandated a devalued yen). Called the *endaka* phenomenon, this caused Japan's companies to adjust and reduce costs. The currency re-alignment led Japanese companies to move their manufacturing and assembly processes offshore to low-cost Southeast Asian locations. Another factor affected the competitiveness of "Made In Japan" goods: rising wages.

Did "metal fatigue" overtake Japanese management? Enormous wear and tear dulls even the sharpest metal. As once-robust corporations became overworked and fatigued, institutional barriers to reform became evident. Banks and companies became interwoven. Their leadership made assumptions—based on the society's conservative outlook—that real estate prices would forever rise. The "land myth" (*tochi shinwa*) had enormous impact, as we will see.

Older people were entrenched throughout corporate hierarchies. Slower decision making was an inherent feature of the system that had performed so well. When older management retired from corporations, they became senior executives in subsidiaries and in *keiretsu* companies, enabling them to retain influence within the corporate group.

It is perhaps no accident that the explosion of information technology (IT) coincided with the first signs of economic weakness in Japan, the world's number two economic superpower. Developments in IT change the style of communication and decision making, alter the flow of information, and necessitate rapid policy making. All of these forces ran counter to the Japanese model.

Ironically, the enormous accumulation of wealth by Japan's export-minded companies led to the collapse in 1989–90 and to the financial bubble. Acceptance of the "land myth" meant that huge amounts of money were channeled into residential and commercial property. Revenues derived from the never-ending export boom, rising GDP, and newly found affluence fueled artificial real estate prices, propelling speculation—and the bubble itself.

The era of globalization, heralded in part by the multinationals' search for new markets, arrived. Overseas, under conditions found outside Japan, the old model was forced to endure new tests. The system that had performed marvelously during a period of stability experienced difficulties. The 1990s was an era of unprecedented change. The new economic environment forced change at a *rate* which strained established traditions. Therefore, the Japanese business system faced obstacles caused by uncontrollable circumstances.

It has been eleven long years of recession and stagnant growth. Downsizing, lay-offs, the end of lifetime employment, and other harsh realities replaced the comfortable social contract. At the same time, unchanging factors such as a lack of natural resources remain challenging. Moreover, Japan is an aging society. In only seven years, those over sixty-five will constitute more than twenty percent of the population; a mere five years later this share of the total population will increase to twenty-five percent. This factor, and a leveling birthrate, will eventually cause the population to decline.

Noted economist Paul Krugman has demonstrated that inputs of labor, capital, and productivity are essential components of sustained economic vitality. In Japan's case, these inputs can no longer be expected. Even the legendary high savings rate (fourteen percent, compared to America's negative savings rate), a source of capital investment, is no longer assured. We cannot expect further improvements in the level of mass production efficiency.

The only avenue remaining for my country is to use creativity. The Japanese education system—which emphasizes egalitarianism and compromises gifted students—is geared to pre-1990 "stable" conditions. Creativity and individualism are required in the new, less stable environment. It is encouraging that new entrepreneurially minded corporations are sprouting up across Japan today. They employ people whose goals and aspirations differ from those prevailing in the era of lifetime employment.

Consider Internet-based Softbank, and Rakuten, an online-based auction service. There is also Mangazoo, an information provider, selling popular *manga* comics and anime products. In these firms, young people dress casually in jeans. Attitudes such as loyalty to the company have been shattered during the past few years. There is no president or CEO; the institutional culture is akin to what one finds in Silicon Valley.

These companies can contribute much to Japan's long-awaited recovery. They can make use of software orientation (as opposed to the traditional growth-era hardware orientation) to help at least some segments of Japan's private sector succeed in the era of IT and globalization. The start-ups will tap high-level engineering talent in Japan that otherwise would be underutilized in this period of ongoing economic stagnation. They will provide opportunities for talented, often younger, workers seeking to achieve creativity-based business success.

This so-called "software" approach may complement a manufacturing base, showing how traditional business culture can adjust without making radical changes in Japanese industry. It is fashionable to proclaim that small companies and high-tech start-ups are "the wave of the future." Let me suggest that Japan's economic growth will be based on businesses whose networks are already in place. They can withstand competitive pressures and raise capital. Creating new footloose companies *within* existing corporations and trading companies is essential. Larger traditional companies can benefit from new divisions devoted to creative activities and allowed occasionally—as in the Western tradition—to fail. They can still maintain traditional values supported by the surrounding communities.

I am happy to report that these new directions are under way. Typical examples are the venture capital (VC) mechanisms that have spawned biotech, IT, and telecommunications "superstars" in America and might well achieve similar results in Japan. For example, Itochu, Japan's second largest trading company, has inaugurated a $100 million VC fund, focusing in part on broadband telecommunications and enhanced IT products. Venture capital is still at a fledgling stage in Japan, but larger corporations such as Hitachi are moving into the VC field, forming new subsidiaries.

While Japan focuses increasingly on creative ideas, it should plan to cooperate more effectively with other countries. Many processes associated with "sunrise industries" such as biotechnology are in fact labor intensive, and some developing countries offer considerable pools of skilled labor. The value-added R&D and other functions would be conducted in advanced countries. Singapore, a true high-tech success story among the fabled "Four Tigers," has a low population base. It faces rising costs of production and labor. It has no alternative but to move up the value-added ladder, recasting education to accommodate the new environments created by entrepreneurship and risk-taking.

In today's Japan, however, we will have to maintain traditional job security mechanisms. If a Japanese company begins to institute massive layoffs to secure profit margins, it may lose society's respect.

Recently, Mr. Hiroshi Okuda, Chairman of Toyota Motors, declared: "Business leaders should commit *harikiri* before dismissing their employees." This view is widely shared. Indeed, the venture capital mechanism is a unique approach to ensure aspects of the traditional job security model.

Among the other transformations taking place is the way in which workers and managers are evaluated. The seniority system as it existed is no longer practical. Competence must be incorporated into the equation in order to maximize efficiency. Other changes involve accountability and transparency: The main banks no longer function as auditors for companies with which they are connected. Non-conglomerate members are encouraged to sit on corporations' boards of directors. I think extending this concept to Japan's multinationals is useful. For example, if a Tokyo-based multinational does thirty percent of its business outside Japan's borders, non-Japanese might then comprise thirty percent of the board of directors.

As mentioned before, the "Made in Japan" trading company is an expression of historical and cultural factors. As importers of raw materials, *sogo shosha* maintained extensive international networks. The eight largest trading companies controlled as much as thirty percent of all exports and fifty percent of Japan's imports. Total sales of this group is US$723 billion, or approximately twenty percent of the country's GDP. Not surprisingly, the *sogo shosha* have suffered during the protracted recession. Yet, in an increasingly globalized environment, they are perfect intermediaries and middlemen: Itochu is now the world's leading distributor of equipment manufactured by U.S.-based high-tech giant Sun Microsystems.

The Western (and American) business model may not be successfully adapted to either Japanese business or Japanese society. America's model tends to effectively account for times of change and transition, times when—to quote the expression—companies may "thrive on chaos." Japan's strengths (and its model) were born in a period of stability. Wisdom may in time tell us how to best use the different aspects of each model. Japan's own cultural and social conditions will be critical to its efforts to bring about economic recovery.

Yet, introducing creativity remains essential. Japan can play a more important role than simply that of "opening its market" to Asia's developing countries: In the past half-century, Japan showed her neighbors how to use export-driven strategies to achieve unprecedented growth. Now the Japanese must show these countries how to make the inevitable transition up the value-added "ladder" and undergo shifts in their own business strategies.

Different Shades of "Crony Capitalism": Not All Asian Values Are Alike

Tion Kwa

Crony capitalism is a phrase much used since 1997 to describe business in Southeast Asia. Yet there remains something unsatisfactory about commentary on it. Crony capitalism has been derided—justifiably— but perhaps too easily, without a thorough understanding of the forces behind it. Much of the lack of understanding has to do with news reports on the matter. The problem is that too many commentators have no real idea of what it means to run a business in Southeast Asia. Too many descriptions of crony capitalism's venality, as such, are trite; you don't have to go too far out on a limb to opine against it.

Certainly, one would not wish to defend a system of patronage that generally tends to allocate capital inefficiently, and whose sum total of attributes constitutes an antithesis to the virtues of free markets. Yet one still needs to understand crony capitalism. Although its time is well past, for many years it did serve to expand southeast Asia's economies.

Personally Speaking . . .

I am the son of a crony capitalist and only recently learned that I was named after Indonesia's General Nasution, who was Minister of Defense in the Sukarno administration. Though my family is Straits Chinese from Penang, Malaysia, my father was involved in business in Indonesia and Thailand, principally in the mining industry. I was named after the general because my father's close friend and business associate in Singapore—a man I have not seen since childhood and whom I had known then only as "Tuan"—was, I was told, General Nasution's brother. The general died only recently, outliving my own parents; I had thought him dead earlier. And as far as I know, Tuan, too, has passed on.

As such, there is no one to whom I can turn to put to rest the nagging suspicion that the name I ended up with was in a way given me to massage the ego of someone that could have aided my father's business ventures. You see, sometimes you can't do business in Southeast Asia in any other way than through so-called crony capitalism.

Suppose you have determined that a particular site in, say, Sumatra has large deposits of high-grade tin ore. Though your financial backers will bankroll the mine and associated infrastructure, you may still be stymied. What is required is a local player—one with contacts. Then you can successfully negotiate mineral rights issues with authorities. You'll need water, a workforce, and so on. Alone, you won't get very far. You need friends with connections.

Today, it is fashionable to stand on the principle that such connections and influence are abominations. But the fact is that sometimes, and certainly in my father's time, you could not do business any other way. Would my father have liked to be free of cronyism? Without a doubt, yes. Perhaps he would have been more successful had he not been constrained by certain norms. The truth is, the blanket indictments of Asia's capitalists as being unable to profit without cronyism is unfair. Many of Asia's businesses would have relished the opportunity for real competition.

The Varieties of Crony Capitalism

I left Malaysia in 1981, in the twilight of my parents' years. For the next fifteen years I returned only twice. The first was a one-month stay in 1985. Almost ten years later I returned to work in Kuala Lumpur, staying a year and a half. By then, the petty cronyism my father witnessed had much receded. Grand Cronyism replaced it.

My extended absence magnified in my eyes the country's little—and not so little—changes. By 1995, the country I had left in my teens had been transformed almost beyond recognition. Instead of being a sleepy backwater to Singapore, it was distinctly modern. While a drive from Penang to Kuala Lumpur used to take all day, it now took four hours on the North-South Highway. Applications for telephones lines took months to be processed before, but in 1995 I walked into the local Kedai Telekom, or "Telecom shop," collected a new phone number, took the phone home, and service began instantly. (When I was growing up, a shortage of phone lines resulted in my family sharing a party line with my aunt's family down the road. We couldn't contact each other; nobody could use the phone when someone else on the party line had it engaged. However, we could listen in on each other's calls.)

In downtown Kuala Lumpur in 1995, an inner-city rail transit system was just about to open. Car ownership had soared and private hospitals offered a level of care comparable to more developed parts of the world. From a sleepy government town, Kuala Lumpur had emerged with new-found vibrancy.

More importantly, all this development presupposed there were people with more money to spend—whether on ubiquitous mobile phones or at restaurants in newly fashionable precincts. While the elite had always gravitated towards Britain, more people were traveling farther than London; the world had become smaller for more Malaysians. Indeed, world fashions and tastes were no longer just something to be read about in the newspaper; they were as much apparent in the country. Most impressive was the sense of a general prosperity, not only among the urban class but for rural dwellers as well.

This was largely the result of crony capitalism. Malaysia is known for its government's propensity for handpicking those to develop choice pieces of infrastructure and those allowed to expand into targeted industries. Contrast this with Indonesia, also known for its penchant for cronyism. But even before the devastation wreaked upon it by the Asian Crisis, the country's standard of living remained far below that of Malaysia. Indeed the gulf between the two countries' income levels failed to close despite the pre-1997 go-go years of Indonesian economic expansion. While Malaysia expanded the breadth and depth of its middle class, few except the rich grew more wealthy in Indonesia; the gaps between the rich and poor yawned wider. What wealth percolated to ordinary folk didn't travel much further than Jakarta and a few other key areas. As Malaysia's population grew more prosperous, Indonesia's remained at low income levels, despite the handful of Maseratis crisscrossing Jakarta's streets.

The difference between the two countries is crucial to understanding the economic dynamics in Southeast Asia. Indonesia's economic expansion was marked by unalloyed greed. The best pieces of the economy are widely alleged to have been reserved for friends and kin of the Suharto family. The claim goes like this: if you were suitably connected and could think up a government scheme to help you make money, the government obliged. A national car project? Perfect for one from the country's first family. It is also widely believed that the Suhartos and their closest friends treated Indonesia as a fiefdom.

In Malaysia, while licenses were disbursed with an equal disregard for competition, there was one crucial difference. Privately, Malaysian officials will admit that the "right" people and business groups were handed the plums of the economy. The point they make is that a country rushing to expand its economy and catch up with the developed world has no time for the experimentation that free competition entails. There are "crony capitalists" in modern Malaysia because these are the people considered most likely to succeed—and thereby raise the financial prospects of the rest of the country. "Cronies" are picked for their abilities, with the idea that if they are freed of the need to compete for projects and licenses, they may devote their complete energies to the businesses they are entrusted to manage. A crucial point: "ability." Cronies were chosen with high expectations of success, to profit themselves as well as their workers and suppliers upon whom they depend. Cronyism was part of a national development project. In contrast, Indonesian cronyism was marked by rent-seeking behavior. The crucial difference between the two is intent, and in this distinction is certainly two different versions of Asian values.

A Caveat

In Malaysia, the plan generally worked out in the manner that was anticipated. Despite the 1997–98 economic crisis, the country remains one of the few Asian magnets for migrant workers from the Philippines, Indonesia, Thailand, and South Asia. This means Malaysians are wealthy enough to refuse the country's lowest-paying jobs. Yet there remains the question of whether the national interest could have been better served by greater open competition. After all, despite the fact that there have been successes logged under the model, there have also been monumental failures. Malaysia probably could have profited better if more economic agents were let loose. Indeed, a great deal of financial and business competency in the country has been being frustrated by a lack of opportunity. Free of paternalism, Malaysia would likely have prospered even more than is the case. Whether in Malaysia or Indonesia, unarguably the time has come for a more efficient form of capitalism in Asia.

Expropriation and the Asian Corporation

Larry H.P. Lang and Leslie Young

The Asian financial crisis was widely attributed to "crony capitalism"—domination of the corporate sector by politically well-connected families. There is now a significant database of 3,000 corporations that can be used to study this issue.

The overwhelming majority of East Asian companies (75 percent) are affiliated to a group, subject to ultimate control of an entity that also controls large numbers of other companies. In Japan 83 percent of firms are group affiliated; in the Philippines, 74 percent; in Hong Kong, Indonesia, and Singapore, more than 60 percent; only in Thailand are group-affiliated companies in a minority (42 percent).

To analyze group ownership structure, one must identify the ultimate owners. Less than one-tenth of Japanese companies (nine percent) are controlled by families, while almost four-fifths are widely held. By contrast, the proportion of corporations under family control is 48 percent in South Korea, 48 percent in Taiwan, 62 percent in Thailand, and two-thirds both in Hong Kong and in Malaysia.

Another measure of family control is the share of total market capitalization held by top families: at the time of the crisis, approximately one-sixth of the total market capitalization in Indonesia and the Philippines was controlled by the top family; half the market capitalization in each was controlled by the top ten families. Concentration was high in Thailand and Hong Kong, where the top five families controlled one-fourth of market capitalization. In South Korea, Malaysia, and Singapore, twenty-five percent of market capitalization was controlled by the top ten families. By contrast, family control in Japan was insignificant.

Looking at pre-"contagion" East Asia, the top fifteen families control companies with the following percentages of market capitalization (as a share of 1996 GDP): Hong Kong, 84; Malaysia, 76; Singapore, 48; the Philippines, 47; Thailand, 39; Indonesia, 21; Taiwan, 17; Korea, 13; and Japan, 2.

Thus, controlling shareholders of large corporate groups can expropriate—in effect, steal—control of group-affiliated firms from minority shareholders. Indeed, exploitation of minority shareholders can drive business activities. This could have played a key role in precipitating the 1997–98 crisis.

Secrets of the Great Pyramid

In this type of corporate pyramid, a private holding company sits on top, a second tier holds the most valuable assets, and a third tier holds the group's publicly-listed companies. The latter transfers cash to companies at the top. Shares of third-tier companies are sold to the public, with proceeds passed up the pyramid via internal transactions. Less profitable assets are passed down the pyramid.

Pyramiding magnifies the degree of control possible despite a low level of ownership, providing both the ability and the incentive for controlling shareholders to exploit minority shareholders. In Figure 1, a family owns 51 percent of company A, which owns 51 percent of company B, which owns 51 percent of company C, which owns 30 percent of company D. The family also owns 21 percent of company D through a separate, wholly owned vehicle, company F.

The family therefore controls 51 percent of the shares of D (30 percent through C and 21 percent through F). However, its ownership stake is only 25 percent. This is because of the pyramiding. The family controls 30 percent of D via the A-B-C chain, but its ownership stake is a mere four percent: 51 percent of 51 percent of 51 percent of 30 percent.

The family can expropriate minority shareholders by paying low dividends to D's shareholders, selling assets from D to F at low prices or purchasing goods and services from F at high prices. Such transactions

Figure 1

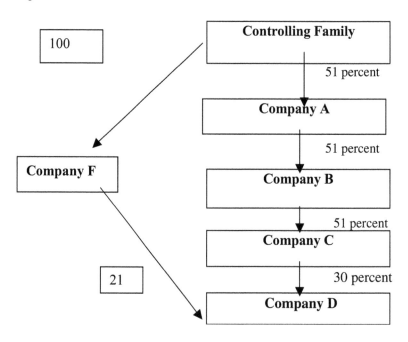

benefit the family because of its low ownership of D and high ownership of F. For example, if an asset sold from D to F were under-priced by $100 million, then the loss to the family (through its ownership of D) would be $25 million. Yet, its gain through company F would be $100 million—leaving a profit of $75 million: the fruit of the expropriation of D's minority shareholders.

In this case the controlling family's ratio of ownership to control rights in company D is 25 to 51, or 49 percent. In general, a company where the controlling shareholder has a low ratio of ownership to control rights is near the corporate pyramid's base; minority shareholders are thus more exposed to expropriation.

Larry Lang, along with Stijn Claessens and Simeon Djankov of the World Bank and Joseph Fan of the Hong Kong University of Science and Technology, studied this issue. Lang and the others discovered that such companies have significantly lower market valuations per dollar of asset compared to industry peers. This indicates that shareholders downgrade such companies for being more exposed to expropriation.

This pattern is found in every East Asian economy in our sample, except Singapore and Malaysia. Singaporean corporate regulation is stringent. For example, any loan to a related party of more that US$5,000 must be secured, a rule absent elsewhere in East Asia.

Degrees of Control and Ownership

Our research with Professor Mara Faccio of the University of Milan found further evidence of expropriation in the pattern of dividend behavior. A corporation was "tightly controlled" if all links in the chain exceeded twenty percent. "Loosely controlled" meant all links were between ten and twenty percent.

Investors appeared alert to expropriation risks within tightly controlled groups. To offset their concerns, higher dividends were paid by corporations affiliated to those groups. The controlling shareholder had a lower ratio of ownership to control rights. This indicates capital markets—except in Thailand and Indonesia—are generally capable of policing expropriation within tightly controlled groups.

Yet, investors seem less alert to expropriation within corporations that are loosely affiliated to a group. Such corporations pay lower dividends if they are lower in the corporate pyramid and the controlling shareholder has a lower ratio of ownership to control rights.

Weak control links are not visible to minority shareholders. Therefore, controlling shareholders face minimal surveillance from capital markets. They retain resources within the company by paying lower dividends. These resources can then be expropriated by unfairly priced transactions with other companies in the group.

Failures of capital market policing are of little consequence in Europe, where loosely affiliated corporations comprise only three percent of listed corporations. In Asia, however, they comprise fifteen percent. Minority shareholders have fewer rights in Asia, where regulators are less effective in enforcing those rights. Therefore, control of a corporation is possible with a smaller proportion of its shares, a situation that obviously facilitates expropriation.

The size and complexity of Asia's dominant corporate groups pose impediments to shareholder control of such abuses. The six largest groups in Asia control twenty-three percent of all Asian corporations and seventy-eight percent of those that are loosely affiliated; the twenty-two largest groups were found to control one-third of all Asian corporations and five-sixths of those that are loosely affiliated.

The low transparency of sprawling, loosely affiliated groups makes it difficult for minority shareholders—and analysts—to discover where control resides, let alone identify unfair intra-group transactions. Apparently weak formal group linkages may be reinforced by non-transparent linkages through nominee accounts (common in Asian markets) and through collusion with other large shareholders. Dividend behavior provides evidence of collusion: we found that the presence of another large shareholder (holding more than ten percent of a corporation) raises dividend rates in Europe but lowers them in Asia.

In another study with Professor Mara Faccio, we concluded that given weak legal institutions, debt serves to facilitate managerial expropriation by permitting controlling shareholders to expand control of resources. These may then be expropriated via unfair transactions with related parties. Those who suffer from the expropriation include minority shareholders, creditors left holding worthless debt as well as taxpayers paying for bail-outs (to prevent systemic collapse).

Nearly all (97 percent) of loosely affiliated firms in Asia have access to related-party loans through banks controlled by their group. More than one-fifth of Asian corporations and 87 percent of Asian loosely affiliated corporations were controlled by six groups comprising more that 50 firms plus a bank. Within these groups, outside shareholders and creditors—both borrowers and lenders—would have difficulty learning of their exposure to expropriation.

Victims of expropriation can include group-affiliated banks. With underdeveloped bond markets, bank loans are still the most popular form of debt. Families control a significantly higher proportion of publicly listed banks in East Asia than in Europe. Figure 2 shows that families control 50 percent of publicly listed banks in East Asia; in Hong Kong and Malaysia it is 73 percent; it is 82 percent in Indonesia and 88 percent in Thailand.

Weak capital market institutions opened the door to expropriation of minority shareholders by the controlling shareholder/manager. A case in point is the swathe of empty, half-finished apartments littering Bangkok—evidence, not of too little business acumen, but of too much (see Figure 3). Apartments were built by a construction company D, which operated low down on a corporate pyramid. The land and concrete were bought at exorbitant prices from companies A and B higher up the pyramid. Loans and loan guarantees to foreign banks were provided by a bank E low in the pyramid, with top managers from the controlling fam-

Figure 2 Percentage of Listed Banks Owned by Families in East Asia

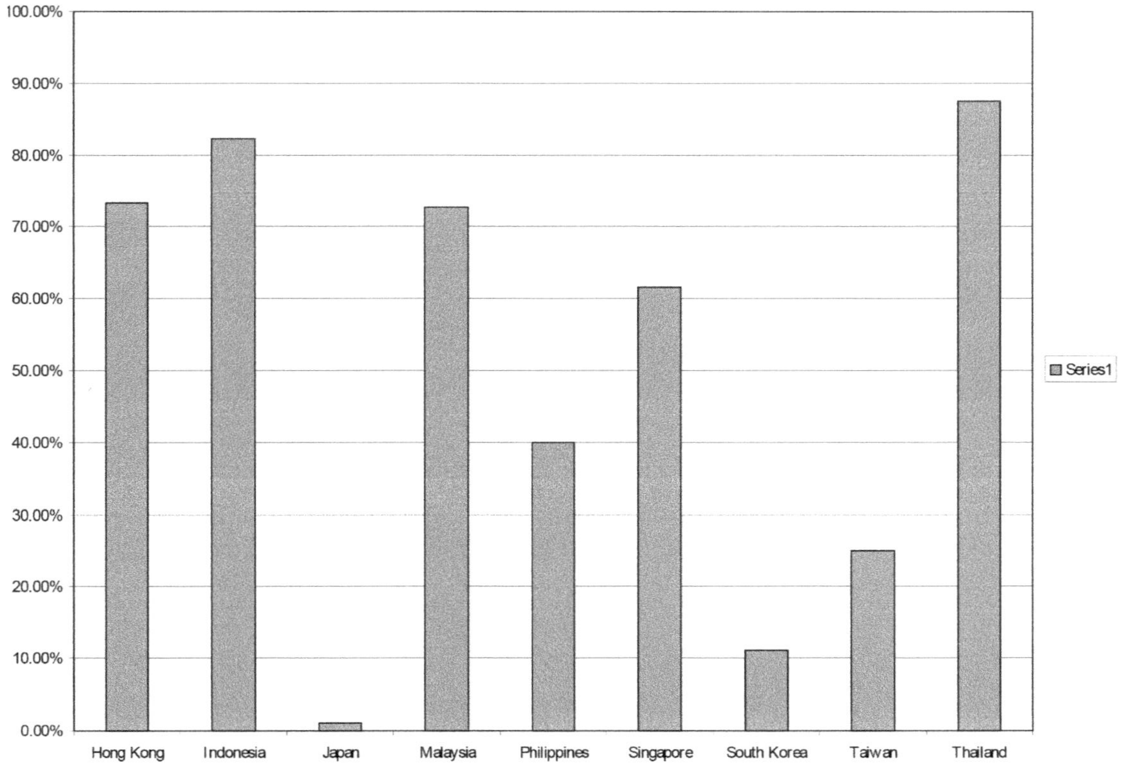

Figure 3   **Expropriation in Thailand**

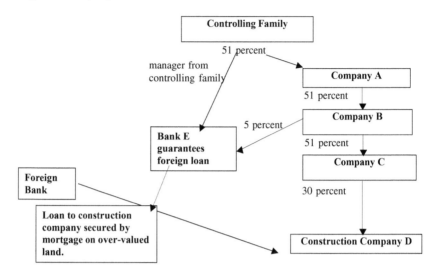

ily, despite its low equity stake. Since the family had small equity stakes and limited liability in company D and bank E, their collapse in 1997–98 left intact the family's prior gains from expropriation.

This example shows how a limited liability corporation can be abused. This concept provides a legal and accounting vehicle for financial transactions and ownership of property, while limiting beneficiaries' exposure. Emerging economies borrowed this concept from mature economies but did so without legal or accounting systems. Laws and regulations need to reflect this reality, so minority shareholders and creditors can forestall and punish expropriation and value-destroying investment.

Suggestions For Improvement

(1) Controlling shareholders who are also managers must act in the interests of all shareholders. The law should acknowledge their conflict of interest, exacerbated by the stronger family obligations and weaker sense of fiduciary duty in Asia. In any dispute with minority shareholders, fraudulent intent should be *presumed* if there are violations in use of funds, related-party transactions, insider trading, or covenants on disclosure of balance sheets. In such cases, the controlling shareholders should be required to demonstrate that their actions were in the minority shareholders' interests. Failure to do so should be taken as proof of fraud.

(2) Because of Asia's weak sense of fiduciary duty, leveraging of voting power by managers/controlling shareholders via the pyramiding of company holdings is abused. Therefore, proven fraudulent intent by the controlling shareholders should lead to dissolution of the corporation as a unitary legal entity such that it can no longer vote as a bloc on decisions related to the corporations it owns.

Thus, if corporation A holds shares in corporation B, then in voting on B, shareholders in A must vote as individuals, although proxies could be solicited. This would force controlling shareholders with fraudulent intent to own more shares in B to be sure of retaining control, thus reducing discrepancies between the control and cash flow rights (which create incentives to expropriate value from B).

(3) Limited liability protects minority shareholders from management decisions. Controlling shareholders who are also managers do not need such protection, and it should be withdrawn upon proof of fraudulent intent. Creditors and outside shareholders should be able to cut through to personal assets of the manager/controlling shareholder, as well as all trusts of which they are the beneficiary or settlor. Transfer of property to settle a judgment should be immediate, even if the judgment is being appealed.

(4) The difficulties of organizing dispersed minority shareholders and creditors would be reduced by adapting features of Western law.

(5) Since effective, independent legal systems are yet to emerge in many Asian countries, the professional civil service can play a role to limit expropriation of minority shareholders and creditors. The Hong Kong Independent Commission Against Corruption (ICAC) is a useful model. It responds to tip-offs and, when sound evidence is presented, initiates investigations. ICAC anti-corruption efforts have earned the confidence of the Hong Kong citizenry. Developing an analogous Independent Commission Against Corporate Corruption to spearhead regulatory investigations might address problems of corporate governance in Asia. Such a commission should be pro-active—not waiting for the next "contagion"—and target random independent firms whose respective profiles (in which the controlling shareholder has a low ratio of cash to control rights) make them likely tools for expropriation.

Lesson Unlearned: Resurgent Asian Exchange Rate Instability

Michael Kurtz

After a year of impressive exchange-rate performance, monetary policy mistakes crept back into relevance in East and Southeast Asia in 2000 to a degree that could affect the region's financial health past 2001. Asian currency watchers noted that in November 2000, just as "ASEAN plus 3" leaders assembled to discuss beefing up currency-supportive multilateral foreign exchange (forex) swap agreements—the Chiang Mai Initiative—several economies were returning to every-man-for-himself, competitive devaluationist exchange-rate policies. This was fueled by both internal factors (such as structural weaknesses) and external factors (high oil costs, a weak Euro, U.S. interest rate policy, global tech stock declines, and concerns over a "hard" American economic "landing") that collectively caused Asian governments to backslide on currency values. Yet in 1999 the *most* volatile regional currency lost a mere three percent on net (see Table 1). This phenomenon was seen both in the less-developed Asean member countries as well as in tech-heavy "Tigers" Taiwan and South Korea.

The phenomenon signaled neglect of the lesson that the 1997–98 Asian meltdown was fundamentally a *currency* crisis and that the collateral

Table 1

	Full-year 1999	Full-year 2000	Q4 2000	Q1 2001
Thai Baht	−3%	−15%	−3.0%	−3.0%
Philippine Peso	−3%	−20%	−7.0%	+0.9%
Indonesian Rupiah	+12%	−27.5%	−10.0%	−6.5%
Singapore Dollar	−1%	−4.5%	0%	−4.0%
Korean Won	+4%	−11%	−11.5%	−5.2%
Japanese Yen	+11%	−11.5%	−4.8%	−9.5%

damage—high inflation, higher capital costs, magnified foreign debt burdens—resulted from sliding exchange rates. It also pointed to the fact that the region's policy-makers still accord exports top priority at the expense of politically sensitive—but needed—domestic structural reforms (which would spur meaningful domestic growth).

Sources of Pressure

East Asian forex performance was shaped in 1999 by the U.S. rate-tightening cycle that continued through the 50 bps (a half percentage-point) May 2000 interest rate hike and subsequent retention of tightening bias through December 2000.The Fed's tightening exercise saw Asian currencies lose out as investors sought better relative returns in U.S. dollar-denominated assets.

Asian economies also confronted trade-account pressures from tenaciously high oil costs while doubts regarding electronics exports and the health of the global technology sector mounted. As earlier assumptions were revisited, markets discounted for potential degradation in the balance of payments. On trade accounts, Asian consumers demanded more American dollars to buy oil, while global export markets demanded less local currency to purchase Asian exports. On the investment side, global portfolio managers saw less attraction to regional assets: lower export expectations undercut equity values. Funds pulled capital out of regional markets, further boosting demand for U.S. dollars (USDs).

Policy Responses

In many cases, Asian governments' priority conversely was one of lowering interest rates, a policy not without merit but one carrying unwelcome exchange-rate side effects. Other governments raised rates alongside the Fed to offset forex damage but higher interest rates meant reduced growth expectations in light of a rise in the cost of capital—and thus lower levels of offshore investment.

Thailand's central bank's self-proclaimed "low-interest-rate policy" expressed the sense that it was more critical to preserve low borrowing costs for a still-struggling financial system and corporate sector than to defend the exchange rate. With the U.S. Fed still hiking rates, the increased relative cost of holding U.S. dollar-denominated debt spurred a surge of repayment of Thai corporate overseas borrowings (refinanced more cheaply onshore). This accelerated to an estimated US$1 billion outflow per month—adding to USD demand and so pressuring the baht lower.

Another case is that of Taiwan. By late October 2000 its stable exchange rate was relaxed to give *local* exports a price advantage internationally (Taiwanese exports comprise forty-plus percent of GDP), as well as to shore up a shaky financial system through the provision of New Taiwan Dollar (NTD) liquidity. The local stock market declined some forty-five percent from April to December (2000) after domestic political uncertainty increased and the domestic economy had fallen into the doldrums as the negative wealth-effect undercut consumer appetite. Further, domestic credit extension slowed as alarming levels of bad debt were unearthed in the island's financial system. These bad loans motivated local banks to retrench in order to protect asset bases. New stimulative fiscal policy was not an option because annual government borrowing reached statutory limits. With only modest danger of collateral inflation damage, policy-makers chose the monetary approach, injecting more NTD liquidity into the economy to lubricate the financial-system machinery and to weaken the currency in an ostensibly "export friendly" fashion. But this advantage was immediately offset as Korea continued with its own "tit-for-tat" won depreciation.

No Free Lunch

There are definite—and often economically debilitating—costs when exchange rate instability is introduced. Chief among them:

- Trade transaction costs increase as importers and exporters are forced to hedge against currency risk exposure, creating frictional trade impediments on the margin.
- Inflation picks up as exports grow more expensive in local-currency terms.

- Boosts in trade competitiveness from currency depreciation are temporary, as costs of imported components for export goods rise and price-level adjustments cause the terms of trade to re-equilibrate in real terms.
- Offshore investors look elsewhere: Why would multinational corporations put capital into a local economy—or portfolio managers channel funds into a local market—when, upon repatriation, dollars could be reduced substantially in value by exchange-rate translation effects?
- Conversely, local costs of existing offshore debt are augmented by the same translation effect, placing added burdens on corporate and public-sector debtors.

Indeed, significant capital outflows have been seen in Thailand, Taiwan, Korea and elsewhere since mid-2000. Investors rationally expect to encounter less beneficial exchange rates if they delay in withdrawing capital.

Benefits of Stability Demonstrated

Not that the region has been without positive examples: China, the Hong Kong Special Administrative Region (SAR), and Malaysia boast not merely stable but actually fixed exchange-rate regimes versus the USD. Malaysia held the ringgit successfully at 3.8/USD since September 1998 and—despite widespread criticisms of its capital controls policy—managed through much of the subsequent period to effect gradual liberalization without suffering outsized drops in equity values.

China and Hong Kong, on the other hand, remain USD-fixed at parities that prevailed before the Asian crisis, having opted for deflation over policy inconsistency. The reasons are compelling: the SAR boasts Asia's second largest stock market, and the PRC looks to engage in a massive program of state-enterprise privatization in coming years. Thus both are sensitive to the need to minimize policy risk to capital formation. This benefit comes at a price: unable unilaterally to loosen a monetary policy linked to a strong USD, China and Hong Kong confronted two years of deflation that only in recent months has shown signs of abating.

One can draw connections between the stability offered by fixed-rate regimes and better performance on local capital markets: over the full-year 2000, Hong Kong's benchmark Hang Seng Index was down a relatively low 12 percent, and Kuala Lumpur's exchange just 16 percent (comparing not unfavorably, for example, to respective Dow and Nasdaq losses of 9 percent and 40 percent, respectively). Locally denominated Shanghai "A-Shares" index *rose* by 48 percent. (Other factors share the credit: China's ongoing progress toward WTO membership, her reduced dependence on exports as a percentage of GDP, and her lower sensitivity to soaring oil costs.) Indeed in a region-wide comparison of local equity markets in USD terms (the only meaningful standard against a background of shifting local currency values), it is Asia's three fixed-exchange rate economies that chalked the best returns in 2000 (see Table 2).

Neither the Will Nor the Way

Unfortunately, perceptions of inherent benefits of stable exchange rates seem to have taken a back seat to other imperatives. Rumors from time to time have cropped up in several capitals that authorities are considering a Malaysia-style fixed exchange rate—or a Hong Kong–style currency board; but it is hard to imagine the rest of East Asia reconsidering currency stabilization. This is especially true if concerns regarding yen instability or tapering export growth persist, as politically powerful export lobbies will become more vocal. Washington has not played a constructive role, as the Treasury Department mantra under both Secretaries Rubin and Summers was that currency stability is achieved through "solid fundamental economic policies and strong domestic demand-led growth." The fatal flaw in this position, and one that China and Malaysia obviously grasp, is that *the suggestion that currency stability should follow growth overlooks the irreplaceable role of currency stability in promoting capital formation and growth.* Similarly, Bush economic adviser Larry Lindsey in a widely-noted April 2001 magazine article portrayed Asia's pre-crisis stable exchange rates vs. the dollar as harmful and distorting.

Washington also played a major role in quashing talk of an ASEAN-wide currency unit that began in February 1998 with an energetic shuttle-diplomacy campaign by Malaysian Prime Minister Mahathir Mohammad. Philippine then-President Joseph Estrada assented to the idea at the July 1998 Manila ASEAN summit, but lack of consensus caused the plan to be shelved at the December 1998 ASEAN meeting in Hanoi, when heads of state instructed officials and experts to "study the issue very carefully."

The year 2000 saw new initiatives when the concept of a mutual, indigenous guarantor of currency stability was revived at the May 2000

Table 2

Regional Equity Returns, Full-year 2000 (US Dollar Terms)

Stock Index	Full-year 2000 returns (US$ terms)
Shanghai 'A-Shares' Index	+46%
Hang Seng Index	–12%
Kuala Lumpur Stock Exchange	–16%
Singapore Straits Times Index	–28%
Nikkei (Japan)	–34%
Philippine Stock Exchange	–48%
Taiwan Stock Exchange	–50%
Stock Exchange of Thailand	–52%
Jakarta Stock Exchange	–56%
Kospi (Korea)	–57%

annual Asian Development Bank meeting in Chiang Mai, Thailand. Strong lobbying by Tokyo led to the notion being resurrected that an IMF-style body might be organized, funded, and managed exclusively by East Asian countries. Japan's "Mr. Yen," Eisuke Sakakibara, suggested the facility begin with $20–40 billion in start-up capital, from which members could draw during speculative attacks against their currencies. But as talks progressed, enthusiasm for regional monetary solidarity faded. Several ASEAN members voiced reservations about Japanese financial hegemony. Agreement on details of possible cooperation modalities proved elusive, and the United States registered its opposition, fearing loss of policy influence. Thus the final agreement looked rather tepid compared to the original ambition.

Even if the will to collectively pursue more stable currency regimes were present, any meaningful Asian regional monetary vehicle must be larger. The November 2000 "ASEAN Plus Three" meeting in Singapore offered modest progress in that direction, drawing in the deep pocket participation of Japan, Korea, and China. But it is likely that even the $20–40 billion originally envisioned for start-up capital would not be enough, given that total IMF (and associated package) aid to Thailand, Indonesia, and Korea in 1997–98 amounted to over $110 billion. It is unlikely that Japan would foot the cost as unilateral lender-of-last-resort without conditions similar to IMF disciplinary measures. Yet Japan, mired in a decade of its own economic malaise, is not necessarily in a position to impose economic advice on others. Indeed, *no* regional monetary body among Asian states can effectively discipline against macro-mismanagement and excesses. This is especially true within ASEAN, where comments on one another's internal politics is considered taboo. Yet ASEAN member Malaysia, as recently as April 2001, maintained its opposition to an IMF role in the arrangement, further delaying convergence and implementation.

The limitations of the Chiang Mai Initiative are symptomatic of the game-theory dilemma facing East Asian countries on matters of exchange-rate policy: With economic and political interests still too disparate, the temptation remains to view one another as competitors, not partners. The exchange-rate approaches seen since mid-2000 demonstrate this fact. The consequences, not only for offshore investors but also for local inhabitants looking to rebuild lost living standards in the wake of economic upheaval, are not encouraging.

Is East Asia's Economy Back on Track?

Junji Ban

Was the Asian economic and financial crisis a bad dream? Glittering skyscrapers, citadels of concrete and steel, bustling streets with vendors and consumers, super freeways crisscrossing Shanghai. A few months ago I sat in my room at the Shangri-La Hotel in Pudong and looked across a vast canal at the skyline. Here, in overlooking the planned high-tech and manufacturing complex next door to Shanghai, it was easy to see why China's GDP is growing above the level of eight percent per annum.

Elsewhere in Asia I have recently felt the same optimism. Passing through passport control at Shenzen (in Southeastern China) to enter Hong Kong I witnessed an endless sea of tourists from Taiwan and the Philippines. It made me wonder if the Asian financial crisis—the heralded "contagion"—was just an unreal nightmare.

What I saw seemed a far cry from the way credit rating agencies mercilessly downgraded East Asia's financial institutions three years earlier. The contagion's causes are well known: accelerated money flows, lack of disclosures, lack of deregulation, loss of investor confidence, and weak financial sectors of those countries combined with lingering impacts of Japan's weakened economy. But solutions such as IMF prescriptions in Korea appear to have succeeded.

Miracles Two Years Later

Asian economies are returning to growth, returning to an upward trend. Yet there is a clear differentiation between two groups of countries. One includes the established "Tigers"—Hong Kong, Singapore, Taiwan, Korea, Japan, and China. A driving force of economic recovery is found in information technology (IT)–related stimulus. Malaysia may also be in this category.

But Thailand, Indonesia, and the Philippines are not yet enjoying real recovery. They are not fully exposed to the activity associated with IT. The forces of IT provide momentum to an array of technology-related industries and to manufacturing. Supported by the strong economic performance in the United States, they are pushing exports of new generations of high-tech goods and consumer products. Also, exports of Asian-made IT-related products to Japan and Europe are rising steadily.

Private-sector consumption and improvements in employment as well as increasing wages are contributing to the recovery. At the same time, private-sector investments are rising in countries where IT plays a growing role in economic development. Private investment lags in Malaysia, Thailand, and Indonesia.

Sporadic Financial Revitalization

Reform and revitalization of financial sectors differ from country to country. The level of non-performing loans (NPLs) differs vastly; for example, Taiwan's NPL is a mere five percent while Malaysia, Hong Kong, Singapore, and the Philippines are in the range of seven to fifteen percent.

In Korea and Malaysia huge amounts of public money had been injected into the financial sector with positive results. For Hong Kong and Singapore, thanks to sound conditions, solid banking practices, and well-managed financial sectors that existed before the contagion struck, there is less risk of danger.

Thailand and Indonesia NPL statistics are difficult to come by, but banking officials of Thailand indicate (as of July 2001) that the NPL level is above thirty percent. Efforts made by Bangkok officials are praiseworthy, but the situation requires close monitoring. Ongoing problems in Indonesia are more serious. Political instability is a continued factor in investors'—and in potential creditors'—perceptions.

Another important determinant of the region's overall economic situation is private consumption. Nearly nonexistent during the height of the region-wide crisis (1997–98), private consumption is increasing. Rising oil prices—plus increasing exports of petrol and natural gas to energy-thirsty nations—saw the value of Southeast Asian energy exports increase by thirty-five percent since 1999.

What Lies Ahead for Asia?

The degree to which the U.S. economy can hold up—and the role of America as "importer of last resort"—will profoundly impact Asia's economies. But "Made In Asia" exports keep inflationary pressures under control in America's ever-expanding economy.

The collective appetite of America's consumers is being reduced, with negative impact for IT-related hardware industries—as well as those of other products made in the Asia-Pacific region. Hong Kong and seven countries—Korea, Taiwan, Singapore, China, Indonesia, Malaysia, and the Philippines—account for forty-two percent of all IT-related hardware imports by the United States. Similarly, in other export industries upon whose successes the region's fortunes are based, high shares of these products are sold to an America approaching an inevitable slowdown.

As financial sector restructuring proceeds—although its speed may differ country-to-country—Asia itself is changing. A very important factor is the change of economic structures—and the successes in developing value-added products—in export-dependent countries.

An economic and financial recovery led by domestic economic performance is one new possibility. Continuing deregulation and improvement in financial sector transparency are other elements of overall recovery. If these do not take hold, hoped-for gains will not materialize. In that case, lackluster non-Asian markets—as their inward imports are reduced—may shake East and Southeast Asia's industrial base, creating the fatal seeds of crisis yet once more.

East Asia: Triumph and Tragedy

How soon can the Tigers fully recover? The U.S. economic slowdown—and weak consumer demand—deflation in Japan, and depreciation of the yen all contribute to a delayed recovery from the 1997–98 contagion. Average economic growth for the region will be far below projections of only a few months ago (March 2001). The Tigers should average four percent, and China GDP increase in 2001 is now forecast to be seven percent.

Although most experts believed the recovery in East and Southeast Asia would prove robust in 2001, the reality is that these countries are still dependent upon sales of commodities and of manufactured items in the IT sector.

The triumph in 1999–2000 was that some structural reforms did take place: transparency, continued changes in legal institutions, greater attention to corruption, better accounting, and attention to potential "bubbles."

The tragedy in 2001 is that just as reforms were taking place in the original Four Tigers (Korea, Hong Kong, Taiwan, Singapore) as well as in the cluster of would-be Tigers (Malaysia, the Philippines, and Thailand), other events took place. Foremost is the end of a ten-year American boom. In addition, the great Internet collapse, Japan's continued weakness, and stock market gyrations in both America and Japan have conspired to reduce East and Southeast Asia's chances for robust recovery.

As Julian Weiss notes in the Introduction to this book, "Without strong domestic markets and the ability to spawn consumer demands, the region is captive to an export-led growth that is no longer capable of sustaining economic development."

With nearly one-fourth of their exports headed for the U.S. the Tigers are experiencing weak export volumes. Japanese markets might have compensated for some share of these (formerly America-bound) exports, but not at this time. Europe, the third hoped-for growth "engine," offers few prospects for Asian manufacturers seeking markets for the ever-mounting goods churned out across the East and Southeast Asian production "hot house."

If China absorbs a greater share of foreign investment—and if WTO benefits are not shared by China's neighbors — it will certainly affect chances for a quick rebound on the part of the People's Republic's neighbors.

There is one other factor affecting economic growth: investors and financial analysts remain too concerned about even the slightest move of stock exchanges. After simultaneous interest rate cuts in Japan and the United States, declines on Wall Street and on the Nikkei Index have stopped. In Japan, the reintroduction of a zero interest rate monetary policy and increasing the money supply has helped. In America, a springtime market rebound coincided with the season of rebirth. Stock market players should realize the importance of the long-range view, and avoid over-reacting to short-term trends. I recall a line in one popular Western rock tune of 1960's, "What goes up, must come down."

America's problems will drag on Asia; the current account imbalance, negative savings rates, soaring consumer debt load, and heavy concentration on equities (as a share of all income), underscore the need for the U.S. to address its own macroeconomic situation.

Conditions before the Asian crisis in 1997–98 differ greatly from the present situation. For example, most of the affected countries have more foreign currency reserves compared with that time. There may be bumpy roads in future, but there were also bumpy paths in the past. Regardless of past moves, Asian economies are advancing forward. Pessimism is counterproductive. In a few years people will reflect, "The year 2001 was a rough year" but they will concede, "We learned a lot." The wounded Tigers are now charging their batteries, waiting for the new jump-start.

Towards a Yen Bloc in Asia

C. H. Kwan

Introduction

Interest in forming a yen bloc in Asia is rising. There is growing recognition of the limitation of the Asian countries' traditional exchange rate policy (pegging currencies to the U.S. dollar). Also stimulating these discussions are the implementation of Japan's ambitious financial reforms (the "Big Bang") and the euro's emergence, challenging the dollar in the international monetary system.

The term "yen bloc" refers to countries using the yen as an international benchmark currency and maintaining stable exchange rates against it. This proposed yen bloc is analogous to the former Sterling Area, and the Economic and Monetary Union (EMU) in Europe.

Traditional approaches to studying the use of the yen as an international currency more widely known as the "internationalization of the yen" (the two expressions will be used interchangeably), has been framed in terms of "Japan versus the world." In comparison, a yen bloc would be more limited in geographic scope but would involve closer policy coordination and economic ties among member countries.

With most of their international transactions denominated in U.S. dollars and their currencies pegged loosely to the dollar, it is fair to say that Asia's developing countries belong to a *de facto* dollar bloc. Taking this conclusion as our starting point, here we try to seek answers to further questions: Is the formation of a yen bloc desirable, and if so, is it possible?

The answer hinges on the implications of forming a yen bloc for both Japan and its Asian neighbors.

A Japanese Perspective

If the benefits of an Asian monetary union exceed the costs, Japan would likely pursue a yen-bloc policy, removing barriers hindering its realization. Tokyo has been reluctant to promote the yen as an international currency, fearing that larger fluctuations in demand would destabilize the Japanese economy and make it difficult to conduct monetary policy. The changing international environment has prompted a new perspective. The official approach to promoting the yen (as an international currency) has come to focus more and more on its increasing role in Asia.

With Asia now replacing the United States as Japan's largest trading partner, stabilizing the yen's effective exchange rate through the formation of a yen bloc should help reduce the vulnerability of the Japanese economy to fluctuations in the yen–dollar rate. No country today is attempting to stabilize its currency against the yen as part of its exchange rate policy, thus rendering the yen more volatile than either the U.S. dollar or the deutsche mark in effective (trade-weighted) terms (see Figure 1). A yen bloc would give the yen a certain built-in stability against other Asian currencies, since countries participating in it would seek to maintain a stable rate of exchange for their own currency against the yen. As a group, the countries of Asia are now Japan's single largest export market and source of imports; if the yen were to remain stable against other Asian currencies, then its effective exchange rate against the currencies of major trading partners would fluctuate less. In fact, a yen bloc in Asia would eliminate exposure to fluctuations in the yen–dollar rate for nearly forty percent of Japan's exports and imports.

At the microeconomic level, the creation of a yen bloc implies that Japan would bear less exchange-rate risk in both current-account and capital-account transactions. More of Japan's trade would be denominated in yen instead of in dollars, thereby reducing the foreign-exchange risk involved in international trade. At the same time, Japan's expanding role as a net creditor nation also makes wider use of the yen desirable, as it would help Japan stabilize the value of its overseas assets. Japan is now the world's largest creditor country, with net foreign assets amounting to US$819 billion (on a net basis).

Figure 1 **Effective Yen, Deutsch Mark and U.S. Dollar**

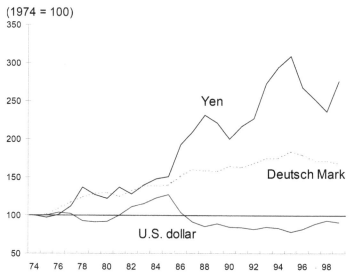

(1974 = 100)

Source: Compiled by Nomura Research Institute based on IMF, International Financial Statistics.

The mirror image is the emergence of the United States as the world's largest debtor country, with external liabilities totaling $1.47 trillion (see Figure 2). Never before has the world's leading creditor country had most of its overseas assets denominated in the currency of the world's largest debtor country. This unprecedented situation has become a major source of instability in the international financial system, as symbolized by the gyration in the yen–dollar rate. Indeed, Japan has suffered immense capital losses in yen terms since the early 1980s by investing heavily in dollar-denominated assets, as the dollar has followed a downtrend against the yen.

To stabilize the value of Japan's overseas assets, the formation of a yen bloc would be desirable, as most of Japan's capital transactions with Asian countries would become yen denominated.

The flow of capital and goods should accelerate among countries participating in the yen bloc because of the diminished foreign exchange risk. This would bring Japanese financial institutions new business opportunities in financing yen-denominated trade transactions, developing their brokerage business in Asian securities, underwriting yen bonds issued by companies in other Asian countries, and listing of Japanese companies on Asian stock exchanges.

Figure 2   **Net International Investment Position**

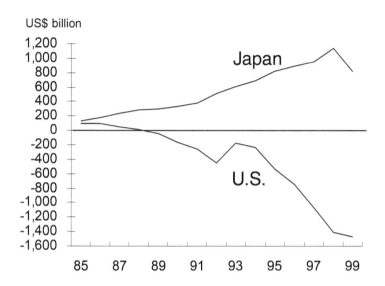

US$ billion

Source: Compiled by Nomura Research Institute based on Japanese Ministry of Finance and U.S. Department of Commerce statistics.
Notes: 1. The direct investment position of the United States is evaluated at market value. 2. The sharp decline in Japan's net external position in 1999 largely reflected the capital gain that accrued to foreign investors as stock prices in Tokyo rallied.

Promoting the use of the yen as an international currency should be useful in other ways. It could reduce the vulnerability of Japan's banking sector to fluctuations in the yen–dollar rate. This is because the Bank of International Settlements (BIS) capital adequacy ratios of Japanese banks would not be influenced by fluctuations in the yen–dollar rate if their overseas lending is denominated in yen instead of in dollars.

An Asian Perspective

With their currencies pegged loosely to the dollar, Asia's developing countries are highly vulnerable to fluctuations in the yen–dollar rate. An appreciation of the yen usually leads to stronger economic growth and rising asset prices in these countries as it promotes exports and capital inflow. Symmetrically, a depreciation of the yen is usually accompanied by a slowdown in economic growth and lower asset prices (Figure 3).

The onset of the latest region-wide financial crisis happened against

Figure 3   **The Yen–Dollar Rate as the Major Determinant of Asian Economic Growth**

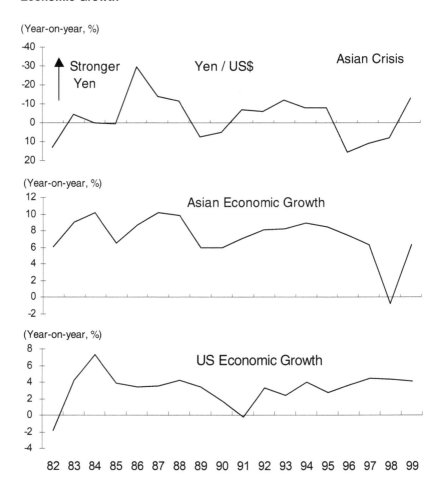

Source: Compiled by Nomura Research Institute based on official statistics.
Note: Asia = NIEs + ASEAN + China

a background of a sharp depreciation of the yen against the dollar. It led—understandably—developing countries in Asia to re-examine the traditional policy of pegging their own currencies closely to the U.S. dollar. To insulate themselves from the adverse effect on macroeconomic stability of a widely fluctuating yen–dollar rate, these countries should peg their currencies closer to the Japanese yen. They can do so by targeting a basket of currencies in which the yen carries substantial weight.

The "optimal" weight assigned to the yen in a currency basket that seeks to stabilize economic growth should be high for countries competing with Japan in international markets. It should be low for those countries with trade structures complementary to that of post-Industrial Japan. Other things being equal, the Asian Tigers, Singapore, Hong Kong, Taiwan, and Korea—also called Newly-Industrializing Economies (popularly called NIEs)—are more appropriate candidates than either the non-Tiger Southeast Asian countries (in the ASEAN region) or China when it comes to joining a yen bloc.

The volatility of Asian currencies against the yen seems to be a major factor restraining the yen as a potential regional currency. What if the Asian countries shift from their traditional regimes—pegging loosely to the dollar—to new regime wherein they peg currencies closer to the yen (or raise substantially the weight of the yen in their currency baskets)? Then, reduction in foreign exchange risk would favor more extensive use of the yen as a regional currency at the micro level.

A growing number of Asian importers and exporters would prefer to invoice in yen instead of in dollars. Borrowers and investors—including governments and central banks—would have more incentive to hold a larger proportion of their portfolios in yen-denominated financial instruments. At the same time, trade and investment between Asia and Japan should increase. A shift from pegging to the dollar to pegging to the yen (albeit loosely) should represent a major step towards the formation of a yen bloc.

Barriers to Be Overcome

Even if the formation of a yen bloc is desirable for Asia and Japan, a question remains as to whether it is possible. There are barriers to be overcome, although chances to implement such a bloc improved after the Japanese government's stance shifted. Tokyo was passive; now it is proactive and senses the vulnerability of the dollar-pegged system.

In Japan, since the asset-price collapse—the famous burst of the "bubble"—in the early 1990s, concern has mounted that erosion of Tokyo's role as an international financial center may reduce the role of the yen as an international currency. Yet wider use of the yen in Asia and elsewhere is needed to enhance the quality and sophistication of the

Tokyo financial market. Without assigning a key role to the yen, the financial "Big Bang" (deregulation and the opening of once-closed Japanese financial markets) could at best turn Tokyo into another Wimbledon championship, where most of the victors among the competing sports enthusiasts are foreign players.

Traditional approaches to studying the internationalization of the yen identified barriers to the yen's use in international transactions. For example, Japanese companies invoice customers in the currencies of export destinations (pricing to market) to maintain market share. This, combined with the fact that most Japanese imports are primary commodities (usually invoiced in dollars), limited the yen's role in denominating trade. At the same time, shallow money markets, distorted by a complex system of withholding taxes, make it difficult for residents and non-residents to park liquid working balances in yen-denominated short-term instruments.

To enhance the attractiveness of the yen as an international currency, the Japanese Ministry of Finance took action in December 1998. New policies included competitive price auctions of financing bills (FBs), abolition of both the withholding tax on interest income for non-residents and the securities transaction tax, and introduction of thirty-year government bonds and one-year treasury bills. In addition, an advisory group within the powerful Finance Ministry called for further measures to improve the repo market (by promoting transactions based on repurchase agreements instead of cash-collateralized lending and borrowing). They wanted steps to assist the government bond market (by introducing five-year government bonds). Other actions, including enhanced services offered by the Bank of Japan to its overseas counterparts, were announced and in time have been implemented.

For the Asian countries, pegging their currencies to the yen implies that their macroeconomic performance (inflation in particular) would depend on conditions in Japan. Following the "bubble," the Japanese economy has suffered its longest recession in the post-war era, and all agree that if the yen is to emerge as Asia's key currency, Japan needs to revitalize its economy as soon as possible. Thanks to government action, stability of the financial system has been restored, and the Japanese economy has shown signs of recovery.

Finally, the political aspects of this issue cannot be ignored. So far, the idea of a yen bloc in Asia has been widely dismissed as premature— even irrelevant—because most Asian countries, recalling World War II, are reluctant to give Japan a more prominent regional role. The Japanese government hesitates to take a higher profile in Asia, or in the world. However, recent monetary integration between Germany and France, and formation of a de facto deutsch-mark bloc in large parts of Europe (which suffered under German occupation in World War II), suggests that political barriers are surmountable.

Political opposition may arise from the United States if the formation of a yen bloc is interpreted as posing a challenge to the dollar's status. The United States has welcomed the emergence of EMU in Europe as a win-win game between the two sides of the Atlantic. Therefore, the U.S. might take a similarly receptive stance towards a yen bloc.

The political cost of a yen bloc in Asia is falling while the potential economic benefit is rising. The concept will mature when the economic benefit surpasses the political cost. Recent progress in financial cooperation among Asian countries is significant. Steps include the establishment of a regional financing mechanism involving a set of bilateral agreements to swap official reserves with local currencies during times of crisis (the Chiang Mai Initiative). This indicates that the time for cooperation towards a yen bloc may not be too far away.

Part III

The High-Tech Sphere

Taiwan's High-Tech Horizons

Brian Kuang-ming Cheng

Taiwan has emerged as a major force in some aspects of the high-tech industry, especially in production. Annual production value of our information technology (IT)–related hardware products is more than US$200 billion (making Taiwan the third-largest producer in the world), and high-tech goods account for a substantial percent of all manufacturing output. Technology-related items are three-fifths of "Made in Taiwan" exports.

Activities at our California-style R&D parks and among our breed of venture capitalists impact global IT. What trends are shaping the island's high-tech industry? Recent assumptions concerning high-tech market segments—that there is a semiconductor glut, that industry profit margins are shrinking, that new capacity is not being built, and that Taiwan's companies lag, in many respects, behind Korean and Japanese rivals—are wrong.

With those myths dispelled, let's examine Taiwan's high-tech industry. With a production value of US$40 billion in 1999, Taiwan's computer-related manufacturers are the world's largest suppliers of motherboards, monitors, keyboards, scanners, computer mice, and power supply systems. This East Asian island is a leader in production of desktop personal computers (PCs) and CD-ROM drives. "Made in Taiwan" notebook PCs were estimated to have an impressive forty-nine percent share of the entire global market.

Table 1

Outlook for Taiwan's Hardware Industry

Year	Production value	Growth rate
1999	39,881	18.1%
2000(f)	45,735	14.7%
2001(f)	52,169	14.1%
2002(f)	57,582	10.4%

Source: Institute for Information Industry, Taiwan.
(f): forecast
Unit: US$Million

Chips off a New Block

Apart from hardware, dynamic random access memory (DRAM) chips are a major revenue-earner for Taiwan's IT industry. Semiconductors are "hot," and the island is home for two large foundries—Taiwan Semiconductor Manufacturing Company (TSMC) and United Microelectronics Corporation (UMC). They process silicon into wafers, then into semiconductors, and both are operating at virtually full capacity. TSMC is building its first twelve-inch wafer plant in the Tainan Science-Based Industrial Park, located in southern Taiwan. That plant will be the largest single fabrications facility in the world, with 190,000 square feet of manufacturing space (the size of four American football fields).

The TSMC is also the world's first chip foundry making custom semiconductors under contract to chip designers, forging relationships with electronics giants such as Motorola and Acer Group. TSMC is gaining business from a proliferation of independent semiconductor houses that lack fabrication capabilities. As a result, TSMC registered sales revenues of $2.3 billion in 1999. Second-ranked UMC is well positioned and has merged with four of its subsidiaries to cut costs.

What trends are driving the semiconductor industry? Until recently, the PC and peripherals linked to it were semiconductor industry drivers. When PC sales grew, semiconductor output rose. Now, cellular phones or personal communications devices are emerging as the drivers. However, shortages of high-end microprocessors, commodity memory chips, and other semiconductors are possible. Motorola and others have decided that the billions needed to set up in-house foundries are better spent on designing circuitry for "cutting-edge" mobile phones. As a result, they are subcontracting ASICS (application-specific integrated chips) to TMSC and its competitors.

High-capacity foundries are changing the industry landscape, and the market will undoubtedly get bigger.

Taiwanese companies are well known for flexibility, adapting quickly as customers' demands change. This is part of the reason they will command thiry-five percent of all semiconductor products in 2010—a sharp increase from the seven percent they hold today.

With a fifteen-percent share of global DRAM market, Taiwan is the world's fourth-largest producer of these types of chips. She might move to second place very soon. The global DRAM chip industry is "dynamic" in more ways than one, and Taiwan-based companies face major obstacles in seeking footholds in DRAMs. Taiwan's DRAM manufacturers are launching strategic alliances with foreign partners and obtaining technical expertise. For example, Taiwan's Winbond Electronics Corporation signed a licensing agreement with Japan's Toshiba Corporation. Under the pact, Winbond was allowed to use 0.175- and 0.15-micron processing technologies developed by Toshiba to produce 64-megabyte, 128-Mb, 256-Mb and 512-Mb DRAM chips. (A micron equals one-millionth of a meter.) Using newly acquired 0.175-micron processing technology, Winbond developed a 256-megabyte DRAM chip, making it the first Taiwan company—and the fourth in the world—to produce these highly advanced chips.

But there are obstacles ahead. Memory chip manufacturers are captives of overseas competitors who have engaged in extensive "dumping" for the past two years. According to the Taiwan Semiconductor Industry Association, the island's DRAM industry suffered US$4 billion worth of lost sales in 1999 due to foreign competition (and dumping).

The Software Side

Taiwan's software industry development contrasts with successes of its IT hardware sector—an area in which the island has remained a world leader. Taiwan lags behind software front-runners. More than 1,000 software companies are operating on the island, but these combined make up a scant twelve percent of a total of $19 billion worth of IT production. The government and the private sector are launching initiatives to boost the island's software industry. Hopes are placed on Nankang Software Park's

Table 2

Outlook for Taiwan's Software Market

Year	Production value	Growth rate
1999	95,437	30%
2000(f)	123,385	29%
2001(f)	152,881	24%
2002(f)	180,859	18%
2003(f)	226,937	25%

Source: Institute for Information Industry, Taiwan
(f): forecast
Unit: US$Million

*Estimate for year 2000 software production: According to the Institute for Information Industry, the output of Taiwan's software sector will rise 35 percent to US$4 billion in 2000.

ability to accelerate the pace of software R&D. Located in suburban Taipei, it is Asia's largest software research park. Some fifty local manufacturers have already moved into the Nankang Software Park, located in northern Taiwan, and $6.5 billion worth of production is expected within four years.

Manufacturers are shifting from hardware production to software development. According to a report by the government-sponsored Institute for Information Industry (III), software is a $3 billion industry. Even if III estimates that domestic software output will increase by twenty-five percent in 2002 are correct, the production value of Taiwan's software will be only one percent of the worldwide total. To sharpen software's competitive edge, government-sponsored training programs seek to groom 22,000 specialists within three years, and $180 million or more in low-interest loans will be made available for local software companies.

Telecommunications and the Internet

Telecommunications is a $2.1 billion industry, and ever-surging demand for mobile phones fuels wireless products. This amount is equal to the value of Taiwan's Internet-related production. Given consumers' seemingly insatiable appetite for "smart" household appliances and the liberalization of global telecommunications markets, Taiwan's Internet sector should grow. The government is spending $460 million to increase production values of local wireless telecom and broadband network com-

Table 3

Outlook for Taiwan's Telecommunications industry

Year	Production value	Growth rate
1999	2,148	8.9%
2000(f)	3,312	54.2%
2001(f)	4,738	43.1%
2002(f)	6,921	46.1%

Source: Institute for Information Industry, Taiwan
(f): forecast
Unit: US$Million

panies. Wireless telecom items should reach the $6 billion level by 2005. Taiwan might become a global production base for mobile phones— and the leading supplier of wireless data communications equipment— by 2002. The long-term goal is to establish wireless technology as the driving force of the island's semiconductor, IT, and software sectors.

Taiwan is Internet crazed. Companies are scrambling to add dot.com, cyber-this and e-that to their names, hoping to emerge as potential Internet players. The island's e-commerce activity will surpass $1 billion in 2002. The III reports there were 4.5 million Internet users in Taiwan at the end of 1999, while on-line shoppers in Taiwan will spend $266 million by 2002. Taiwan will be the world's leading supplier of portable Internet surfing devices such as palmtop PCs, personal digital assistants and mobile phones with Internet-access functions.

A major problem facing Internet companies is to establish name recognition (and hence credibility). Many dot-com companies may be swallowed up by established retailers seeking new business opportunities and ways to augment distribution.

Officials in Taipei worry about a lack of e-commerce zeal among small and medium-sized companies, which remain a cornerstone of the island's economy. Business-to-business ("B2B") e-commerce among and between IT companies totaled only $1 billion in 1999. Some companies are short of cash and have not embraced the Internet.

Challenges in the New Era

Taiwan's high-tech firms face challenges; some result from rapid evolution of advanced technologies. Others arise from competitors in the People's Republic of China (PRC) and from would-be high-tech kingpins in Southeast Asia. At some point the PRC will surpass Taiwan in IT output. The best chance for Taiwan is to boost innovation and value-added production. Another possibility is to have companies such as TSMC and UMC inaugurate elements of system design for the next wave of post-PC devices such as CD-ROM drives, CD-ROM disks, light-emitting diodes and liquid-crystal displays. The value of these (Taiwan-made) products should reach $17.4 billion in 2002 and—along with photo printers, digital cameras and digital discs—become increasingly important exports.

Environmentally friendly and portable, LCDs will gradually replace cathode ray tube monitors in the coming post-PC era. Although Taiwanese manufacturers of IT products are relative newcomers to the LCD industry, they have unprecedented opportunities to become major suppliers of thin-film transistor liquid-crystal displays (TFT-LCDs) for global markets. TFT-LCDs make up one-third of the total production costs of notebook PCs. Japanese and South Korean producers—likely TFT-LCD competitors—curtailed expansion plans. Taiwan can reach twenty percent of the TFT-LCD global market this year, surpassing the thirty percent level by 2005. The island will become the world's second-largest TFT-LCD supplier after Japan.

One potential hurdle is that of generating continuous investment: foundries cost US$1–1.5 billion; even upgrades (to keep in step with technological advances) are costly. But the most difficult part is acquiring engineering talent and management expertise. As other authors in this book observe, in East and Southeast Asia human capital is a much more significant issue than financial capital.

Taiwan's IT Companies in China

More than 100,000 Taiwan-owned and managed businesses operate on the Chinese Mainland, many of them in high-tech industries. These factories turned out $11 billion worth of IT products in 1999. Taiwanese investors have pumped $15 billion into China, and many hope a growing bilateral economic relationship will yield harmony. Ironically, many businessmen complain that Mainland officials target Taiwanese-owned factories for violations of labor standards and customs rules. The Chinese market cannot be ignored, and Mainland investment is critical for Taiwan's IT companies. Establishing operations in the PRC's industrial zones provides access to China's markets, a large pool of cheap labor, and considerable engineering talent. Computer giant Acer is among those building factories that are transforming China into a global IT supplier. Evidence of this high-tech migration is obvious in Suzhou, a special economic zone in Jiangsu Province (near Shanghai). Taiwan companies are shifting production of low-end motherboards, monitors, and keyboards to the PRC. In 1999, one-third of "Made In Taiwan" computers were assembled in on the Mainland.

Understandably, Taipei is attempting to maintain a delicate balance in its ties with Beijing. Taiwan's IT makers strive to sell to the PRC without becoming dependent on it. Despite political tensions, the integration of Taiwanese industry into the Chinese economy benefits both sides. The PRC is challenging Taiwan's manufacturing prowess in PC assembly and in the production of related components. This will prompt Taiwan to move from computer hardware and printed circuit boards to products born of creativity and "cutting edge" technology.

Use of the Internet is growing in China, and the on-line population in China should reach twenty-seven million this year. Although only $42 million in e-commerce transactions were registered last year, a $4 billion market is seen by 2002. Few doubt that the Internet is changing the Mainland and Chinese society.

For Taiwan's dot-coms and Internet service providers, making money in China is not easy. Beijing censors apply brakes to those traveling along the information highway. The Taiwan dot-coms edit content on their Websites to avoid official displeasure: the business strategy is to shift from content to infrastructure. Taiwan software makers in the PRC hope to persuade investors there to use the Web to outsource back-office functions such as billing, e-mail, customer databases, accounting, and shipping. "B2B" e-commerce isn't the answer: few Chinese consumers have credit cards, making on-line transactions difficult. The PRC lacks a large base of affluent consumers (only two million citizens have a disposable annual income of US$20,000 or higher). People are using the Web for sending e-mails and "surfing" for free information, not for commerce.

Taiwan will be doing other things to assure it is at "the cutting edge." Steps to better link the manufacturing sector with high-tech—making it a formidable support industry for the growing list of our successful technology-based companies—is one priority. Obtaining advanced technologies and original equipment manufacturing orders from abroad is necessary. Whether the island can make the leap to new products or advanced R&D is debatable; Taiwanese firms are increasing investments in China to remain competitive—not spending money on R&D.

As other authors observed, the knowledge-based economy is essential for Asia's survival and competitiveness. This is certainly true for Taiwan, perhaps even more so than for its neighbors. Taiwan has not escaped the current high-tech slump: Acer's stock plummeted eighty percent by March 2001 and others are suffering losses. But the island's nimble companies can weather the storm. M-(mobile) commerce could be the next wave. Already, Taiwan is a serious competitor to Japan's and Korea's thin-film transistor-liquid crystal display technologies.

Asian E-Commerce: Waiting for Takeoff

Richard Martin

When the Chinese government announced new regulations on Internet ventures, groans from would-be Internet entrepreneurs could be heard from Guangzhou to New York. The rules were anti-private enterprise and could strangle Mainland e-commerce: Internet businesses were required to register with the powerful Ministry of Information Industry; foreign investment in on-line enterprises was effectively banned. Chinese Internet firms were prohibited from listing on overseas stock exchanges, while Byzantine regulations countered the fervor that fueled Internet growth in the West.

Yet, foreign investment in Chinese dot-com companies continued unabated; by the end of 2000 nearly US$200 million in foreign capital had flowed into Web "portals" and e-commerce startups in the People's Republic of China (PRC). Almost nine million Chinese are on-line, and state investment in Internet infrastructure has proceeded at a rapid pace. The unquenched thirst in China for Internet opportunities—along with the hard-to-control nature of the Internet itself—made the Communist Party's attempt to regulate Internet commerce seem meaningless.

The situation in China was emblematic of the state of electronic commerce across the region. Obstacles to a thriving Internet economy in Asia are manifold: in the less-developed parts of the region, such as Indonesia, the Philippines, and the Chinese hinterland, basic infrastructure is not yet in place for reliable telephone service (much less Internet connections). Government intransigence and corruption stand directly in the path of a free Internet economy. Rigid social structures run contrary to the anti-hierarchical world of cyberspace. Even in sophisticated economies like Japan and Taiwan, ill-advised government policies, a lack of venture capital, and decaying business structures cause e-commerce development to lag.

Still, the prospects glow brightly on a distant but real horizon. Government and corporate resistance to Net-inspired change is crumbling swiftly. The spread of cell phones (in Japan and South Korea) and set-top boxes for televisions (in the PRC) hasten Internet usage without the need for cumbersome personal computers (PCs). Strong math and science educational systems might provide some societies a competitive advantage in software and telecommunications. Internet entrepreneurs are springing up in unlikely corners, and e-commerce can overcome non-existent infrastructure, government corruption, and entrenched business interests.

"E-commerce" is broadly defined. People in Xinjiang, in western China, or along the Indonesian archipelago, won't be ordering books and CDs over the Internet for years. But the wider effects of the Internet economy—huge investment in telecommunications, growth markets for PCs and cell phones, and the overturning of rigid social systems—can hardly be overstated. E-commerce in Asia is more than selling goods and services on-line. It's about remaking economies still recovering from the disastrous crash of 1997–98.

In 1993 I visited Marawi City, on the island of Mindanao in the southern Philippines. It was during one of the rashes of kidnappings that periodically flare up around the lawless Sulu Sea. The hotel proprietor—an amiable though fierce-looking young man—made no bones about his hometown's isolation. Philippine Airlines had cut service to Marawi City, and phone service was sporadic at best. Few people had even heard of the Internet. An e-mail connection for my laptop was out of the question.

Seven years later, the Philippines was a hotbed of homegrown Internet technologists. The most famous was a young hacker who in 2000 rocked the cyber-world with the destructive "Love Bug" computer virus.

What's more, the Philippines had become a major center for outsourcing by American Internet firms. America Online has most of its help-desk call-in support handled from a site at the former Clark Air Force base, two hours north of Manila. Young Filipinos answer calls from around the globe twenty-four hours a day, getting a crash course in technology.

The Internet was slow to gather momentum in the region, but by last year it was taking off rapidly. The most striking thing about this expansion is its high variability. According to A.C. Nielsen, sixty-two percent of all households in Singapore—where high-speed Internet connections are a government priority—owned a PC in 1999, and twenty-four percent of the population used the Internet. In Indonesia and Thailand, on the other hand, less than five percent of households had computers, and the percentage of the population on-line was negligible. In China, the most promising country in the region for e-commerce, only sixteen percent of households owned PCs in the urban areas of Guangzhou, Shanghai, and Beijing. Few households elsewhere in the country have PCs.

The first wave of e-commerce in Asia will not consist of buying and selling on-line but in selling basic hardware and connections to bring people on-line. With sixty-one percent of the world's population, Asia accounted for only around eighteen percent of worldwide PC sales in 2000. That's changing rapidly. American companies such as Dell and Gateway are expanding Internet direct-sales models to Asia. Most of that growth is Internet-fueled. Many PCs sold in Asia now come with pre-installed "one-click" Internet connections.

The second phase of the e-commerce wave is not far behind. Forrester Research predicts Asia will experience e-commerce "hypergrowth," with numbers of users growing exponentially, by 2003. Japan will lead the way, with US$364 billion in e-commerce sales by then. The PRC will reach the same level of growth until 2007. Asian e-commerce will overtake Europe by 2004, according to data presented at the October 2000 World E-Commerce Forum in London.

Country Scenarios

Singapore should be an ideal laboratory for turning a vibrant economy based on shipping and value-added manufacturing into an e-commerce dynamo. The country's population is highly wired. Singapore leads the world in computer-based education and boasts the highest rates of PC ownership and Internet connectivity in the region. It already leads Asia in high-tech exports, with $65 billion in sales in 1999. Moreover, the government has launched a public drive to make Singapore a center for electronic commerce, and revenues doubled from 1998 to 1999, reaching $206 million.

Singapore has launched an overall program to become the communications hub of Asia. The government's networking plan calls for "Singapore One" to be the "world's first implementation of a multimedia broadband network," linking every household, business, and school to the Internet. Besides building a state of the art network, the government has announced plans for a novel "Internet I.D. card," which will authorize Internet accounts for banking, e-mail, and transactions. The government has also authorized funds to help small and medium-sized firms go electronic. Half of all businesses will be doing business online, generating $4 billion in revenue.

The only obstacle to this "wired island" vision is its statist model: in the United States and Europe, the Internet has grown organically, with little government planning or regulation. Indeed, the Internet has shown itself remarkably resistant to authoritarian models of all kinds: witness China and Malaysia's efforts to stifle internal dissent on the Net, or the recording industry's attempts to control digital music exchanges such as Napster.

What's more, government selection for public funding of Internet startups is risky. In some ways, the dot-com shakeout that ravaged U.S. Internet companies last year could be the best thing for the industry's long-term health. Whether e-commerce can be mandated from the top-down is an open question.

In many ways Japan, the region's most highly developed economy, epitomizes opportunities for—and barriers against—e-commerce. Internet users in Japan surged past the twenty million mark in 2000, many of them tech-savvy consumers. The country's telecommunications infrastructure is unmatched, and the Internet promises to break through outmoded business structures and irrational pricing regimes.

The high cost of telephone service in Japan has hampered the build-out of the Internet to residences. Around seventy percent of Internet usage is confined to office PCs, and the government has shown no sign of opening up the Internet service industry. That has driven the majority of e-commerce growth in Japan onto cell phones and other handheld devices, where DoCoMo (Internet) service has proven popular. Launched in 1999, DoCoMo's Internet mode boasted some fourteen million users in twenty-four months. The growth of e-commerce in Japan will depend on how many consumers will buy goods over devices with tiny screens and keyboards.

Still, Japan shows promise: The Ministry of International Trade and Industry predicts that electronic commerce will reach 70 billion by 2003, with consumer purchases increasing fifty fold.

Given the unique aspects of Japanese society, e-commerce could take unlikely forms. Japanese consumers are notoriously averse to credit cards, and only twenty-nine percent of Japanese homes have PCs. A vast network of convenience stores—of which there are as many as 50,000 nationwide—could serve as e-commerce sites with Internet kiosks allowing customers to pay bills, make travel reservations, buy theater tickets and purchase goods on-line.

Since 1993 the PRC government has invested some $50 billion in telecommunications and Internet projects, including a fiber-optic grid spanning the nation from Shanghai west to Urumchi and from Hong Kong north to Beijing. More than two million new phone lines are being laid every month, and mobile phones are multiplying. The enterprising and far-flung overseas Chinese community supplies a ready-made international market—and source of capital—for Mainland e-commerce ventures. Hong Kong's low tariffs and world-class infrastructure make it an ideal virtual entrepôt. The PRC government clearly views the Internet as economically important, although state control is essential in its view.

No spectacle is more entertaining than the rise and remarkable fall of China's portal sites, such as China.com, Sohu.com, and Sina.com. Several of these have been listed, through licensing agreements, on overseas stock exchanges, inspiring mob scenes from would-be investors and enjoying fabulous run-ups before share prices collapsed after the U.S. market correction in April 2000.

Many non-Asian hardware manufacturers are setting up on-line sales channels, laying a foundation for future electronic commerce in the PRC. Barriers remain high: government control, absence of national credit cards, unreliable distribution systems, and poor on-line security have combined to delay China's e-commerce revolution. Currently, transactions total no more than $10 million per year and will likely not increase significantly until the end of this decade.

Forrester Research predicts e-commerce in Asia will reach $1.6 trillion by 2004, with the vast majority of that amount coming from the Four "Tigers" (Hong Kong, Taiwan, Singapore, Korea). As mentioned above, the type of commerce witnessed will differ greatly from the West's experience. The region's shipping trade, flourishing tech-hardware sector, and growing services firms will be the primary beneficiaries of Asia's e-commerce revolution, Part I.

Part IV

Defense/Security

Security in the Region: An Asian Perspective

Daljit Singh

The shift of global economic power towards East Asia has been striking. In 1960 the region accounted for only four percent of the world GDP; by 1995 it accounted for a quarter. This shift is expected to continue, though more slowly because large regions like China (population 1.3 billion) and Southeast Asia (population 500 million) are still in the early stages of industrialization.

Yet East Asia's economic prospects could be jeopardized if the region's politics and security are not carefully tended. The risks become obvious when East Asia's security and political environments are compared with those of North America and the European Union (EU), two other poles of global economic power. The latter comprise mostly mature, developed societies with stable political systems. The prospect of a major inter-state war among countries within the EU is remote.

Asian Security Challenges

The same cannot be said of East Asia, which is the only part of the world with serious strategic tensions between major powers—especially between China and Japan and between China and (beyond the region) the United States. If the Taiwan issue is mismanaged, the U.S. and China could find themselves at war in short order, with incalculable consequences for the future of the Asia-Pacific region. The international community has lived with the danger of a major war on the Korean Peninsula for the past half century; these fears continued well beyond the Cold War's end. Japan-China relations remain poisoned by history and contemporary rivalry.

Above all, the security challenge in Asia is structural, involving a more "normal" Japan and the rise of new powers, principally China but also to a lesser extent India. The rise of these powers has to be managed peacefully if the international community is to avoid a repetition of the horrendous consequences witnessed in the first half of the twentieth century. They arose from failure on the part of the major powers to peacefully manage the rise of Imperial Germany and Japan.

Unlike the EU or North America above the Rio Grande, much of East Asia is still part of the developing world. The wide differences in economic achievement, ranging from Japan, Hong Kong, and Singapore at one end of the spectrum to countries like Laos, Cambodia, and Myanmar at the other, are matched by an enormous diversity in political systems, political development and quality of administrative structures and governance.

Rapidly growing "Developing Asia" is in the throes of a historic transition from rural-based development and society, on the one hand, to modern industrial and service economies on the other. Any failure to manage the resulting societal change could cause major domestic instabilities, with spillover effects on interstate relations, as, for instance, through large-scale migrations of peoples. Or instability could impel regimes to ride the tiger of nationalism for self-preservation.

Among the fundamental longer-term security uncertainties are the following:

- What kind of China will a powerful China be? Will it be a benign great power or not?
- What will the U.S.-China relationship be like? Will China accept that East Asia is large enough for both China and the United States or will it seek to evict the United States from the region? Will the United States, in turn, allow China larger space and influence in Asia?
- Will the United States keep its Asian alliances in good shape and continue to maintain credible regional military power?
- Will Japan remain anchored in the security alliance with the United States, or will it rearm and assume an independent military posture?

- Will China and Japan become reconciled, or will their rivalry intensify?
- Will North Korea forego the development of nuclear weapons and long-range missiles and reunite peacefully with the South?
- Will the South China Sea disputes be resolved peacefully in accordance with the United Nations Conference on the Law of the Sea (UNCLOS)?
- Will China formally renounce its claims and ambitions regarding the South China Sea? (Represented by a U-shaped line enclosing nearly eighty percent of the Sea's surface area.)
- Will the Association of Southeast Asian Nations (ASEAN) recover its credibility, or will it become increasingly irrelevant?
- What will happen to Indonesia?

In the next few years, factors to watch will be the changes in Korea and their impact on the U.S. presence in the region and on Japan; the dynamics in the Taiwan Strait—and their effects on U.S.-China relations; and domestic developments in China as leadership changes and other shifts occur. In addition, events in Indonesia must be monitored carefully because of that country's strategic importance.

Institution Building and Cooperative Security

Despite the strategic and security uncertainties, Europe's pre-1945 past need not necessarily be Asia's future. For one thing, the possession of nuclear weapons by all the great powers in Asia (except Japan) makes a major war between them less likely. There is also a good deal of awareness among the ruling elites, including those in China, that a major conflict would destroy hopes for economic development and modernization on which the power and prestige of a country ultimately is founded. Yet it would also be naive to dismiss the dangers; miscalculations can occur, and leaders may not be fully in control of the forces pushing a country off the edge.

A number of steps have been taken since the end of the Cold War to build confidence and cooperation in interstate relations. At the bilateral level, the most significant developments have been the regular political and security dialogues between old adversaries China and Japan and between South Korea and Japan. Also institutionalized since the end of the Cold War is dialogue between China and ASEAN.

At the multilateral level, two important institutions have been established. The Asia-Pacific Economic Cooperation (APEC) forum was established in 1989 for economic purposes. However, its annual leaders' meeting enables heads of government to come together in an informal summit and pursue their bilateral agendas in separate meetings on the side. The ASEAN Regional Forum (ARF), set up in 1994, is a cooperative security mechanism. One of its objectives at the time of its inception was to engage and integrate China, a rising power, into the regional and international order. The ARF today has twenty-three members: the ten ASEAN countries and the five major powers in Asia (the United States, China, Japan, Russia, and India) as well as the European Union, Australia, New Zealand, Canada, South Korea, North Korea, Mongolia, and Papua-New Guinea.

Furthermore, in the past few years steps have been taken towards East Asian regional cooperation. These were fostered through the "ASEAN Plus Three" process, the Three being the Northeast Asian countries of Japan, China, and South Korea. The process involves regular meetings at significant levels (senior officials, ministers, and heads of governments). These meetings provide another vehicle, in an Asian setting, for engagement and confidence-building between China and Japan—as well as between Japan and South Korea.

Their Value and Limitations

It is clear that while dialogue, cooperative security, and institution-building all have their value, their present capacity to prevent or resolve conflicts is weak. The ARF is not in a position to deal with any security crisis apart from discussing it. The unanimity rule of decision-making gives any country, and especially the big powers, a veto against any concrete action to prevent or resolve a conflict that is against their interest. China has so far not allowed the ARF to move to even the most limited preventive diplomacy.

The only organization which has helped to prevent interstate conflict between its members in the past is ASEAN, which was established in 1967. But ASEAN is a subregional organization, confined to Southeast Asia. The major sources of strategic tension in East Asia lie outside its scope. Its capacity to manage the principal strategic relationships in East Asia, through its leading role in the ARF, is feeble. Even within Southeast Asia, ASEAN's international standing has suffered in recent years because of problems caused by its expansion (since 1995) and by the political fallout of the regionwide economic crisis.

ASEAN succeeded in keeping the peace among the original five members (Singapore, Thailand, Malaysia, Indonesia, and the Philippines) for thirty years. There was a commonality in their pre-dispositions and aspirations which the much larger and much more heterogenous ARF does not possess. The original five ASEAN members were relatively at ease about territorial boundaries and the distribution of power within the geographical area. After Sukarno's Indonesia failed at attempts to foster sub-regional hegemony, there was no hegemonal threat from within the ranks of the Association.

The ARF, on the other hand, is not marked by a similar sense of comfort about the status quo within the geographical area of the Forum; its principal strategic tensions are intramural.

When the ARF was first established, most East Asian countries regarded America's forward military deployment and its bilateral alliances with Western Pacific countries—and especially with Japan—as the bedrock of security in the Asia-Pacific. The ARF was intended only to supplement them. These realities have not changed since then. Maintenance of this U.S. role is crucial, for otherwise there would be an extremely destabilizing scramble by the Asian powers to fill the perceived vacuum.

Already, Korean reconciliation and the prospect of eventual reunification are causing anxiety in Asia. This is because American military power on the Korean Peninsula has for the past half century served to contain the historic rivalries and animosities among China, Japan, Korea, and even Russia.

Cooperative security, both multilateral and bilateral, arguably may help ease tensions and cushion the sharp edges of hard security arrangements based on deterrence and balance of power. In this sense, even "talk shops" have value up to a point, especially if they help to clarify each other's intentions and thereby prevent miscalculation. But there is also the danger that they can cause strategic confusion and myopia if participants are allowed to be lulled into believing that, as it pertains to the East Asian environment, cooperative security is the main answer to security problems.

The American Role

The strategic realities outlined above show that there are as yet no Asian solutions to the major security problems of Asia. The humanitarian tragedy in East Timor in 1999 and the consequent United Nations (UN) intervention illustrated this at another level. The role of the United States and of the international community through the UN will remain crucial for a long time. And given the global importance of Asian economic and security developments, it is also right and proper that approaches and solutions to Asian problems be consistent with global norms and rules. Indeed, one problem that the international community has to grapple with in East Asia is that the foreign relations reflexes of some of the rising powers may not always be in accord with international norms and practices.

East Asia's economic success story owes much to the post-World War II role of the U.S. as a guarantor of security in the region. Access to the vast American consumer market, combined with East Asian virtues (industriousness, frugality, love for learning, and a penchant for organization), contributed to the region's historic economic prowess. Enlightened self-interest to contain communism dictated America's approach.

Now it transpires that American military engagement and security commitments will continue to be critically needed to keep the peace in East Asia. The United States, in its own interests, cannot afford to be shut out from this economically dynamic region—one emerging as the biggest market for American products and services. Washington must continue helping to keep the Asia-Pacific region open to all while also sustaining a liberal international trading order. This is also in the interest of most Asian countries.

Because of Asia's growing weight in world affairs, war and peace in the region and political and economic initiatives taken there will have global repercussions which America, on the other side of the Pacific, will not escape. America's forward military presence, alliances and "soft power" provide it with substantial clout, including the ability to help steer changes in East Asia in a benign direction. It should not be discouraged from this enterprise by perceived differences in values or perceived ambivalence of some Asians toward America.

The good news is that although differences in basic values remain between the West and some countries in Asia, overall trends are proceeding in the right direction: towards market-oriented economic systems, democracy, and greater respect for human rights. Further, such differences have not weakened the sense of realism of most East Asian states in wanting the continuation of the U.S. military presence in the region.

America's preponderance of power can breed fear and resentment, leading others to gang up in order to curb perceived arrogance and unilateralism. In the face of contemporary realities, America should "carry a big stick" but "walk and talk softly," keeping to existing alliances, especially those with Japan, Korea, and Australia. Washington should work closely with friends and allies while reaching out to all, including potential rivals. The espousal of human rights and democracy is important, both to sustain domestic support for American foreign policy and to bring about a better world. Yet such espousal cannot be the foremost priority in America's Asian policy, and it should be exercised with sensitivity, bearing in mind strategic considerations as well as the unique situation in each country.

The decision to admit China into the World Trade Organization reinforces a wise American policy to engage rather than isolate China. America has to gradually create space for rising powers in Asia, whether it be in China, Japan, Russia, or India, while being active enough to ensure—together with allies and friends—that none abuses its power.

Dragons' Dance: The Evolving Security Situation in Northeast Asia

Peter Brookes

An Uncertain Future

In the twenty-first century, Asia will replace Europe as the center of global political, economic, and security gravity. The countries of Northeast Asia will be at the core; unfortunately, the region's security environment is fragile and fraught with potential instability. The region is less stable than many had anticipated in light of the end of the Cold War. The Taiwan Strait and the Korean Peninsula are two of the world's most dangerous military flashpoints. Intra-regional rivalries could prove increasingly dangerous. Defense budgets and advanced weapons acquisitions are on the rise. Some countries already have nuclear weapons while others are capable of quickly adding them to their arsenals. Regrettably, the region has yet to develop a multilateral security framework for addressing mutual concerns and initiating confidence and security-building measures. Despite the prospects of growing interdependence, the question writ large is: will the major powers manage—or mismanage—the current peace.

The China Conundrum

The rise of the People's Republic of China (PRC) is clearly the key question in Northeast Asia's future. The Soviet Union's collapse increased

China's relative power in East Asia, making the PRC the nation offering the region both the greatest hope and the gravest concern. Indeed, Beijing is dissatisfied with being a secondary global power and is consequently unwilling to accept constraints on its expanding international influence. Asserting Chinese claims over Taiwan, the South China Sea, and the Senkaku (Diaoyu) Islands are integral to Beijing's regional goals. Chinese success will upset the current balance of power between continental Asia, dominated by the PRC itself— and maritime Asia— dominated by the United States and Japan. In fact, China may aspire to become the regional hegemon, imposing permanent strategic subservience upon Japan—and demanding an end to the U.S. presence in Asia.

China's conventional and nuclear force modernization program is buttressed by the fastest-growing defense budget in the region. The PRC has purchased advanced weapons systems from Russia that increase its military power projection capability. These new Chinese acquisitions include: KILO-class diesel submarines; advanced SU-27 fighter aircraft; sovremenny-class destroyers; and strategic SA-10 surface-to-air missile batteries. In addition, the PRC is developing a prodigious theater ballistic missile arsenal, and its strategic nuclear force is increasingly sophisticated and dangerous.

China's military build-up is directed primarily at Taiwan. Beijing's stated goal is to regain control of Taiwan, preferably by peaceful means. The Chinese interest in unifying with Taiwan is the foundation for Beijing's concern over America's forward military presence in the Western Pacific, the U.S.-Japan security alliance, and the deployment of missile defense systems by the U.S. and its allies. China currently lacks the capability to conduct an amphibious invasion of Taiwan, much less an occupation of the island. Nevertheless, Beijing is developing other military options including a naval blockade and an overwhelming ballistic missile strike against critical Taiwanese targets.

Taipei is addressing the situation by requesting additional advanced weapons systems to counter the growing asymmetry in military capability between itself and the mainland. Unfortunately, the increased militarization of the Taiwan Strait by either party increases the risk of both miscalculation—and conflict.

The Korean Question

The long-divided Korean Peninsula remains the Cold War's last frontier. The misnamed Demilitarized Zone separating North and South is the most heavily fortified border in the world. Events—including the June 2000 KIM-KIM Summit—have not fundamentally altered the security situation on the peninsula. In fact, the North's capacity to undertake large-scale military operations against the South—and against American forces on the Peninsula—has increased over the last two years. Furthermore, the North's rulers will quietly pursue a nuclear weapons program while using its missile arsenal and proliferation practices as bargaining chips for international concessions.

Despite the North's economy being in a state of near-collapse, Pyongyang will move slowly toward a political rapprochement with Seoul as long as it is deemed profitable. Diplomatic "brinkmanship" can be expected and miscalculation by the enigmatic Pyongyang regime cannot be discounted. North Korea's recent emergence from self-imposed isolation may, or may not, foster a new political and security environment in Northeast Asia. Barring an authentic opening or change in leadership by Pyongyang, the situation on the Peninsula will remain tense.

The Japanese Equation

The Cold War's end did not bring Japan the security environment it had envisioned. Challenges to Japanese security include: North Korea's nuclear and ballistic missile programs, China's rising military power, and questions about America's future security role in the region. These concerns have encouraged Tokyo to focus on the state of its own security forces. The Japanese Constitution's Article Nine forever renounces war as national policy, but grants the right to maintain self-defense forces. The "peace constitution" restrains security policy and is the source of significant debate within Japanese society today. A constitutional revision commission is reviewing possible changes in policy regarding collective self-defense and the use of military power. Japan's interest in reconnaissance/intelligence satellites and ballistic missile defense are evidence of a more assertive—and autonomous—security posture.

Within the region, there are some concerns that Japan is reverting to a 1930s-style foreign policy—militaristic, expansionist, and internationally forceful. In all likelihood, in the absence of a significant provocation, any change in Japanese defense and security policy will be measured, incremental, and transparent.

The Missile Defense Dilemma

Arguably no other issue affects Northeast Asian security more than the question of missile defense. Some fear missile defense will trigger a spiraling arms race. Others regard these systems as a force for stability, limiting threats from the burgeoning missile arsenals of China and North Korea. China's short-range ballistic missiles are capable of striking Taiwan, South Korea, and Japan. Meanwhile, North Korea is capitalizing on medium-range missiles while clearly aspiring to build ICBMs capable of striking the continental United States.

If Washington—and others— ignore these missile programs, the consequences are potentially dire for regional stability. Disregarding them raises questions about America's security guarantees, weakens alliances, and encourages other countries to consider alternative defense strategies (e.g., missile programs or weapons of mass destruction). China has demonstrated significant hostility toward missile defense. Beijing is also concerned that the transfer of missile defense to Taiwan will encourage Taiwanese independence, undermine Beijing's military threat toward the island, and trigger a revival of the U.S.-Taiwan military alliance. Understandably anxious about the burgeoning Chinese missile threat, Taiwan sees missile defense as a logical and imperative response. Similarly, the August 1998 launch of a North Korean long-range missile over Japanese territory encouraged Tokyo to begin cooperating with the United States on missile defense. For itself, South Korea is unlikely to pursue missile defense since Seoul feels there is a greater threat from North Korean conventional forces than from missile attack.

The United States as Balancer

Washington plays a critical role in maintaining peace and stability in Asia. America's presence provides a framework for a security structure that offers protection to allies and reassurance to others. Washington serves as a strategic counterbalance to the historic mistrust that exists between many of the regional capitals. The United States' absence would create a dangerous competition for power and resources. Yet, Washington's long-term commitments to the region are often questioned by Asian policy-makers. The ongoing shifts in regional equilibrium require America to review its security posture and policies in Asia in order to maintain a balance of power conducive to peace and stability.

The Future?

The tectonic plates of power across Northeast Asia are shifting, and the consequences of the ongoing changes are unclear. Security uncertainties will likely encourage regional powers to hedge in order to protect their interests. They will use diplomatic, military, economic, and any other means imaginable to achieve unilateral advantages at the expense of their neighbors, resulting in fear, misperception, and possibly conflict.

Northeast Asia lacks an institutionalized multilateral security arrangement to promote transparency, confidence-building, and long-term stability. Such a security framework could transform competition and uncertainty into cooperation and stability. The security dynamics in Northeast Asia are at a critical juncture. A failure to address perceptions of rising mutual insecurity may lead to another tragic conflict in East Asia—one that, like others, could have been avoided.

Part V

Quest for Civil Societies and Political Harmony

Democracy in the Balance

Roland Rich

East and Southeast Asia will be the laboratory for democracy in the twenty-first century. It will be in Asia that the big questions about the universality of democracy will be answered. And it will be in Asia that the proposition that democratic governance can lift both living standards and promote human rights will be best tested.

Asia encompasses a vast area and a great diversity of political systems. It has vibrant democracies, states in transition to democracy from authoritarian systems, feudal monarchies, and single party states wishing to practice capitalism, and in North Korea and Burma it has two dictatorial systems of government. Within this great ferment there are China, the world's most populous nation and an emerging superpower resisting democratic change; India, more a continent than a nation yet still able to make democracy work; and Indonesia, the largest Muslim country in the world, now attempting to reinvent itself as a democracy.

The region is diverse economically, with countries at the "cutting edge" of technology and others scraping by on subsistence economies. There are long-established market economies and other countries in transition. One finds dictatorships with economies in such bad shape that they have few options other than to fall back on autarky or international charity. Within this great diversity, the popular demand for democracy has shown itself to be present throughout Asia. Whether on the streets of Rangoon, in Tiananmen Square, or at the hundred thousand polling booths in Indonesia, the people of Asia have demonstrated their wish for democracy. How that wish translates into reality will be a great test for democracy in the world.

A Difficult Path towards Democracy

It has taken half a century to come to this critical point in Asian history. The post-colonial period, which essentially began with the end of World War II, saw many countries flirt with democratic forms of government. Either in imitation of the political systems of colonial powers or, as in Japan, through imposition by the victorious United States, multiparty electoral democracy was the method of government initially attempted.

The early post-colonial years saw a great intellectual and political effort to make democracy work. Constitutions were drafted, parties formed, and elections held. Great statesmen and champions of democracy emerged in this period: Mahatma Ghandi and Jawaharlal Nehru in India, U Nu in Burma, and Ramon Magsaysay in the Philippines. Yet it was only in India that democracy took firm root among both the people and the political elites and has remained to this day the dominant form of government, interrupted only briefly by Indira Ghandi's imposition of emergency powers, over which the Indian people turned against her.

With the benefit of hindsight, we can today better understand the unbearable weight that democratic systems in the region had to shoulder during the period of nation-building, often reconstructing societies out of unjust colonial infra- and social structures and the ruins of war. Burdens of leadership had to be carried by young nationalists who were untested administrators. Leaders emerged in the anti-colonial struggle, but their talents were not always the talents needed to forge a new society. The people they were leading were struggling for survival and were often illiterate. They molded themselves into nations from the ethnic jigsaw puzzles that history and colonialism has bequeathed to them.

But perhaps the greatest burden was the Cold War ideological contest. The new countries' initial reaction was to reject the push to join sides. Asia was in a sense the birthplace of the Non-Aligned Movement, which was formed in Bandung, Indonesia, in 1961. Two of the Movement's major founders were Asian countries (India and Indonesia). Here was an attempt to opt out of global rivalry by finding a third, independent way.

Non-alignment had a certain logic and for two or three decades enjoyed considerable success. But it never developed an ideology for the economic and political organization of society to challenge the two great ideologies of the era: capitalism within a liberal democracy, as opposed to communism led by a single party. Mao's China claimed to be a natural ally of non-alignment and loomed as a hulking presence in the region. Ultimately, the ideological battle came to Asia in the brutal reality of the Vietnam War. The Vietnamese may have considered they were fighting a continuing battle for independence—but in Washington, Moscow, and Beijing the battle was for ideological and strategic superiority.

By the 1970s and throughout most of the 1980s the twin pressures of nation-building and ideological confrontation forced democratic governments from power. The autocrats of the period were either heads of communist parties, such as Mao Zedong in China, Kim Il Sung in North Korea, and Phan Van Dong in a unified Vietnam, or military dictators, like General Ne Win in Burma and General Suharto in Indonesia. Civilian leaders understood the new self-serving rules of the game only too clearly, and Ferdinand Marcos in the Philippines, Park Chung Hee in South Korea, and Zulfikar Ali Bhutto in Pakistan demonstrated their disregard for free elections.

Democracy was in bad shape in the 1980s, being practiced only with difficulty in India and virtually ignored elsewhere. Japan, Malaysia, and Singapore went through the processes of elections, but their leaders ensured, through the powers of incumbency and the cynical manipulation of the law, that opposition parties were in no position to exert a significant challenge. The word itself was losing its meaning by being appropriated by the most dictatorial of regimes. North Korea, where the leadership had deified itself, was formally called the Democratic People's Republic of Korea. The Khmer Rouge, who were to calmly kill two million of their own people, called their country Democratic Kampuchea.

Certain leaders in the region developed an ideological construct that claimed to explain why liberal electoral democracy was not suited to Asia. It left these leaders in the comfortable position of having a near-monopoly on power. It put great store in relativist notions of national mores, downplaying universal norms, and challenging the ideal of universal democracy.

Ideology and Culture as a Challenge to Democracy

The 1980s saw the eclipse of democracy and the rise of "Tiger" economies. For over a decade Asian countries like South Korea, Malaysia,

Singapore, Thailand, and Taiwan registered the world's fastest growth rates. A new-found confidence in their systems of government led them assertively to laud those systems. Democracy did not figure large in these analyses. In its place were ideas based on Confucianism, Asian Values, and the need for strong government.

These views found an echo in Asian societies partly for reasons of national pride (in economic achievements) and partly because of widespread disquiet with aspects of Western society. Issues such as violence, racism, dislocation of family life, disparities in income distribution, unemployment, promiscuity, and wastage were freely discussed in the Western media and tended to show life in the West as dangerous, capricious, and uncertain. It allowed the leadership of many Asian countries to portray themselves as the bulwarks stopping the ills of the West from infesting Asian society.

Asians were told to support strong governments committed to economic growth, giving leaders time to transform Asian societies into modern successful states. Here was a formula for government involvement in virtually all aspects of life: interventionist policies with respect to industry were one side of a philosophy that also called for social engineering policies. Decisions on subsidies and bailouts, ethnic university quotas and entry of foreign workers, labour conditions and women's rights were made by a small group whose vision of society—however altruistic—was not subject to significant political or popular reviews.

Supporters of this system pointed to impressive results and developed a theory of governance specific to Asia. Acknowledgement must go to Singapore's Lee Kuan Yew for having the courage to articulate this view and defend it. The argument was that Asian societies differed from those in the West and needed distinct governmental forms. Asians put more value on societal harmony and the advancement of the group than on individual rights, and they were prepared to make trade-offs for the benefit of society as a whole. This self-sacrificing attitude would avoid the fractiousness and petty political intrigue prevalent in Western countries, while individuals would benefit from high growth rates. Some commentators called this a flow-on from Confucianism; others referred to it as a part of "Asian Values."

The premise: cultural specificities should predominate over universal values where this was judged (by the leadership) to be in the national interest. Ideals considered as strongly pronounced in Asia included respect for elders, strong family ties, the encouragement of education, and interpersonal politeness. The error in this argument lies in the tendency to translate "different values" as "different rights and a different form of government."

It is not plausible to argue that the various Asian civilisations are just like everybody else. There are clearly aspects of many Asian cultures that put a high value on issues such as community harmony, social order and respect for the leadership group. Such differentiations need to be acknowledged, yet they should not preclude respect for universal rights. Universal rights deal with basic issues that flow from one's inherent dignity as a human being, and they sit very comfortably with different cultural traits around the world. One of those universal values is everybody's right to participate in decisions that affect them. It is articulated in Article 21 of the Universal Declaration of Human Rights. From it flows basic reasoning for democratic forms of government that might apply in Asia—as they do elsewhere.

Democracy Returns

Two events brought democracy back into sharp focus in Asia: the end of the Cold War and the East Asian economic and financial crisis. Communist regimes, in spite of all the self-serving propaganda about representing the working people, had no domestic legitimacy. Their leaders never subjected themselves to a true electoral test.

With the end of the Cold War came the end of global ideological confrontation and the acceptance of market systems within liberal democracies; this was the most proven form of government. Much of Asia was quick to hear the message.

The People Power revolution in the Philippines, which swept Corazon Aquino to power, was a harbinger of a democratic movement that would sweep across Asia. In Burma, Aung San Suu Kyi's National League for Democracy convincingly won the national elections only to have the military refuse to hand over power. In China the students built the goddess of democracy in Tiananmen Square. In Thailand, the revered King Bhumibol Adulyadej publicly humiliated the military coup leaders and installed Anand Panyarachun to lead the country back to democracy. In South Korea the rule of the ex-Generals came to an end with the election in 1992 of Korea's first civilian president. In Japan, complete domination by the long-ruling Liberal Democratic Party was broken, allowing the citizenry genuine electoral choices.

The East Asian crisis of 1997–98 exposed the weakness of the argument that Asians accepted benevolent autocrats in the name of rapid economic growth. The crisis demonstrated that economic growth built on political repression was ultimately unsustainable. The most obvious abuse of unfettered political power was best seen in Indonesia, where the Suharto regime became synonymous with the battle against "KKN," or Corruption, Cronyism, and Nepotism. (While Singapore never tolerated corruption, its neighbours came to see it as a normal benefit of political life.) The next round of people-power revolts in Asia swept Suharto from the scene, eventually to see Abdulrahman Wahid elected as president.

In South Korea, noted human rights activist and recent Nobel Peace Prize laureate Kim Dae Jung became President at his fourth attempt. But in Malaysia the threat posed by Prime Minister Mahathir's deputy, Anwar Ibrahim, was snuffed out by jailing Anwar on trumped-up morals charges.

Much of Asia had thus rejoined the mainstream of world politics, and accepted free and fair elections as the political norm. By year 2000 the causes exciting Asian people were democracy, human rights and the fight against corruption. Popular sentiment was buttressed by important new academic work. Nobel laureate Amartya Sen argues cogently that democracy has become a universal value. He explains that democracy is essential to the functioning of modern society because it incorporates key values: it has intrinsic value in allowing people to participate fully in the social and political life of their nation; it has instrumental value in directing political attention—and energy—to voters' needs; and it has constructive value by maintaining a political dialogue that allows society to learn and progress. Concurrently, research undertaken by The World Bank and others demonstrates that democratic governance encourages sustainable economic growth.

What Will the Twenty-First Century Bring?

Having seen many post-colonial democratic systems in Asia falter, there are no grounds to wax triumphant when analyzing the future. Democracies need to work hard to retain broad popular support. Leaders can all too easily squander their mandates if they are viewed as corrupt or incompetent. The first responsibility of the leadership of those Asian countries in transition to true democracy is to build confidence in the system and thus fulfil the ambition that democracy will bring with it good governance.

The greatest threat to the consolidation of democracy in Asia is money politics, which casts a pall over virtually all the functioning democracies. Vote-buying and gift-giving are the faces of money politics seen by electors. But this is only part of a wider range of corruption wherein huge amounts of money can change hands to pull together government coalitions, win commercial contracts and secure party finances. While some electors may see some trickle down benefits in politics, it is those same electors who as taxpayers eventually foot a large—and undisclosed—bill. Thailand, a country that admits to being beset by money politics, is leading the way in combating corruption with an innovative new constitution that prescribes a regulatory branch of government to oversee the politicians, and with freedom of information legislation allowing the media to play its necessary watchdog role.

Unless countries such as India, Indonesia, Japan, the Philippines, South Korea, and Taiwan are similarly pro-active in their efforts to minimize the influence of money politics, their democracies could lose popular support.

Francis Fukayama proclaimed the end of world history to be marked by the victory of market-based liberal democracy as the only viable form of government. Yet there remains a potent challenge to that thesis in Asia. The challenge is mounted by the People's Republic of China (PRC), a nation shedding itself of Mao-era idiosyncrasies and maintaining the Communist Party as the sole source of political power while allowing some degree of economic freedom. As we witnessed in Tiananmen Square, the army will ultimately deal with any challenge to the monopoly of political power. Indeed, as we have so sadly seen in the recent repression of the Falun Gong, even organised spiritual groups will be taken as a threat to the Party's monopoly of power.

Can China succeed? Can a single-party system run a market economy? Will the Chinese people be satisfied with economic reforms unaccompanied by political reforms? These are key questions, and I feel compelled to answer each in the negative. Some argue that the Confucian tradition predisposes the Chinese people to accept strong central government. But scholars could argue for decades about what the Confucian legacy means for the PRC. Many aspects of the Confucian tradition, such as support for meritocracy and loyalty to family rather than to the State, tend to militate against an unquestioning obedience to a central political authority. The Chinese people will judge its government in part on its economic success. To successfully manage a sophisticated market economy, a government must not control the decisions of economic actors but rather allow them to initiate transactions on the basis of accurate information. Neither proposition can hold true in China where the authorities cling to central control over all the important decisions and refuse to tolerate a free press.

Another crucial question for the future of democracy in Asia is the impact of Islam. There are many countries in South, Central, and Southeast Asia with either Muslim majorities or significant Muslim minorities, but the key country in this regard must be Indonesia, a country of 220 million people, some ninety percent of whom are either practicing or at least nominal Muslims. The liberal democratic model from the West is secular. Can this model be incorporated successfully into Indonesian society? I believe it can and that modernist Islam will best strike a balance between the institutions of government and a Koran-based moral code. Democracy requires a tolerance of minorities, an equality of political rights regardless of religion, ethnicity or gender, and participation by all parts of society. The challenge for Indonesia's leaders is to find an amalgam that meets the aspirations of its Muslim majority but remains true to universal democratic (and human rights) values.

The challenges posed by the consolidation of emerging democracies, China's continued adherence to Communist Party control and the need to find a blend between Islam and democracy are onerous. But there are many positive factors. The ideological debate is very much on the side of democracy; popular sentiment clearly favors democracy; and the international community militates in favor of democracy. These are powerful forces. I believe democracy will find an enduring place throughout Asia in the course of this century.

Part VI

Ecology, Energy, and Resources

Dateline 2005: Hong Kong Disappears in a Cloud of Particulate Dust

Fred S. Armentrout

It is the year 2005, and instead of Hong Kong having become the "World City" that was the espoused goal of its first post-colonial government, under Chief Executive Tung Chee-wah, it became something quite different. Hong Kong—what is now called the Special Administrative Region (SAR)—has fallen off the map of preferred regional headquarters' destinations for transnational corporations. Those businesses sought to take advantage, sometime in 2001, of the wide-open China and Taiwan markets that resulted from World Trade Organization (WTO) accessions. They might have located in the SAR, but did not.

Is This Hong Kong's Fate?

"It *can* happen here," is the message being repeatedly brought to the attention of today's Hong Kong government and local business communities by the Business Coalition on the Environment.

In June 1999, Alex Arena, then managing director of Pacific Century CyberWorks and an architect of the SAR's information infrastructure development plans, sounded the alarm. Speaking before the American Chamber of Commerce (AmCham) in Hong Kong, Arena included a lengthy explanation of difficulties faced by his company in recruiting "dot.com" computer engineers. These companies considered leaving Silicon Valley and relocating to Hong Kong. But trading a clean, campus environment lifestyle for the SAR was a major disincentive.

That same year, respondents to AmCham Hong Kong's annual "Business Outlook Survey" indicated quality-of-life and air quality were major factors affecting continued investment in Hong Kong (ninety percent and eighty-seven percent respectively). Yet, they rated the pair of factors low as regards levels of satisfaction (seventeen percent and four percent). Anecdotal reports reveal that executives with young children point to the same issues, declining to renew their corporations' contracts if residency in Hong Kong is required. These complaints do not keep most businesses from coming to the SAR, but companies look for better alternatives to a combination of high business operation costs, an unhealthy environment, declining local English-language proficiency and a location that looks increasingly like another dirty Chinese city.

This is not the image of a "World City" standing apart from other Asian cities competing for the same image (and the same business). Hong Kong's regional competitors—Singapore and Shanghai among them—are working hard to qualify for the mantle. At the margins, even Shenzhen, the heartland of the bustling Southeast Chinese coast, feeds off access to Hong Kong and is a less-expensive combination of industrial/residential suburbs. The Shenzhen–Hong Kong boundary accommodates traffic from 30,000 diesel-driven goods lorries daily.

Post-colonial Hong Kong must reinvent itself into a more affordable, pleasant posting for both residents and expatriates. The Hong Kong Trade Development Council describes the city-state as the world's largest service economy (with services accounting for eighty-five percent of GDP and eighty-five percent of employment). To maintain a solid service economy, the SAR must embark upon workforce training and take steps to attract knowledge workers.

Massive public investment in physical transformation enhanced the trade services infrastructure, fueling airport and container port expansion as well as rail and telecommunications projects on a truly "world" scale. At one point Hong Kong had more deepwater dredges deployed on-site than were working in the rest of the world combined. Local quality-of-life—and investment in human resources development—declined during this period.

The remarkably successful post-Mao history of the British entrepôt colony was based on its location and efficient transport, on the rule of law, on low taxes, and upon a quality workforce. Also helping were the wholesale export of light manufacturing to cheaper Chinese Mainland operations and massive infusions of overseas Chinese capital. "Round-tripping" of foreign direct investment (FDI) from the People's Republic of China (PRC) entered the SAR via shell companies easily purchased in Hong Kong. Receiving special tax concessions, most of this money went to Guangdong Province, where seventy percent of FDI comes from Hong Kong.

The Environmental Equation

A sustainable environment never entered into the equation. "People often condemn colonial Governors for having occasionally talked much, but done little, on environmental issues," say Wong Koon-kwai, a Hong Kong Baptist University geographer, and Man Chi-sum, CEO of Green Power, a local non-government organization (NGO), in a chapter on the subject in the 1998 edition of the popular—and often contrarian—*The Other Hong Kong Report.* The authors conclude that both colonial and post-colonial administration assume "protecting the environment [in Hong Kong] cannot be done at development's expense. Environmental protection is conceived as [action toward] minimizing adverse effects of projects."

To the SAR government's credit, it does issue daily air quality announcements based on roadside readings taken in heavily-trafficked urban districts. Public reaction to readings reported on nightly television news have punished the new government for what many insist was the colonial government's "big lie": namely, that Environmental Protection Department (EPD) annual environment indicators contained flaws. The indicators are based on measurements of five pollutants for which Hong Kong Air Quality Objectives (AQOs) were established. The problem was that, save for a single roadside station in Mongkok (Kowloon peninsula), the EPD reported only ambient pollution levels, with monitoring equipment installed on top of buildings, seventeen to twenty-five meters above ground. This situation provided politically useful fodder to attack Hong Kong–owned manufacturing plants in Shenzhen for re-exporting air pollution—especially to Hong Kong. The PRC's lax controls were also decried.

A study by William Barron and Nils Steinbrecher notes:

> Hong Kong has gotten by environmentally . . . by "exporting" much of the environmental impacts of our development to Guangdong, South East Asia and beyond. Hong Kong now needs a land area several hundred times its actual size to support itself. Already the environmental damage caused by Hong Kong's style of development in Guangdong is coming back on the SAR in the form of air and water pollution imports from the (Chinese) Special Economic Zones.

In 1998, the government of Chief Executive Tung Chee-wah ended this charade by installing roadside readers in urban white-collar districts (Causeway Bay and Central). Figures from the first week of roadside monitoring indicated pedestrians in urban Hong Kong were breathing air up to 172 percent more polluted than had been previously recorded from the rooftops. Only EPD civil servants were surprised.

In his 6th October 1999 annual Policy Address (equivalent to the State of the Union address in the United States), Mr. Tung noted "this problem, which is affecting our health, is already serious and may get worse." Air pollution kills about 2,000 Hong Kong people a year, according to the World Health Organization. The total number of hospitalization days of patients with respiratory diseases in public health care rose from 802, 385 in 1996 to 994,612 three years later. In its *Clean Air for Hong Kong* report, released in 1999, the Planning, Environment and Lands Bureau estimated that air pollution–linked health problems are "costing HK$3.8 billion (or US$540 million) a year in medical expenses and lost productivity."

Government reports do not focus on all pollutants. Christine Loh's Citizens Party released a study in June 2000 noting the reports exclude volatile organic compounds and heavy metals, which cause respiratory illnesses and are known or suspected carcinogens and mutagens. Diesel exhaust, benzene, and Polycyclic Aromatic Hydrocarbons (PAHs) are "the largest single class of known chemical carcinogens," claims this report. Levels found in Hong Kong exceed those in Beijing, Guangzhou, and other Asian cities.

Significant drops in Hong Kong's year 2000 competitiveness ratings were linked to pollution. Swiss think tanks International Institute for Management Development (3rd to 14th) and the World Economic Forum (3rd to 8th) both cited pollution as a major reason for their reduced ratings of Hong Kong.

Addressing the Problem

Is there a "green" faction in Hong Kong? EPD is well staffed. Popularly elected Legislative Councillor Christine Loh, universally regarded as the SAR's premier environmental champion, has other allies. The SAR has sophisticated academic support from The Centre of Urban Planning & Environmental Management of the University of Hong Kong. (Centre scholars include William Barron and Nils Steinbrecher.) The city-state's polluting industrial sector has virtually disappeared in the past fifteen years as a result of a massive transfer of technology and management expertise to factories in the Pearl River Delta region of Guangdong Province to the north and northwest of Hong Kong. Government leaders have influential support in the Legislative Council's "democratic camp" and have enforcement machinery in place. They can avail themselves of high-quality intellectual support for modeling: they are given easy access to international NGO advice and may access economic and technical assistance from abroad.

So What's the Problem?

There are several problems. The first was stated most clearly by William Barron in "The Environment and the Political Economy of Hong Kong" (in *Managing the New Hong Kong Economy*, ed. by David Mole, Oxford University Press, 1996). Barron found that Hong Kong's role as a physical transshipment center led (and still leads) planning priorities. Some US$14 billion in mega-projects—a re-cast port complex and a new international airport—were responses to foreign investor jitters over the July 1, 1997, hand-back of Hong Kong to China. They were pursued with an eye on a glorious British exit and shiny new capital projects. Opponents, noted Barron, cautioned that "the environmental costs of the terminal construction and cargo transport through Hong Kong" would be enormous.

Such was the price for frenetic public works activity in a city already in a state of constant reconstruction—due to the fact that real estate transactions generate half of its government's income. Some examples: about half of the city's solid waste comes from construction and demolition activities, directly linking the pace of development to the absorption rate of its quickly filling landfills; construction activities are the largest users of water in the territory and none of it is recycled; trucks comprise about forty-five percent of the diesel vehicles in Hong Kong; dust and noise are residents' constant companions. Local jokes hold the flying construction crane to be the SAR's "national bird" and the percussive pile drivers' thuds its "national anthem."

Barron pointed to a fundamental contradiction. The colonial

government's espoused environmental priorities and the harsh environmental impacts of economic goals were at cross-purposes. In fact, environmental purity is implicitly ranked low on the government's agenda. Christine Loh draws the same conclusion. In 1999, government spending on the environment was only 1.7 percent of recurrent public expenditure (HK$3.5 billion, US$500 million). In 2000, the amount was 1.9 percent of recurrent expenditure—tiny when compared to education (21.3 percent), health (14.6 percent), social welfare (14.1 percent), or security (12.2 percent).

Is a Political Backlash Developing?

Barron predicted a clash would come when "reclamation works have reached such a scale, even at only a fraction of their ultimate planned level, that they directly and visibly affect a large part of the population." He warned, "how damaging it can be to allow a few civil servants to impose their own personal preferences on the . . . landscape we all share."

In 1998–99, reaction was strong to redevelopment plans for the former Kai Tak Airport environs of Southeast Kowloon and to the intended reclamation of Hong Kong's central business district. The SAR government's pro-development initiatives were blocked in Legco (the Legislative Council). A local joke asserts that the government intends to transform the visually magnificent Victoria Harbor into a canal, as its contents have become an open sewer. Planners were ordered back to their drawing boards by Tung Chee-wah.

Government's Role

The second problem is that environmental management in Hong Kong is still exercised by command and control. Despite Hong Kong's much-touted *laissez-faire* approach to economics, economic incentives are rarely used. Bans are the simplest such tool. Environmental policies—bans on livestock farming in urban areas, high-sulphur fuel for power generation, and incineration as a solid waste strategy—are often less efficient than are economic incentives. Yet they are easier to implement and more predictable in outcome. This pleases civil servants.

The Environment for Civil Servants

The third problem involves civil servants. Controlling them is a major preoccupation of Tung Chee-wah's "executive-led" government. Civil servants are the closest thing to a direct "political constituency" to which the Chief Executive must answer. They are the group who are most discomfited by more public transparency and legislative influence. The civil service is unionized. Together, civil servants and public body officials comprised some ten percent of the more than three million eligible voters in the year 2000 Legco elections (their spouses, adult children, and extended families also vote). Civil servants' salaries are high; this prevents corruption. Hong Kong civil servants rank among the highest-paid in the world. (Amid much grumbling they have suffered a pay freeze for the past three years. Yet, the entire population suffered enormous economic losses. This was the most difficult economic period witnessed in the lifetimes of most residents.) They have added perquisites for senior officials inherited from the colonial regime, "localization" of these perks include: spacious housing (in the world's most expensive housing market) or housing purchase schemes, cars and drivers (the government maintains a fleet of 7,000 vehicles), long leave-accumulation entitlements, education allowances for themselves and their children and other perks. These perquisites are mostly the preserve of the 37,500 middle and senior ranking posts.

The term "iron rice bowl" originates in China and refers to the PRC's employer-worker, cradle-to-grave social contract. It also exists in the SAR, even in the face of incompetence. This was demonstrated during the past few years in scandals affecting housing, public health, and other agencies. Unless convicted of criminal conduct, failed civil servants are transferred, not fired.

Patten Politics

Chris Patten was the territory's first professional politician to serve as governor. His predecessors had all been foreign office diplomats. The construction of a viable political environment before and after the inevitable hand-over to the PRC in 1997 was entrusted to him by his political patron, Prime Minister John Major. However, a joint liaison group (JLG) was the instrument of direct negotiations between the UK and PRC on Hong Kong's future for almost fourteen years, from 1984 to mid-1997.

The Basic Law, drafted and approved by China's National People's Congress (NPC) resulted and provides certain guarantees under the "One Country, Two Systems" approach, devised by Deng Xiaoping. Christine Loh summed up the governance situation as follows:

> Three years into being an SAR, the . . . design of Hong Kong's post-97 political system is showing the cracks of age. You have heard the Chief Executive lament that there was no government party in Legco. You have heard the Chief Secretary wail about how civil servants should not be held politically accountable. . . . Legislators complained . . . they had no power. The public appears to be disillusioned. . . . So, no one is happy.
>
> Mr. Patten's shrewd division of political policy-making from the apolitical and highly efficient functions of its civil service . . . raised the credibility of the government to its highest point . . . [H]e left behind a legacy of legitimacy seldom . . . seen by an appointed colonial regime. Thus, ironically, Mr. Patten, a patronage appointee of a colonialist government . . . stands in the hearts of most of its people as Hong Kong's most democratic leader to date.

This view of an idealized civil service was also an article of faith of the world's press and of the local business community, largely due to the forceful presence and stately bearing of its leader, Chief Secretary Anson Chan. Now, she and her colleagues are saddled with unrealistic expectations of both efficiency and political independence from the public—and from overseas observers. On the other side, civil servants desire to preserve personal privileges and departmental fiefdoms.

What of the high standards of the civil service? Only recently have the environmental protection, transport, lands, customs, and planning departments of government begun to even talk to each other about cooperating on the environment.

Results of Inaction

Consider the runaway use of illegal diesel fuel smuggled in from the Chinese Mainland. Fuel tax revenues dropped over seven per cent between 1997 and 1998. In the first five months of 1999, Guangdong and Hong Kong Customs officers seized 1.8 million liters of illegal diesel. Locally, raids resulted in the closure of 237 illegal filling stations in 1998. Such low-grade diesel fuel is estimated to be ten times more polluting than fuel sold in Hong Kong. Its illegal sale to transport lorries, taxis, and minibuses is big business, saving drivers up to US$450 a month.

Christine Loh accompanied customs officials on a raid of an illegal diesel filling station on Tsing Yi island and filed the following report:

> *28 Jan 2000:* . . . the Customs Department took me on a raid. . . . [A]rrests were made. The land was actually government land, leased out to a company for use as a public open air carpark. Customs raided that same place

a dozen times before. The Lands Department is the landlord. . . . I called the Director of Lands, who within three days told me he was going to revoke the tenancy. From Customs' point of view, Lands was not helpful enough. [If the location was] used continuously for illegal purposes, Lands should make it hard for criminals to operate.

. . . I have discovered that there are 55 other carparks under government leases, where illegal fillings have taken place in 1999. In all of these places, seizures and arrests were made and Lands informed. As far as I know, illegal filling is still going on in those places. I have now given the list to the Director of Lands and await his reply. . . . Customs has plenty of evidence of continuous wrongdoing.

25 Feb 2000: The Lands Department confirmed in writing that the 55 sites I pointed out are indeed government sites where illegal activities are taking place: "Wholesale cancellation [of leases] would create other problems, not least the loss of several thousand vehicle parking spaces," was the reply.

Hellooo!

This flippant reply to an elected legislator on a matter of blatant, organized, and repeated criminal activity was astounding and in direct contravention to two of the Chief Executive's announced priorities: air pollution control and preference for public transport.

It also reflects on other civil service practices. Barron best summarized why public pessimism dogs Tung Chee-wah's promises to clean up street-level air pollution by 2005: "This predicament in which the government's own agenda works counter to its professed concern for the environment . . . stems from the absence of an effective mechanism by which the particular interests of government's economic planners may be objectively weighed against broader concerns."

Not only do the relevant civil service departments have their own agendas to advocate—often under the guise of consultation with the public—but agency hubris does not permit a unified approach to attaining the specified goals of those separate agendas. Meanwhile, Patten's "poison pill" defense of his own legacy was to leave the SAR with very high public expectations of citizen participation in government—expectations he would never have to fulfill. This political masterstroke made him a liberator on the world's stage, yet he represented a modern anathema—a brazen colonialist empire, however benign it may have grown with age.

Are There Solutions?

There are ways to address a sound environmental policy. Wong and Man have suggested the creation of a "Green Plan" to educate and involve the public. They also suggested an inter-departmental Sustainable Development Committee modeled on that in Singapore. There is no shortage of ideas, talent, or money in Hong Kong. What's absent is the "vision thing." A popularly elected leader would appeal directly to the public that empowered him to overcome recalcitrant legislators or civil servants.

Tung Chee-wah has no such mandate, nor has he worked to build one that might offset his limited constituency of 800 electors, all chosen by Beijing, to where pessimists assert he runs when in doubt. Indeed, he ran there on the "right of abode" issue, and the perception is that the SAR's judiciary independence has been weakened as a result. The issue centered on the Basic Law's provision of "right of abode" to all children of Hong Kong people. Significant numbers of those children, often bred in second families in Mainland China, have made claims for entry. The SAR government used inflated figures to assert that millions of children would tax the social service and education rolls. These scare tactics won public support for opposition to new migrants' entry.

When its case still failed before the Court of Final Appeal, the SAR government turned to the National People's Congress (NPC) in Beijing for an "interpretation" of the original intention of the Basic Law. The NPC duly gave an interpretation that pleased the SAR government and kept the would-be migrants out. Therefore, how "final" is a decision by the Court of Final Appeal in Hong Kong? Only years of acceptance of even-handed rulings that go against government will convince anyone in Hong Kong that Tung Chee-wah's government did not intend to trample the spirit, if not the letter, of freedoms and autonomy promised in the Basic Law.

No one in Hong Kong believes Tung Chee-wah to be a bad man. His government has in fact initiated very positive programs and changes; but it is built around crisis intervention, patching cracks in someone else's vessel of state. Perhaps the best summing-up was foreshadowed by John Walden, writing in *The Other Hong Kong Report* in 1997:

> If the state of the Hong Kong community reflected in this year's calendar seems no less turbulent than it was almost a decade ago . . . the reason is not that Governor Patten sabotaged a smooth transition to Chinese rule

[but because] both Chinese and British negotiators made [the] false assumption that a smooth transition could be achieved on terms negotiated and implemented without the participation and consent of those most directly affected by the deal—the people of Hong Kong.

The environment—as well as other issues—is entwined in the resulting mix. Instead of building a new and improved statecraft of local design, Tung's self-perceived task has been to bail out the emergency survival dinghy tied to the stern of *H.M.S. Status Quo*. For better or worse, all around him the Hong Kong public is left learning to swim.

China, Energy, the Environment, and Climate Change

Seth Dunn

China's rapid industrialization created an environmental crisis, and scientists have extensively and exhaustively documented the nation's litany of ecological woes (as outlined by Dr. Elizabeth Economy elsewhere in this book). The reality is more complex than is presented. It is true that China is the world's second-leading emitter of greenhouse gases, including the most important of these gases, carbon dioxide. But it is also the case that China's historical and per capita emissions remain well below those of the industrialized world. Furthermore, China—with its dense urban populations, low-lying coastal regions, floodplains, and agriculture-dependent regions—is among the most vulnerable of nations to the negative impacts of a changing climate.

Coal with Chinese Characteristics

China was the first to utilize coal on a commercial basis—for iron production during the Han dynasty though large-scale exploitation would wait until Great Britain's launch of the Industrial Revolution. The country has now become a major consumer of coal, which accounts for close to seventy percent of its overall energy supply. One-third of this amount goes to supply three-quarters of the nation's electricity; the other two thirds are devoted to domestic uses and industry. Coal is also the most carbon-intensive fossil fuel, making China's coal dependence—accounting for eighty-three percent of its carbon emissions—a major factor in climate change.

The People's Republic of China (PRC) coal conundrum is an ironic twist on British economist William Stanley Jevons' classic nineteenth-century work, *The Coal Question*. Jevons predicted that as Britain's coal mines became depleted, her empire would decline. But for twenty-first-century China, it is coal dependence—not depletion—that endangers global environmental welfare.

Human health in China is affected by coal use. Beijing is nearing the pollution levels measured in London shortly before the tragic 1880 "coal smog," which took 2,200 lives. Millions of children in Beijing, Shanghai, and other mega-cities are exposed to this deadly mix, as well as to the smog-causing nitrogen oxides also released during coal-burning. Roughly 800 million rural poor rely on coal for cooking and heating; exposure to coal smoke increases lung cancer risks dramatically.

The World Bank estimates the total cost of air and water pollution in the PRC is eight percent of GDP, or more than US$50 billion per year. Acid rain covers more than forty percent of the country, destroying $10 billion worth of forests and crops. Thousand-year-old sculptures from the Song Dynasty have been corroded. Ground-level ozone has cut China's wheat yields by as much as ten percent in some regions. China's sulfur emissions are projected to overwhelm farming soils in South Korea and Japan by 2020. Dust clouds from PRC-based coal combustion have reportedly reached the west coast of the U.S.

On top of this is the specter of global warming: growth in carbon and greenhouse gas emissions over the next decade is expected to increase global temperatures by between 1.9 and 2.9 degrees Celsius, raising sea levels by an average of 46–58 centimeters. More frequent and intense weather extremes, prevalence of infectious diseases, altering of species population and migration patterns, and other impacts are forecast. China will be especially hard hit.

Famine and Floods?

As in other parts of temperate Asia, climatic patterns in China range widely from region to region. To the north is a humid, cool, temperate climate; to the south, a tropical monsoon climate; and in the inner regions, a desert or steppe climate. In the populated middle coastal regions, humid and temperate conditions prevail. East Asian monsoons account for most PRC rainfall—and its major floods. Over the last century, the region's average annual temperature has increased by more than one degree Celsius. Annual precipitation has also risen.

Should global carbon dioxide levels double during this century, China's average temperature may increase by between one and two degrees Celsius. One of the most certain impacts of warmer temperatures is a decline in ice cover: at this higher temperature estimate, all of the permafrost in northern China is projected to disappear, as could the Qing-Zang plateau. Already during the last century, some 2,000 glaciers in the Eastern Himalayas disappeared. Central Asia's Tien Shan Mountains have lost twenty-two percent of their glacial ice volume since the 1960s. Since the 1970s, the Duosuogang Glaciers in the Ulan Ula Mountains of China have shrunk by sixty percent.

Climate change also entails shifting precipitation patterns: greater winter runoff and lower summer runoff, extra runoff from melting glaciers, and more frequent and severe flooding and droughts. While it is not clear how climate change impacts monsoons or El Nino, Northern China's Huaihe River basin—with current water shortages—would be especially susceptible to alternating bouts of flood and drought.

China's agricultural yields may be affected. While in the short term warmer temperatures may increase crop growth, these productivity gains will be overtaken by reduced water availability. Rice, wheat, and maize production are projected to decline. The Huang-Hai Plains, the central and southern Yunnan Plateau, the middle and lower sections of the Yangtze River, and the Loess Plateau will be hit hardest by the dual threats of drought and waterlogging.

The deltaic coastal regions of China, the country's major economic hubs, face potential problems. The Yellow River, Yangtze River, and Pearl River deltas are already experiencing subsidence from groundwater extraction or land reclamation. Rising sea levels will exacerbate this problem, causing saltwater intrusion. Sea-level rise and more frequent—and intense—tropical cyclones could create coastal storm surges. Erosion, property loss, and the displacement of millions of Chinese are possible. A one-meter sea-level rise—the IPCC's latest estimates range from ten to ninety centimeters—would cause China's largest city, Shanghai, to lose one-third of its area. This would displace one-third of its seventeen million inhabitants.

The Great Carbon Diet

China has much to gain by bypassing the path taken by today's industrial nations—and by evolving a low-carbon energy economy. Chinese negotiators like to point out that they emit one-seventh as much as Americans on a per-capita basis and historically have only contributed a fraction of the climate burden. Their American counterparts typically respond that population growth and coal use are likely to make China the leading contributor to the problem. In talking past each other, both sides miss the fundamental challenge: to "decouple" economic growth from carbon emissions—a long journey along which China has taken its first steps (ending subsidies, allowing freer markets to determine coal prices, passing legislation, etc.).

The PRC's coal use may continue to fall in the wake of power and energy privatization; forces of international competition accompany China's growing involvement in global trade. Decoupling of carbon from China's economy is underway: Chinese carbon intensity, measured in tons per million dollars of economic output, is now *lower* than that of the United States (see Figure 1).

From Hydrocarbons to Hydrogen?

Fortunately, China has abundant energy resources that are cleaner than coal. Use of natural gas, the lowest-carbon fossil fuel, has expanded by fifty percent since 1990, and recent discoveries of new gas fields and mounting urban air quality problems are prompting a boom in pipeline construction. The Shaan-Jing pipeline, which serves Beijing, was completed in 1997. Chinese officials and companies are now planning a major "west-east" pipeline project from the Tarim Basin (in the Xinjiang Uygur Autonomous Region) to Shanghai; three other gas transport projects—from Sebei to Lanzhou, from the Sichuan Basin to Hubei and Hunan, and from Shaanxi to Hebei and Shangdong Provinces—are also being planned.

The PRC is endowed with abundant renewable energy resources. Its wind resource is world class, and installed capacity has quadrupled to 240 megawatts since 1996. Wind farms in Inner Mongolia could provide nearly twice the nation's current electricity needs. With modern turbines mass-produced in China, and electrical storage systems, these farms could be competitive with coal-based plants in delivering power

Figure 1. Coal Consumption, United States and China, 1950–1999

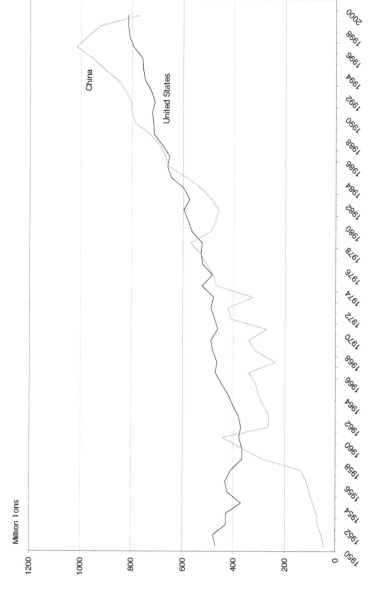

Million Tons

China

United States

Source: U.N., EP, Amoco

to distant markets such as Beijing and Harbin. China's solar hot water heating market is the world's largest, with more than five million square meters of heaters installed. The solar photovoltaic market is small but growing rapidly, with 200,000 home systems in place. There are 60,000 micro-hydro plants in the PRC; these account for a quarter of rural electricity use.

Less exploited possibilities include geothermal power, ocean and tidal energy, and gasification of biomass (such as crop residue) to generate power in micro-turbines. Existing use of solar, wind, biogas, small hydro, and tidal energy already displaces some 223 million tons of carbon—twenty-six percent of current emissions—that would otherwise have been produced by coal-fired power plants. Challenges in realizing a "clean energy" strategy include reform in the power sector, lack of private capital for commercial applications, and an inexperienced renewable energy industry.

How much of China's renewable resource is actually tapped will depend also on technical progress. Chinese scientists have expressed growing interest in hydrogen as an energy carrier. In June 2000 Beijing hosted the Thirteenth World Hydrogen Conference, where Nobel physics laureate Carlo Rubbia of Italy announced that Italy and China would cooperate in the use of hydrogen. Part of the project will explore the use of coal to produce hydrogen, with the excess carbon emissions to be sequestered underground. The hydrogen, which can be produced from fossil fuels but eventually will be derived from renewable energy, can then be used to operate fuel cells to serve as power plants for homes, businesses, cars, and even as batteries in portable electronics.

Under a more optimistic scenario, China and other developing countries could "leapfrog" industrial nations' fossil-fuel-based energy systems, thereby taking the lead in harnessing renewable resources and creating vibrant new industries while contributing to environmental protection—local, regional, and global. International cooperation, like the Italy-hydrogen initiative, can accelerate this process.

Another Superpower Struggle

But as much as they might foster cooperation, environmental issues can also be sources of conflict. U.S.-China relations on climate change are emotionally charged. Prior to the 1997 Kyoto talks, an editorial in *China Daily* opined that "There are those who are unwilling to see China progress and who are trying to contain its development by pointing their fingers at the world's environmental problems." Noting that on a per-capita basis the U.S. emits eight times as much carbon as China, the lead negotiator in Kyoto charged that "In the developing world only two people ride in a car, and yet you want us to give up riding on a bus."

The U.S. Senate passed a resolution forbidding Washington from agreeing to Kyoto Protocol emissions reduction targets that did not include specific commitments from developing nations to limit their own. The resolution was viewed by Beijing as hostile. The U.S. diplomatic focus has turned to achieving the "meaningful participation" of developing nations—though the meaning of that term remains ambiguous.

The challenge for both countries is to do less finger-pointing and more hand-holding. For to cut world carbon emissions by sixty to eighty percent during this century—as many scientists believe is necessary to avoid serious climate dislocations—will require more cooperation and less conflict between two leading emitters, the United States and the PRC. With a forty percent share of global carbon emissions these two will shape our children's and grandchildren's climatic future.

Battelle National Laboratory researchers estimate that had each nation kept its energy intensity at 1977 levels, China's emissions would be double what they are today, with U.S. emissions twenty-five percent higher. The United States and China should expand avenues of collaboration on these issues. The China Council for International Cooperation on Environment and Development, a high-level consultative body, has emphasized energy efficiency and the use of renewable resources in its recommendations to Chinese leaders. The China Project of Harvard University's Committee on Environment is engaged in cooperative research with Chinese institutions on energy issues. These—and other—efforts are important. A U.S.-PRC agreement to work together is one hopeful sign.

There is scope for further U.S.-China cooperation. A bilateral panel convened by the Academies of Science and Engineering in China and the United States has explored the prospects for greater collaboration in the energy futures of both nations. The group recommends "increasing cooperation between the two in the accelerated use of advanced energy technologies"—notably energy efficiency, natural gas, renewable energy, and distributed power generation.

China can market a climate policy consistent with economic interests by leveraging its need for clean energy technologies to argue for WTO membership. It can use its clout as a large carbon emitter to achieve favorable terms under the Kyoto Protocol's international emission trading system and Clean Development Mechanism. The PRC could grab as much as sixty percent of carbon trades between industrial and developing countries.

The third and final challenge is perceptual: to transcend the PRC's reputation as an ecological rogue nation and recognize the scope of the nation's effort to modernize its energy system while avoiding costly end-of-pipe approaches to pollution pioneered in the West.

The Greening of East Asia: The Quest to Tackle Environmental Dilemmas

Elizabeth Economy

Introduction

The Asia-Pacific region suffers from a range of development-induced environmental stress and resource demands. Growing water scarcity, land degradation, and its attendant problem of food scarcity, migration, and public health are foremost among them. Increasing demand for energy across Northeast Asia has enormous implications for the region's ability to cope with acid rain, other trans-boundary air pollutants, and issues such as nuclear waste storage. Moreover, there are the dire prospects of continued population growth—especially in China, where infrastructure to meet basic environmental, energy, and sanitation needs lags.

Most country leaders in Asia acknowledge that these problems are serious and merit far greater attention than they receive. Yet the region has not developed the collective consciousness and commitment necessary to address them effectively. Conflict among countries in the region over issues such as access to water, acid rain, and fisheries resources is commonplace. Only a few countries have demonstrated the political will to tackle their environmental challenges domestically, much less participate in region-wide solutions.

The danger is not only that these problems will worsen but that regional conflict is possible as new problems emerge. The status of the region's most pressing problems indicates that these countries are ill-equipped to respond to the challenge ahead.

The Nature of the Problem

The Asia-Pacific region contains nine of the world's fifteen cities having the highest levels of particulate air pollution, as well as six of the fifteen affected most heavily by sulfur dioxide (which causes acid-rain). Because of China's overwhelming reliance on coal to meet its energy needs, she has five of the world's ten most polluted cities (Beijing, Shanghai, Xian, Shenyang, and Guangzhou). In some Chinese cities, coal combustion results in concentrations of particulates of up to twelve times that of the levels flagged by the World Health Organization. Respiratory problems are severe.

The death toll from air pollution in Asia is alarmingly high—and rising. Particulates in the People's Republic of China (PRC) cause more than 300,000 premature deaths from lung cancer and respiratory infections. In both Bangkok and Jakarta, air pollution is estimated to be responsible for 100 to 2,000 deaths per year. With energy demand in Asia doubling every twelve years, total emissions of air pollutants will likely increase—as will the consequent health hazards.

Acid rain caused by coal burning results in enormous health and economic costs. Levels of acid rain are forty-five times higher than were recorded in Japan during the years of that country's own economic boom. And the PRC's bustling coastal industrial centers "export" acid rain to Japan.

Deforestation contributes to the sand-laden "yellow dust" that impacts northern Chinese cities—Beijing among them—for days at a time. More recently, South Korea has begun to experience the effects of China's yellow dust, including eye and respiratory illness, impaired visibility for airline pilots, and reduced agricultural productivity.

Accelerating deforestation damages local ecosystems, contributes to biodiversity loss, enhances soil erosion and exacerbates damage from flash floods. In Burma (Myanmar), Cambodia, Laos, Thailand, and Indonesia, effective grassroots environmental governance remains poor. In a situation of weak government controls and rampant corruption, loggers fell large tracts of the oldest and most commercially valuable timber. The World

Bank estimates that some 1.4 percent of the region's forest cover is lost annually—a substantially higher rate of loss than elsewhere.

The deleterious effects of unchecked "slash-and-burn" deforestation were seen in the fire haze that resulted from forest fires in Indonesia and blanketed Southeast Asia during 1997. This was the most prolonged period of haze in Asia-Pacific history. In parts of the Philippines, the haze reduced visibility to under twenty meters, causing migratory birds to die, children to develop eye problems, and crops to suffer increased insect attacks. Such forest fires may again envelope the region: Indonesian companies face few sanctions for clearing land by fire and—given the political and economic crisis there—environmental issues are unlikely to receive priority attention.

Impending water shortages, as noted elsewhere in the book, are another challenge. Water tables in China and Mongolia are sinking. Taiwan and the PRC both face salt water intrusion into ground water. Singapore is likely to remain dependent on piped water supplies from Malaysia, while Malaysia's own water supply will reach crisis point in 2010. The combination of deforestation, flooding, and drought also limits its access to clean water, hindering agricultural production. According to The World Bank, by 2025 most of the region will face severe water shortages unless actions are taken.

Storage of nuclear waste affects Northeast Asia. South Korea, Taiwan, Japan and now China have developed substantial nuclear power industries. In January 1997, Taiwan rejected South Korean demands that it not ship its nuclear waste to North Korea for treatment and storage. The PRC intervened to extract maximum political capital from the dispute, offering to take the Taiwanese nuclear waste on condition that the island be considered an "indivisible part of China." One year later, however, Taiwan attempted to capitalize on this assertion of unity by proposing that it store its nuclear waste on Wuqiu, an islet off Fujian province on China's coast. Environmental activists in Wuqiu, Taiwan, and Fujian all protested the deal, forcing the Taiwan Power Company to halt the project.

However, protests by environmental groups—though a positive sign of increasing awareness and activism—remain atomized without a common agenda for long-term, non-crisis-driven environmental protection. As the region becomes dependent on nuclear energy, a regional storage plan is critical.

The Limits of Community: The Asian Response

The development of regional or global regimes to address environmental problems is a time-consuming and difficult task. In Asia, it may require a Herculean effort. As Australian researcher Alan Dupont has noted, effective environmental cooperation tends to occur in response to crisis, or in an impromptu issue-by-issue manner. Several environmental regimes focus on the marine environment. The "second track" Council for Security Cooperation in the Asia Pacific devotes considerable attention to security-related aspects of the environment. It has considered various proposals to safeguard the marine environment and provide for "environmentally responsible defense," but these are all devoted to research, monitoring, and data collection. There is no capacity for enforcement.

Moreover, established regional organizations such as APEC have no ability to monitor the implementation of environmental provisions. Even Japan—the most pro-active environmental actor in the region—takes a cautious attitude towards building regional institutions for these purposes. Tokyo insists there is a lack of historical basis for a regional system, arguing that differences between countries pose problems. Other factors within Asian countries' domestic systems have inhibited the development of effective regional environmental regimes: political systems simply are not structured to encourage environmental protection. Many countries share common characteristics, including close ties between business and government elites, inadequate legal structures, weak environmental protection agencies and fractured environmental nongovernmental communities.

In Malaysia and Indonesia timber concessions requiring low capital investments and almost guaranteeing high returns have been a favorite tool of patronage. The royal families in both countries have been accused of illegal logging practices, and in Malaysian court cases, those punished are typically the workers, not the license-holders.

Throughout the region, the dominant mind-set perceives environmental protection as coming at the expense of economic development. In China, for example, fees for polluting companies are so low that enterprises typically pay them rather than retrofit with advanced pollution-control technologies. Many towns are dependent on the existence locally of a single, high-polluting factory. Local officials often intervene to prevent the fining or closing of a factory, citing the risk of social instability from the unemployment that would result.

In some cases, most notably those of North Korea and Burma (Myanmar), environmental protection is virtually non-existent. In Mongolia, environmentalist efforts are difficult to pursue, despite an active "green" party.

Most countries in the region are undergoing a process of economic and social transition that places greater stress on the capacity to meet environmental protection (as well as other social needs). They now confront a rapidly aging populace, increasing levels of unemployment (notably in the PRC) and slowing growth rates.

Moreover, the role of non-governmental organizations (NGOs) and of the public as environmental watchdogs is grossly underdeveloped. In China, Malaysia and elsewhere, NGOs exist at the governments' discretion. In Taiwan, South Korea, and even Japan, their numbers and impact are limited. Primarily, they focus on NIMBY—*"Not In My Backyard!"* issues, rather than on region-wide ecology-related problems. Nonetheless, genuine NGOs have emerged in the PRC to address biodiversity loss, deforestation, and urban pollution.

International pressures on regional governments have not yet prompted a strong commitment to region-wide action on these issues. While there have been nascent efforts to establish inter-regional working groups and organizations, their scope and efficacy remain limited. Yet if these countries are effectively to tackle the serious environmental challenges facing them, they need collective ties—and the communication embodied in rigorous regional environmental regimes.

Asia's Energy Predicament and Its Implications

Robert A. Manning

Oil-dependent Japan, Korea, and Taiwan were—along with Western nations—slowed by recent skyrocketing energy prices. Energy, encompassing production, distribution, and consumption, is intertwined with the future welfare of these countries and their Asian neighbors. The region's oil demand has driven global markets for the past two decades and even in the aftermath of the 1997–98 economic crisis, is growing at three times the world average.

Energy remains a fundamental issue surrounding the region's growth, affecting regional security, and strongly influencing the macroeconomic environment that shapes East and Southeast Asian economic development. Asia is both a major producer (see Figure 1) and a major consumer and importer (see Figure 2) of oil. It is within Asia and along its offshore regions that investments of more than US$1 trillion in exploration and infrastructure are expected. Asia by 2015 may hold modest new petroleum reserves, yet they will not satisfy the region's own burgeoning demand for oil and gas. This impacts future energy markets.

In a world that literally runs on fuel, countries whose economic futures are based on manufacturing and exports are blessed—or cursed—by energy. East and Southeast Asian countries such as Indonesia,

Figure 1. **Asian Oil and Natural Gas Production**

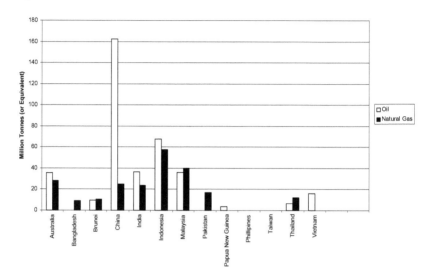

Malaysia, Vietnam, and Brunei are affected positively by price increases. Others—including the Philippines, Thailand, Korea, Japan, and even China (also a major producer) —are net losers as import costs per barrel rise. Prices of commodities that run nations' economic engines also increase. Moreover, energy shocks reduce Western purchases of "Made In Asia" goods.

Asia currently imports about thirteen million barrels per day (b/pd); that is projected to rise to about twenty million b/pd by 2010 and later to roughly twenty-six to thirty-one million b/pd. As the middle class in China grows and urban sprawl increases throughout the region, oil needs and electricity use will increase faster than GDP. China today consumes eight times less energy per capita than the United States and twenty-two times less oil per capita. She and other less-developed economies are less fuel-efficient than post-industrial economies. In the United States, oil has declined from some eight to 1.8 percent of GDP. In the U.S., Europe, and Japan it takes far less energy to produce a unit of economic growth than in China, Korea, Taiwan, or Thailand.

Perceptions and Reality

The last 150 years have been dominated by unsound predictions regarding "inevitable" shortages. I examined the famous Club of Rome report

Figure 2. **Asian Oil and Natural Gas Consumption**

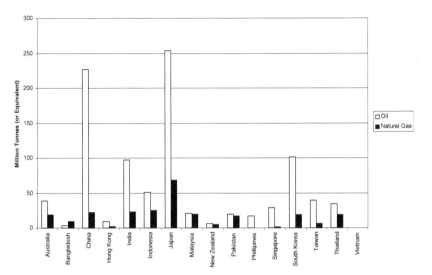

from the 1970s which predicted that by 1990 the world would use up 600 millions barrels of oil—and because that's all we had—supplies would end. They were almost half-right. The world did use 600 million barrels of oil by 1990, but we have 2.3 trillion barrels of proven reserves. Oil is not simply a static resource, to a considerable degree it is something created by investment. The revolutions taking place in this industry—technological, financial, as far as marketing, and in terms of conservation—are having an enormous impact. There is a troubling gap between energy realities and Asian perceptions of it, and hence, Asian views of energy security, as I discovered when researching my recent book (*The Asian Energy Factor: Myths and Dilemmas of Energy, Security, and the Pacific Future*, 2000). For example, energy is frequently seen as a source of tension in and around the South China Sea (particularly in the case of the disputed Spratly Islands). Are policies by the People's Republic of China (PRC) energy-related? No. Dry holes in that area disappoint oil "insiders"; moreover, no major oil company analyst believes there are major gas resources in these disputed territories. South China Sea oil and gas are therefore of marginal significance. Any conflict would be over sovereignty claims and national ambitions.

The Middle East remains critical in the supply equation; two-thirds of known petrol reserves are located in the Persian Gulf states. More than sixty percent of Persian Gulf oil is exported to Asia, and seventy-five percent of Asian imports come from the Gulf. (America is far less dependent on Middle East oil, with about twelve percent of total oil consumed originating there.) Oil exporters Iran, Iraq, and Libya are under economic sanctions, yet those sanctions will likely erode over time: Iraq alone has reserves in excess of 130 billion barrels.

Energy affects other choices. As other chapter authors reveal, there are critical environment-related aspects to Asia's twenty-first-century energy paradigm. Yet energy has the potential to launch new multilateral arrangements which will strengthen the region's economies and preserve peace. East Asia must determine what, precisely, constitutes energy security.

Energy Demand and Its Consequences

Across Asia, energy demand grows by five percent a year. Demand is fueled by a growing thirst for fuel as the region recovers from the 1997–98 financial crisis—an era of sharply declining oil prices. During the 1997–98 "contagion" economic activity—inextricably linked to energy—came to a standstill. Petrol demand was so low that exploration—and investment—was curtailed and the spigots turned off. By 1999 the price per barrel fell to US$8. The investment-exploration cycle is eighteen to twenty-four months, from the first commitment of resources to refurbish production sites or advance virgin exploration, until production comes on line.

In 1998 Asia's lower demand for oil caused one million out of the seventy-five million barrels produced worldwide to have no ready buyer. New investments by oil companies slowed dramatically. Add to all these factors a persistent uncertainty caused by unsettling developments in the Middle East, and you get a picture of the complexities surrounding energy. Should Saddam Hussein withhold Iraq's 2.7 million b/pd, prices could rise into the $50–$60 range. Mergers, refining regulations, a tight oil tanker market—combined with the faster rate of Asian economic recovery—led to price hikes and supply bottlenecks. Prices reached $35 a barrel.

What are medium-term prospects for petrol? According to data provided by the International Energy Agency (IEA), annual oil consumption should increase to 110 million b/pd in nineteen years. Asian consumption will account for fifty percent of the increases—twenty-five to thirty-one million barrels. Asian oil consumption more than doubled from 1985 to 1995 and is projected to double again by 2015. Consumption declined after conservation efforts began to pay off. The United States used 18.7 million b/pd in 1978. Two decades later—with a booming economy and despite relaxed auto fuel economy performance standards—it used the same amount of oil. The U.S. GDP increased by sixty-eight percent during those twenty years.

Technology to the Rescue

New technologies for enhanced exploration are having an impact. Three-dimensional seismic analysis, for example, enables geologists to probe deep inside layers of porous rock. "Virtual exploration" uses advanced computer methods to open vast new areas to serious—and profitable—exploration. These, in turn, make the latest round of doomsday predictions concerning energy shortages unrealistic. Major auto companies have developed gas-electric "hybrid" and fuel cell–powered cars, and marketability by 2005–10 is likely. Fuel cells for powering homes and offices are in the experimental phase. Fuel cells' wider use will ease many environmental and resource concerns.

The petrol sector is high-tech: a person sitting at a computer screen in London is capable of doing "real-time" management of a Caspian Sea oil well. We can get thirty to fifty percent more oil out of a well than before. Offshore technology allows us to go down 3,000–4,000 feet. Over the next decade, oil companies should be able drill to 10,000 feet. A recent U.S. Geological Survey study concluded there are 2.3 trillion barrels of recoverable conventional oil resources available as well as huge quantities of non-conventional shale and tar sands. There might be six to ten trillion barrels of oil available.

Prisoners of Geography

One dilemma facing the Asia-Pacific region is that energy, like water, is not always located in areas where it is needed. In today's transparent, increasingly efficient oil markets, we find transport costs are a significant factor in price.

Transportation across vast distances is essential and increases the oil's cost—impacting price structures for other energy sources as well. The use of indigenous sources to meet local needs—in the PRC and elsewhere—is an efficient solution for energy and transport quandaries. Hydropower is ideally suited for consumers and for industry along the mighty Yangtze River. Coal and domestic oil are available in Northeast China. A pipeline from Sichuan to Wuhan will begin to create a nation-wide gas grid linking the north and the east and coalescing in Greater Shanghai.

Southeast Asian gas suppliers can be linked to the sprawling manufacturing belts of the Southeastern coast, Yunan, and the Southwest.

Japan's Quandary

The Japanese seek to diversify their sources of energy while simultaneously searching for alternate sources. Their strides in "hybrid" autos—vehicles using both batteries and petrol—are impressive. The country's quest to assure uninterrupted supplies is evidenced by diplomatic outreach to Russia, whose Far East contains vast mineral and natural resources.

Let us consider Japan's present energy mix further. The oil demand in the world's Number Two economic superpower is likely to decline. Persian Gulf oil remains the primary energy source, with the United Arab Emirates and Saudi Arabia accounting for forty-nine percent of imports, followed by other Gulf states (twenty-four percent), Iran (ten percent), and Asia-Pacific sources (ten percent). Oil has dropped from seventy-seven percent of Japan's total energy mix in 1973, the year of the first "oil shock," to fifty-three percent; in nine years it will be forty-seven percent. Dependence on imports for all energy supplies dropped from ninety percent to eighty percent during the same time frame. And, as is true of the United States, energy inputs now yield twice as much output (measured by GDP): conservation and efficiency are at work.

Also encouraging is the country's shift to natural gas. This clean-burning fuel helps Japan—where the Kyoto (global warming) Protocols were proclaimed three years ago—achieve reduction of CO_2 emissions. Reliance on natural gas will expand. While Korea built a network of trunk lines (for natural gas) to heat office buildings and homes, Japan has not committed resources to this type of infrastructure. As the world's largest consumer of liquefied natural gas, Japan must build effective distribution systems.

Japan's energy choices have a major impact on global energy markets. Her state-owned corporations conduct joint ventures in exploration, distribution, and pipeline development from Central Asia to Siberia. Tokyo has discovered that market forces are more dependable than industrial policy in securing affordable energy. One-third of Japan's electricity is derived from nuclear power. Accidents, most recently at Tokai Mura in 1999, affect public sentiment, and Tokyo has scaled back plans for new nuclear plants.

China's Energy Role

In 1993—for the first time in 5000 years—China became a net energy importer. The PRC imports 1.3 million barrels a day, an amount that will triple in only nine years. By 2020 the level is projected to reach six to seven million b/pd, depending on the rate of economic growth. China has major coal deposits and is the world's second-largest consumer of coal. It had been the fifth-largest producer of oil—over three million barrels a day. Unfortunately, its energy resources are in the north and west, far from population and industrial centers.

The PRC's oil industry is continually reorganizing; companies are merging and bureaucracies reshuffling. Two of the largest Chinese oil companies, PetroChina and Sinopec, have put offerings on the New York and Hong Kong stock exchanges. Beijing is transforming *state ministries* into *energy companies*; progress towards rationalization and internal market competition is gradually appearing.

As noted elsewhere in this book, there is a shift from coal to natural gas, which China has in abundant supply. Connecting pipelines will stretch from Xinjiang to Shanghai provinces, contributing to a fifteen to twenty percent annual growth rate in natural gas use. Today, natural gas use accounts for two percent of China's energy mix, but this share will increase dramatically by 2020.

Table 1

Chinese Estimates of Future Petroleum Imports (millions of tons)

	2000	2010	2020	2050
Demand	200	260	320	520
Domestic Supply	155	165	180	80
Deficit	45	95	140	440
Deficit met by:				
Substitution Fuels	—	10	51	280
Oil Imports				
Projections 1996*	45	85	89	160
Projections 1999**	35	60–75	130	—

Source: "China's Worldwide Quest for Energy," OECD/IEA Publication, 2000.
*PRC (1996) *China Energy Strategy Study (2000–2050),* Beijing, (in Chinese).
**China Oil, Gas and Petrochemicals Newsletter, vol. 7 no. 24, December 15, 1999, p. 1.

China's *diplomatic* links to the Middle East are, to date, predominantly *commercial* links. In 1997, the Chinese oil companies suddenly out-bid an American-owned rival for rights to Middle East fields. Beijing's state-owned companies had ample cash and were buying oil fields—something the Japanese tried without success. It is a positive signal China is moving into world markets, playing the "oil game." While the PRC engages in troubling exports of military-related technology to Iran and Pakistan, there is little correlation (thus far) between China's "energy connection" and arms exports.

Energy and Military Security

China is a "free rider," as is Japan, both depending on U.S. military presence in the Gulf to safeguard stability and the freedom of navigation in adjacent sea lanes—thus assuring oil supply security. Will China be content to be a free rider—or will she build a blue ocean navy? Such "energy security" actions could lead to a naval arms race. If major powers embarked on this course, energy security would not be guaranteed. Like the British-German naval competition a century before, it would make conflict more likely. If a revolution occurred in Saudi Arabia and oil production were disrupted, aircraft carriers would be of little use, for the threat to energy security does not lie along sea lanes—the lifeblood of a globalized world economy where the MAD ("mutual assured destruction") doctrine prevails. The real threat is short-term disruption of production, and Asia cannot think about energy security in outdated terms.

A practical Asian response is to do what Organization for Economic Cooperation and Development (OECD) member nations did by creating the IEA, launching a strategic petroleum reserve (SPR) as well as systems to share reserves during crises. Japan is the only Asian country with a large (150 days' worth) reserve. Korea, an OECD member, has not yet reached OECD petrol reserve levels. China has begun to develop an SPR.

A New Multilateralism?

Oil issues constitute one of several areas where common interests overlap. Energy could be an integrative force for regional stability. It is not difficult to envision a multilateral mechanism—through existing fora such as the APEC energy working group or other institutionalized coop-

eration. If East Asia begins to rely on gas, as it is expected to do, cooperative development of gas pipelines makes sense. Natural gas in Siberia and in the Russian Far East will be expensive to tap: pipelines are
difficult to lay through permafrost, over rivers, undersea, and through
deserts. Furthermore, as pipelines grow longer than 2,500 kilometers
they tend to become less economical. In any case, international financing would be needed. Before building these pipelines and investing in
energy security, countries require a certain comfort level: they must be
sure nobody along the route will turn off the spigot. (Indonesian natural
gas reserves from the Natuna fields will reach Singapore this year.
Indonesia's estimated pipeline revenues over a three-decade period should
exceed US$1 trillion.)

Only a few pipelines exist; ones in Southeast Asia only extend from
Singapore to Malaysia and to Thailand. Yet, Sakhalin (off the Russian
coast) is a relatively short distance to Hokkaido. The Japanese are involved in Sakhalin gas and oil projects. There is talk of pipeline networks extending from Southeast Asia to Northeast Asia. If it is
economically feasible, pipelines can proceed in bits and pieces (and internally within the PRC).

Perception is the challenge. It is starting to change. The Chinese attitude has evolved, and Japan's MITI accepts the concept of market forces,
with scarcity less the basis of energy policy. Japan's state-owned oil
company spent $41 billion over the past twenty years and has little to
show for it.

Re-Thinking Energy Security

Skyrocketing energy prices, disruptions, and feared shortages are discussed in the context of core national security matters; analysts point to
geopolitical flashpoints along the sea lanes. One-half of world trade
passes through the (three separate) Straits of Malacca. Studies on sea-
lane security show that the likelihood of all three straits being closed in
a conflict is extremely low. Future wars will likely last three to four
weeks, or three to four months. Any sea-lane disruption amounts to a
short-term tax on commerce: closed straits mean that longer distances are
required, and detours around Australia would increase costs. Guarding sea
lanes might trigger an unnecessary Sino-Indian-Japanese naval arms race.

Oil markets are global, not regional. Asian oil imports are seventy-
five percent dependent on the Middle East—and the percentage will rise

considering that two-thirds of world reserves are in the Persian Gulf. Yet, the East Asia-Middle East energy nexus poses intriguing scenarios. Pessimists suggest a Confucian-Islamic alliance confronting the West. There is no evidence of this: Chinese and Japanese oil firms invest in upstream activities such as petrol fields, whereas Middle East players invest downstream, in refining and marketing. Asians seek to assure supply while Gulf States try to assure demand. One can speculate that in the event of another Gulf War the PRC might side with Iraq in the UN Security Council. A price spike anywhere is a spike everywhere; therefore, the PRC has a stake in Gulf States' stability.

Will China, with its enormous demand for energy, drive oil prices up and herald the end of the oil age? Probably not. In 1960 the United States imported 1.8 million barrels of oil a day, the EC, 4.5 million. By the time of the second "Oil Shock" in 1979, America imported nine million, the EC nineteen million. These numbers are above projected demands in Asia. After the second "shock" subsided, oil prices were at near-record lows. Thus, meeting projected Asian demand for oil to Year 2020 is manageable.

Although scarcity is not a concern, several Asian countries face decisions with profound consequences. The oil debate is dominated by myths—oil's disappearance; the Caspian as a new Persian Gulf; supplies in disputed territories within Asia. But conflicts in Asia won't have much to do with oil. How countries in the region learn to cooperate on these issues is an important challenge.

Asia's Quest for Water

Kog Yue Choong

Water sustains natural ecosystems and human health; and in Asia, water holds symbolic and religious meaning. Water is critical to human survival; the fates of entire nations depend on access to water. Shortages not only limit economic growth, but water scarcity is the single greatest threat to human health, the environment and global food supply. Scarcity may even spark violent conflicts within Asia.

Fresh water is not so very abundant. Nearly ninety-seven percent of all water on earth is sea water, while two percent is locked in polar ice caps and underground reservoirs. A scant one percent is fresh water available for human use. Mankind is already using more than half of this amount and, in twenty-five years will require three times as much. For the period 1940–90, withdrawals of fresh water from rivers, lakes, reservoirs, underground aquifers, and other sources increased by more than a factor of four. The World Bank estimates that those without access to clean water will number 2.5 billion—one person in three—by year 2025, unless more attention is given to water supply systems.

Supplying water to people and businesses is a US$400 billion industry, forty percent of the size of the oil industry, and an amount one-third larger than that for global pharmaceuticals.

Water may be to this century what oil was to the last, a precious commodity determining the wealth of the nations. How a country handles water supplies will spell the difference between greatness and decline. Nations keeping their waterworks in superb working order—and operating at low cost—will have a competitive edge.

A country with less than 1,000 cubic meters per person per year of water resources is defined as water-stressed, with insufficient resources to meet developmental needs. Table 1 shows water resources of all countries in the Asia-Pacific region. Using the criterion mentioned, Singapore is clearly water-stressed. Across the region, per-capita availability of water declined by forty to sixty percent between 1955 and 1990. The water stress index must be interpreted cautiously. Shortages depend upon use patterns and efficiency. Tiny Israel supports its population, growing industrial base and intensive irrigation with less than 500 cubic meters per person per year.

The supply of fresh water anywhere is limited by the dynamics of the hydrological cycle, and renewable supplies are an important constraint to the sustainable use of water within a region. Asia has the lowest per-capita availability of freshwater in the world, with parts of Southeast Asia already above the threshold of "high water-stress" conditions (defined as the condition in which the ratio of use to availability exceeds forty percent). Some countries in Central Asia are already using ninety percent of their available freshwater resources. Use of available freshwater resources is twenty-five percent in northern portions of the China and Mongolia. Many other regions will suffer the same fate during the next twenty-five years. China and India both have serious water shortages.

Water shortages may likely become the largest limiting factor to economic growth. And in most countries, water supplies are linked to food supplies, which are dependent on irrigation rather than rain. Asian industry swallows ten percent of the region's fresh water, the agricultural sector some eighty percent. Irrigated rice, the staple food throughout Asian, is a heavy consumer of water. It consumes 7,650 m3/ha, as compared to wheat, which consumes only 4,000 m3/ha. Water shortages might affect China's food self-sufficiency, and should China turn to global grain markets to meet shortfalls, grain prices will increase. This will in turn aggravate social and political instability in many developing countries.

Table 1

Water Resources of Asian Countries

Country	Annual per capita water resources m³	Annual withdrawals internal renewable as percentage of water resources
Afghanistan	2,354	47
Armenia	2,493	32
Azerbaijan	1,069	204
Bangladesh	10,940	2
Bhutan	49,557	0
Cambodia	8,195	1
China	2,231	16
Georgia	10,682	6
India	1,896	21
Indonesia	12,251	1
Iran	1,755	55
Iraq	1,615	122
Israel	289	109
Japan	4,344	17
Jordan	114	145
Kazakhstan	4,484	45
North Korea	2,887	21
South Korea	1,434	42
Kuwait	11	2,690
Kyrgyz	10,394	22
Laos	50,392	0
Lebanon	1,315	31
Malaysia	21,259	2
Mongolia	9,375	2
Myanmar	22,719	0
Nepal	7,338	2
Oman	393	124
Pakistan	1,678	63
Philippines	4,476	9
Saudi Arabia	119	709
Singapore	172	32
Sri Lanka	2,341	15
Syria	456	206
Tajikistan	11,171	18
Thailand	1,845	29
Turkey	3,074	16
Turkmenistan	232	2,378
United Arab Emirates	64	1,405
Uzbekistan	704	355
Vietnam	4,827	8
Yemen	243	72

Source: World Resources Institute 1998.

Impending Water Shortages

Rain in many parts of Asia comes in torrents over a single monsoon lasting from four to six months. The rest of the year is almost dry. As a result, much of the ceaseless runoff flows into the ocean as waste, eroding the uplands—sometimes catastrophically. The monsoon is often erratic; floods and seasonal water shortages occur concurrently. Water demands are fast approaching the limits of resources. According to the International Water Management Institute, one third of Asia's population will experience severe water shortages by 2025. The warning signs include rationing for the 1.8 million people of Malaysia's Klang Valley because of drought (three years ago). Satellite photographs show the entire north of China is drying out: China's Yellow River ran dry and had no outflow into the sea for 226 days in 1997. The North China Plain's water table—in a region responsible for nearly forty percent of China's grain production—fell by an average of nearly 1.5 meters over the last five years. The Chinese Academy of Sciences estimated that economic losses caused by water shortages in cities across the North China Plain ran as high as US$24 billion in 1997, or three percent of GDP.

China's and the developing Asian countries' farm sectors waste water by diffuse irrigation methods. There is also the problem of mismanaged water resources, as evidenced by the thirty-five percent of "unaccounted for water" in Selangor and the Federal Territory of Malaysia. The results have been increased pressure on fresh water resources and a lack of adequate supplies in some localities.

The last 140 years has been one of the most wet periods during the past four millenia. More frequent droughts can be expected as the anomalously wet period ends. The outlook for the world's fresh water supply will be bleak indeed.

Environmental Crisis

The Southeast and East Asian environmental crisis—or crises—was of concern before the onset of the just-ended Asian financial and economic crisis. Other chapter authors in this book have addressed different aspects of environmental degradation. As regards water, decades of rapid industrialization and urbanization without effective environmental management led to deforestation and flood problems in Southeast and East Asia. Major rivers were despoiled, used as waste dumps. The absence of adequate infrastructure to treat wastes—and dispose of them—is evident. Past pollution affects water availability tomorrow. The Asian-born

Green Revolution, which led to greatly improved rice production for thirty years, occurred at a great cost to the environment. Chemicals applied as fertilizer and as pest and weed control mechanisms pollute rivers and lakes through runoff and groundwater through leaching.

Cambodia found traces of arsenic in nine percent of drinking water samples collected in thirteen of the nation's twenty-four provinces. All of India's fourteen major rivers are badly polluted. Of 700 main rivers in China, nearly one-half are significantly polluted, with one in ten considered undrinkable. The culprit: industrial waste. Now, toxins such as DDT are being detected in fish and other marine life in the South China Sea. This pollution removes large volumes from available water supplies.

Considerable water in Southeast Asia is polluted by lack of wastewater disposal, adequate sanitation and proper management of sewage. The problem of pathogenic pollution is quite severe; pathogens come from domestic sewage discharged untreated into watercourses. Half of the lakes in Southeast Asia suffer from eutrophication, and inland water bodies are similarly affected by pathogenic agents. Many rivers carry enhanced nutrient and pollutant loads as a result of changes in land use. Mine residues created "hot spots" of heavy metal pollution.

Pumping water from underground aquifers faster than they can be recharged, or diverting so much water from wetlands or rivers that freshwater ecosystems fail, are unsustainable practices. Depletion of aquifers (caused by over-pumping in parts of Southeast Asia) are removing underground water reserves twice as fast as they are being replenished. When India's aquifer reserves run out, its grain harvest could fall by as much as one-fourth. Other examples of disappearing reserves are found in the diversion of river waters from the dying Aral Sea in Kazakhstan and Uzbekistan. Excessive withdrawals are causing intrusions of sea water into deltas and coastal aquifers in China and Vietnam. There, uncontrolled flow of sewage and fertilizer runoff is hastening eutrophication in some temperate and tropical lakes as well as in many coastal seas. The situation in Thailand is also severe.

Global warming could reduce water supplies because of its impact on climate cycles which produce—and distribute—water. Global warming is causing yearly melting of Greenland ice, the equivalent of 4.5 trillion liters of water. This results in a twenty-three–centimeter rise in the sea level. The impact of global warming has been profound—and its implications are worrisome. There are fears that fresh water supplies such as lakes and reservoirs will be submerged by the rising sea water level.

Since before the globalization era, cities and affluent countries have created ecological footprints which outweigh their relative size. For example, it requires resources from an area many times the size of Singapore to produce the food, water, energy and other resources needed to sustain that city-state and its economy. The need for trade and sharing of resources among the nation-states of Southeast and East Asia will increase. With diminishing supplies of water and other resources, it is certain that rivalries will intensify.

(Although far from East Asia's borders, the tense situation in the Middle East is worth noting. The bulk of the water supply for Israel, Jordan, Lebanon, and Syria comes from the River Jordan and the River Yarmuk. In the 1967 Middle East War, Israel occupied the Golan Heights, including the Jordan River and its watershed. This pre-empted any Syrian or Jordanian plan to change the river's flow and cut off Israel's water supply. Reliable water sources have since ancient times been a priority for Israel. Elaborate projects, such as King Hezekiah's secret tunnel to the pool of Siloam in Jerusalem were constructed to ensure the nation's survival under siege. Currently, Israel depends on the West Bank for twenty-five percent of its supplies, and any peace settlement is closely related to the resolution of Jordan River water rights and the use of groundwater from aquifers.)

Other forces can exacerbate water scarcity. Industries classified as polluting could move from richer countries to poor ones with lower environmental standards, thus exporting dirty industrial processes. Unless rich and poor regions adopt—and effectively enforce—common environmental standards, sources of tension will remain.

Cities and farms are beginning to compete for available water. Last year, there were clashes in China's Henan province as hundreds of villages fought over control of disputed water catchment areas. The northern China drought dried up rivers and drained reservoirs months ago, forcing more than 100 cities to implement strict water rationing. In some villages farmers rioted over rationed supplies and higher prices. Thousands of villagers in Shandong Province (along the eastern central coast) clashed with police after officials cut off water used for irrigating drought-plagued fields.

Conclusion

To avert impending shortages in Asia, water consumption by the agricultural sector must be reduced substantially. Currently available technologies include Low Energy Precision Application, or LEPA, sprinklers for grains, and drip irrigation systems for high-value fruit and vegetable crops.

Correct pricing of water has been touted as the best policy to ensure its proper use. Pricing levels are too low to avoid wastage. However, a two-tiered pricing system—one price for farmers and another for industry and cities—has potential. Effective water management systems must be in place to reduce pollution. For countries with high levels of water stress, sufficient infrastructure is needed to secure fresh water supplies. Policies to encourage recycling and recovery of renewable water are also required.

Feeding Asia in the Twenty-first Century

Dennis T. Avery

The challenge of feeding East and Southeast Asia in the new century will be affected by population growth, but more so by rising incomes for the region's 1.9 billion inhabitants. By 2050 most of those consumers will be able to eat as well as today's Japanese.

Consider the People's Republic of China (PRC), with per-capita purchasing power already at US$3,500—seventy times above the level during Chairman Mao's tenure.

Changing Tastes

Rapid recovery from the "Asian Contagion" (1997–99) underscores the solidity of Asia's export-led growth. The free-trade environment created by the World Trade Organization (WTO) has helped that model. Purchasing power is recovering in Korea and is—at $11,000—the level of pre-crisis 1997. Thailand is moving back to the pre-crisis $3,000–level, and Indonesia may be recovering as it undertakes painful structural reform.

Japan's consumers were once content with rice, vegetables, and fish. Now, their consumption of high-quality protein has quadrupled in five decades and is sixty grams per day; ultra-high meat tariffs and prices prevent it from rising further. The PRC doubled per-capita meat consumption amid giddy economic expansion, and seventy million tons are consumed per year. Ice cream is now the new food fad. South Korea produces no cheese, but mozzarella cheese imports grew twenty-fold during the period 1993–97, reaching 10,000 tons. Indonesians seek varied diets for more and higher-quality food despite risks of spreading erosion. Corn and soybeans are grown on poor-quality soil, some of it exposed to 100-inch rainfall in two-month long monsoons.

Asians will continue to eat rice, vegetables, and fish—but are adding fried chicken, tacos, spaghetti, pizza, bratwurst, and other "foreign" dishes. They are—as part of the ritual of globalization—copying the First World by assimilating foreign food, collecting recipes from over the world. Demand for farming resources will arise from rising acceptance of meat, milk, and eggs. These require three-to-five times as many farming resources per calorie as do cereals. Even the fish for tomorrow's East Asian tables will come from fish farms, fed on corn, wheat, and soybeans. Aquaculture is already popular in the region.

For many years, the International Food Policy Research Institute (IFPRI, affiliated with the International Agricultural Research Network) was skeptical of additional meat for Asian cultures. In 1999, however, IFPRI published *Livestock to 2020: The Next Food Revolution.* This noted that developing countries will increase meat consumption four times as rapidly as the First World during the next two decades.

In 1900 only ten percent of the world's grain production went to livestock; the current level is forty-five percent—and increasing. IFPRI projects developing country meat consumption will nearly double to 188 million tons in 2020.

Lester Brown, in *Who Will Feed China?* wrote that the PRC was running out of gains in crop yields and paving over its cropland. Brown predicted that the country would have to import more than 300 million tons of grain per year from other countries. (Current world grain trade totals only about 200 million tons per year, with little reaching the PRC.)

Although Brown's book indulged in scare-mongering, the reality is sobering: Much of the PRC's increased yields will depend on farming systems more advanced than the fabled Green Revolution's crossbred seeds, chemical fertilizers, and pesticides. The cropland Brown thought was paved over was actually hidden from the taxman. However, China has no additional land for farm production and may lose three percent of cropland to roads, factories, and apartments. The PRC already uses high-yield seeds and has the world's highest rates of chemical fertilizer application.

As noted elsewhere in this book, the western two-thirds of China receives virtually no rain; rainfall in the productive east is dependent on erratic tropical storms that often bring floods or drought. The severity of recent floods along the Yangtze River reveals that too many hilly slopes above this vast interior waterway were cleared. Major reforestation projects are under way.

Many assert that China must import more food. Yet the PRC won't have to import 300 millions tons per year unless grain production is high enough to keep prices low. Consider supply and demand: World production must be high enough to allow market prices to remain low enough, in turn keeping consumer meat demand high. While China must improve its agriculture, it will remain a major growth market for food exporters.

The Biotech Revolution

Several technology-driven developments are worth noting. Golden rice will provide beta carotene, which bodies turn into Vitamin A—preventing blindness and death. Golden rice also combats the chronic iron deficiency of rice-consuming women by disarming the phytate (in rice) that neutralizes iron. And a Taiwanese-Japanese research team in the U.S. has produced a rice plant that—incorporating a corn gene—performs photosynthesis more efficiently, yielding thirty-five percent more rice per hectare.

Acid-soil crops are important: half of tropical soils have high acidity. New methods allow plants to fend off aluminum ions that stunt crop growth, thereby doubling crop yield potential in Indonesia and the Philippines. "Cutting edge" gene mapping allows researchers to identify promising genes from wild relatives of our crop plants. Dramatic fifty-percent increases in tomato test plots have occurred. The PRC may now be a world leader in biotech crop research, with more than 100 gene-altered crops released (double the U.S. number) and more than one million farmers planting them. Slow-ripening tomatoes and virus-resistant peppers were commercialized, and new goals include high-protein rice plus rice plants with fewer stalks and twice as many grains.

Even with these advances, Asia will require substantial food, feed and/or fiber imports. Most of Asia's land is already intensively farmed with modern inputs, and repeating Green Revolution "miracles" by tripling crop yields will be almost impossible.

Technology has to be used in combination with free trade so that densely populated, land-scarce countries may supply consumers with high-quality diets at competitive costs. Governments had been rated on whether their countries were self-sufficient in food. Gone are the days when wooden sailing ships were blown off course for weeks while weevils devoured grain in their holds. And farm imports can help the region keep their manufactured exports competitive: Asia cannot expect to produce food as cheaply as big, land-rich, rain-fed temperate countries such as the United States, Canada, Argentina, Brazil, and France. Major irrigation dams and canals are expensive; greenhouses even more so. Clearing tropical forest—for any purpose—will soon be prohibitively unpopular with Asia's citizenry.

Inevitably, Asia's earning power will be derived from non-farm industries, and ultra-small farmers will adapt off-farm careers, many living within rural communities rather than in the teeming cities.

Support for farm free trade is increasing in the West; price supports have not proven cost-effective, and the United States is phasing out farm subsidies. The WTO farm trade talks endorsed free trade, and the European Union (EU)—long the bastion of farm protectionism—cannot afford to double its current $150 billion in subsidies. The EU will support agricultural trade liberalization—and then be an active competitor in farm exports.

Feeding East Asia in the twenty-first century is an enormous challenge but not beyond the world's capability. With continuing research to raise crop yields and increase meat production efficiency and open markets, the region will be eating well.

Part VII

People, Society, Culture and the Urban Edge

Hong Kong After the Handover: From Elation to Confusion

Chris Yeung

Scene I: Thousands of people queue outside banks to hand in share application forms for tycoon Li Ka-shing's Internet venture, Tom.com, in February 2000. About one and a half million applications are received. Says one middle-aged applicant: "It's better to queue up for one day than work for a whole year." His hopes are dashed. The stock price of the Internet venture dived shortly after it was listed.

Scene II: A political cartoon satirizing Hong Kong's chief executive Tung Chee-hwa as old and silly sells like hotcakes at a springtime book fair. Popularity ratings of the first local Chinese given the task of leading the so-called Special Administrative Region (SAR) of Hong Kong fell to new lows recently. Asked whether Beijing supported a second term for Tung in October (2000), Chinese vice premier Qian Qichen said: "Of course."

Scene III: More than 4,000 people mark the fourth anniversary of Hong Kong's return to Chinese sovereignty with protests against various policies and decisions made by the chief executive. A July issue of *Newsweek* magazine features the SAR, calling it "A City of Protest."

These lively scenes will be remembered because they took place during the past few eventful months, a period that saw the culmination of changes since the handover. As Hong Kong nears the end of the fourth year of Chinese rule under the "one country, two systems" formula, the aftershock of the regional economic recession continues to make an impact on the 6.8 million inhabitants. Although the worst is over, the economy has not fully recovered. And the vital property sector remains weak; in addition, information- and technology-related industries are far less promising than expected. Consumers' mood is at a low point.

In an address at the Chinese University of Hong Kong in December 2000, Singaporean former prime minister Lee Kuan Yew was bewildered by the SAR's doom-and-gloom attitude. He has praised Hong Kong as a model for his own city-state. Lee said, "[P]eople were frustrated, feeling trapped and hemmed in under SAR, unable to get out of their economic difficulties as easily as during the British times. . . . [T]he economy improved, but the mood of Hong Kong is still dark." He asked: "How is it possible that Hong Kong people were happier with their lot for decades under the rule of colonial governors than now?"

Notwithstanding the lack of a formal happiness index in Hong Kong, there is no dearth of anecdotes to reflect the depth of public frustration. Property-industry tycoons blame the government's interventionist housing policy for the sharp fall in prices and the collapse of confidence in the market. (Property prices plummeted by 40 to 50 percent from 1997 to 2001.) Businessmen worry that Hong Kong will pay dearly for bureaucratic short sightedness and inertia; hopes that government would facilitate a World Trade Organization era boom have not been realized. The official hype concerning opportunity for the SAR and its citizens after China opens its (economic) door wider does not provide a clear roadmap of how local businessmen can benefit from these trends.

Some fear Hong Kong will lose status as a gateway to China's 1.3 billion-population market. Professionals are shocked by the drastic fall in per-capita income while pondering the city-state's competitiveness in the new globalized economy. Workers in the semi- and unskilled categories are increasingly vulnerable in the highly competitive job market.

Unlike the perception during past economic recessions, locals are not certain about a swift rebound and fear that, unlike the previous track record, there will not be a phoenix-like rise from the ashes. More importantly, economic turmoil and recent faltering of information technology stocks shattered the SAR's faith in 1990s-style economic "miracles."

The economic woes have exposed the vulnerability of this Tiger. Yet a crisis in governance has occurred at the same time, a crisis caused by the lack of effective political institutions. A spate of policy blunders—characterized by embarrassments, including inoperative cargo transport systems, during the opening of the $30 billion airport and port in 1998 —dented public confidence in the government. And fears of favoritism surfaced after local Chinese leaders took over from colonial rulers. While the former British administration had been accused of favoritism towards British hongs, Tung faced tirades over decisions favorable to long-time friends and tycoons.

On the political front, the chief executive—chosen by a China-friendly 400–member panel—did not build coalitions and consensus, and thus failed to bolster his legitimacy. Faced with severe challenges to his authority, Tung did not adjust his strategy. Worse still, the wave of public discontent with the chief executive was seen as a conspiracy by hardliners in pro-China circles. They countered with a "Support Tung" campaign that further politicized Hong Kong society.

The sharp and vitriolic political rhetoric of the campaign did not solve problems, but deepened a sense of frustration and fostered indifference. A sharp decline in voter turnout in last year's Legislative Council elections shows the depth of public feelings of helplessness: Turnout was forty-three percent, down from fifty-four percent in the 1998 elections. While people did not trust the government, they did not see voting as a means of solving problems because the power of the elected SAR legislature is severely limited under the Basic Law, Hong Kong's post-handover mini-constitution.

According to a survey published in February 2001, only 50.1 percent of residents declare themselves to be happy. Meanwhile, seventy-two percent feel free. A mere twenty-nine percent say the government cares about the needs of the people. Forty-three percent say the society now is very chaotic, while three in four note that the problem of income disparity is very serious. The survey, conducted by a coalition of religious groups called "I Love Hong Kong Campaign," found that public frustration stemmed from social decline. Almost two-thirds of respondents believed media ethics had declined, while most said social morality was deteriorating, and forty-four percent felt family harmony had worsened. These findings show a loss of public confidence in the government. More people are impatient with abuses by the media such as sensationalism, inaccuracies, and unethical practices. Polls reveal more people do not believe what they read in newspapers.

(Nevertheless, this is only one of the two pictures of the Hong Kong media. The other is one in which the media plays the role of an effective and influential watchdog. Senior officials regularly take calls during radio phone-in programs, explaining—and defending—policies in a show of transparency and accountability within a limited democracy.)

Contrary to pessimistic forecasts, Beijing has behaved reasonably well since the handover. There has been no overt interference. But skeptics are worried that the dominating China factor has begun to upset the delicate balance in the "one country, two systems" policy. Senior mandarins factored in forms of political correctness when making decisions that might offend China. Cases abound and include planned visits of the Pope (to the SAR) and of Nobel Prize literature winner Gao Xingjian, a Chinese dissident. Journalists were warned by Mainland officials not to report news concerning separatist activities in Taiwan. Falun Gong has been branded as a cult in China, and its practitioners in Hong Kong have been under growing pressure to stop their activities or face a ban. Described as the conscience of Hong Kong, senior official Anson Chan resigned recently, reportedly because of her longstanding disagreements with Tung and Beijing. This deepened fears about the gradual erosion of Hong Kong's legal systems, practices, and values under the overbearing "one country" portion of the post-1997 handover formula.

Over the past four years, changes in the economic and political landscape have cast a shadow over Hong Kong and over Beijing's promises to the people of Hong Kong. Encapsulated in sixteen Chinese words, the four pledges are: "one country, two systems"; locals ruling Hong Kong; a high degree of autonomy; plus stability and prosperity. More people now feel these are merely well-intended policy objectives, if not empty slogans, that are not necessarily in synch with reality. It would be simplistic to say, though, that people have become nostalgic about the good old days of the colonial rulers.

Hong Kongers are known for their pragmatism. People have conceded the "one country, two systems" formula is the best possible option. Many still believe Beijing wants to make the post-1997 transition a success and that it is also in China's own interest to make the new arrangement work.

The alarm bells have been rung. It is another testing time for the people. Their versatility, resilience, and entrepreneurship helped the territory ride through the 1997–98 "Asian contagion," the worst recession in decades. They remain loyal to a strong self-image and identity. They continue to hold firm in their collective belief in the rule of law, an independent judiciary, the free market, clean government, an unfettered media, as well as in an open and liberal society. Shocked by regional economic turmoil and perplexed by changes in the domestic political scene, Hong Kongers have not yet been able to reorient themselves toward a clear direction. More than ever, the current situation is a litmus test for the SAR's political leaders. They must assist the community to as it tries to understand changing values and systems.

This is because the key lesson learned from the regional meltdown and socio-political controversies resulting from the "Asian Contagion" is that Hong Kong's success should never be taken for granted. There is now a greater sense of crisis and insecurity within the society. The once-eternal "can-do" spirit has been imbued with a more realistic awareness of the problems and challenges facing Hong Kong. Competition comes not only from fellow "Tiger" Singapore, but from a trio of large, affluent Chinese cities—Shanghai, Shenzhen, and Guangdong.

In the face of the need to foster a knowledge-based society, Hong Kong leaders are alarmed by a decline in the quality of local college graduates—both in their abilities and in their actual knowledge. In addition, the problem of a rich-poor gap is worsening. Political elites realize the importance of managing drastic economic and political changes, reinventing the can-do spirit, looking for new directions, and establishing the region's own identity.

Moreover, there is no easy route in sight. Nor is there a strong consensus on matters ranging from the positioning of Hong Kong and government's role in the society to the pace of democracy, and to assorted economic policies. While diversity of opinion is a sign of a pluralistic society, it can be an impediment to progress if public debate does not result in a set of shared goals and a common approach on a forward direction.

In light of the greater economic nexus and new sociopolitical interface with the Mainland, there is an inclination among opinion leaders to argue that Hong Kongers must readjust their mindset toward China. They call on people to think more Chinese and to look at China positively and from a historical perspective. Set eyes on the opportunities, they insist: be patient with the pace of the process of political liberalization.

Amid uncertainties regarding post-recession prospects, Hong Kong people remain cautiously optimistic about their future, with a reasonably strong self-image and a firm belief in the systems, values, culture, and practices of their society. The success of Hong Kong in undergoing its economic, social, and political transformation in the new era will not only facilitate the modernization programs in Mainland China, but provide important lessons for its Asian neighbors and other parts of the world.

Looking Below the Surface: Cultural Subtleties in U.S. and Chinese Negotiations

Deborah A. Cai

In a recent conversation with an American who conducts extensive business in China, I—once again—found myself explaining to a seasoned "China hand" the more subtle nuances of culture that affect negotiations with the Chinese, nuances unfamiliar to this man. I often encounter Americans who make frequent trips to China but do not understand the culture. And I have met as many Chinese who have given up trying to understand people from the United States.

People in these two cultures view the world in fundamentally different ways. Despite nearly a quarter of a century of revived bilateral diplomatic and business relations, there are cultural subtleties that still evade negotiators on both sides.

In this chapter, I will compare Chinese and American perspectives on the foundations of culture. Obviously, making such comparisons within a single chapter relies on generalizations that ignore wide cultural variations found in both countries. The comparisons offered here are between the generalized cultures of these two nations, in the same way that people from China visiting the United States refer to "American culture" and Americans visiting China refer to "Chinese culture." Furthermore, in my comparison I am limiting "Western cultures" to the United States;

Western readers can make inferences based on knowledge of their own cultures. Yet, these caveats are not as limiting as they may seem. (The term "American" refers to the general culture or people of the United States, not of Canada or Mexico.)

Taking the Long View

Effective negotiators understand that international negotiation is a process that takes time. But in negotiations between Americans and Chinese, Americans often report frustration over the length of time it takes to reach an agreement. One reason: Americans and Chinese do not share the same view of time. The Chinese long-range and more holistic view of time incorporates a sense of the distant past and distant future even while decisions in the present are considered. Americans, in contrast, tend to isolate issues, handling them one-by-one, separating them from the larger context of time. In addition, the sense of past and present is much shorter for Americans.

Consider, for example, the reclaiming of Hong Kong by the People's Republic of China (PRC) in 1997. For a full year prior to the actual handover the Chinese nightly TV news provided reports covering the history of Hong Kong, and a gigantic marquee in Tiananmen Square counted down the seconds (literally) until the handover. This stressed the significance of the event. In contrast, American news coverage focused on the economic significance of China's regaining Hong Kong and its implications for democracy in the city-state. What people in the United States generally failed to grasp was that although China had lost Hong Kong to Britain over 150 years before, a sense of humiliation over the loss was still real to the Chinese people. The American perspective tends to view 150 years as time long gone and forgotten. For people in China, reclaiming Hong Kong would finally rectify a significant injustice that had occurred in "recent" history.

Similarly, the Chinese long-range, holistic view of time means that two of the most recent incidents shaping United States-PRC relations in recent years are perceived as closely linked. From the Chinese perspective, the April 2001 incident involving a collision between a Chinese fighter plane and a U.S. spy plane above the China Sea is inseparable from the incident in 1999 when the United States bombed the Chinese embassy in Yugoslavia. American media coverage made little connection between these two events. Americans tend to view them as isolated incidents. For most Chinese, however, these two events are so close in time that they appear closely linked and therefore not coincidental.

The long-range and holistic perspectives of the Chinese—compared with the short-range and specific perspectives of the Americans—can translate into conflict when negotiating. First, the Chinese are in less of a hurry to reach an agreement than the Americans because, from the Chinese perspective, there is time to do what needs to be done. Furthermore, once an agreement is made, the Chinese do not view it as final because an agreement is only one element in the longer process of working out the conditions of the relationship.

In comparison, Americans focus on post-agreement stages of a negotiation. Treating time as a commodity that should not be wasted, Americans tend to rush the negotiation process to reach an agreement because it is not until an agreement is reached that it is possible to "get down to business."

Second, Chinese holism—compared with American specificity—relates to what constitutes a good argument in, or for, negotiation. Western reasoning is primarily abstract and conceptual, with emphasis on specific, detailed scientific and economic facts serving as evidence to support an argument. Chinese reasoning, in contrast, emphasizes general principles over details, and universals, especially those that can be drawn from history, over specifics. Whereas American logic uses inductive reasoning and relies upon data to argue causal relationships, the Chinese are more likely to use deductive reasoning and rely upon context, historical evidence, and metaphorical imagery to support their positions.

Third, the long-range view and holism mean that the Chinese neither separate issues from one another, nor do they separate relationships from negotiation. Instead, the Chinese are more likely to move slowly by first checking out and establishing the nature of the relationship, then negotiating (with all of the attendant cultural complications), and then reaching an agreement. Even then, Chinese are not likely to be ready to "get down to business" in the way familiar to Americans.

Furthermore, American negotiators tend to be unique on the international scene in that they do not emphasize prenegotiation stages of relationship-building (such as attending banquets or sightseeing). They often view this stage as merely socializing or even manipulating; thus they miss the crucial element of relational assessment that takes place during this stage.

The Role of the Individual

Another issue on which Chinese holism and American specificity differ is the role of the individual in society. Chinese culture is generally viewed as collectivistic, meaning the goals and needs of the group to which an individual belongs are valued above individual goals and needs. American culture is generally viewed as individualistic, implying an individual's goals and needs generally are valued above the needs of the group(s) to which the individual belongs. This contrast is often accompanied by suggestions that the Chinese are more concerned about relationships, while Americans are more concerned about individuals. But there are some subtle implications of these values at various relational levels that merit attention.

At a societal level, these values relate to perceptions of human rights as they affect each culture's understanding of the individual's role in society. In the West, the individual has the highest value. Human rights concerns therefore center around individual freedom, as well as rights to express opinions and make choices, even if those opinions and choices create dissent and disruption within society (albeit within a set of legal boundaries that restrict this freedom from harming other individuals). From the Chinese collectivistic perspective—in which harmony and social order, as promoted by Confucius, are especially valued—human rights have to do with the right of the individual to live in peace, not disrupted by another individual's dissent or disruption.

Consider, for example, the poignant images from Tiananmen Square in 1989, and specially the image of a young man standing in front of— and defying—a tank. For Americans, this picture was meaningful because it represented the power of "one" against a much greater force. One Chinese writer noted, however, that this image held little value for people in his own country because it revealed only the foolishness of this person.

Two cultural misassumptions often arise as the two concepts (American individualism and Chinese collectivism) are considered. First, American individualism does not mean that only individuals are of paramount importance. In fact, the concepts surrounding individualism provide constraints on individual actions. For example, a group of Chinese business and political leaders visiting the United States noted the serenity and cleanliness of American suburbs. They were surprised at the sense of community concern in the midst of an individualistic society. But included in American individualism is the sense that one individual is not to disrupt the living or autonomy of another individual—disrupting society, that is one thing; disrupting an individual is another matter. In contrast, the Chinese desire is to maintain harmony within the ingroup and also within society as a whole, but there is less concern for the disruption of individuals in an outgroup.

Second, the Chinese intolerance for individual dissent often is attributed to the reigning communist system. Yet, Chinese culture, although influenced by communism, remains at its core, Chinese. Collectivism and the Confucian values of social order and harmony have as much—or more—to do with avoidance of dissent than do communist doctrines. A response to events and to incidents in the PRC as "communist" deflects attention from many subtleties of Chinese culture.

At the interpersonal level, the concept of collectivism in the PRC is often reduced to an emphasis on *guanxi*, or the importance of relational networks. But *guanxi* does not refer to social networks in accordance with the American concept. For Americans, a large social network means that an individual knows a lot of people, hence is "well-connected." *Guanxi* relationships are better understood as having a "transitive" nature (see Figure 1). The transitive syllogism provides that if A = B and B = C, then A = C. In relationships, "transitivity" means the following: Zhang San (A) has a network of relationships; within that network is Li Si (B), who also has a network of relationships; included in Li Si's network is Zhao Wei (C).

"Transitivity" means that if Zhang San has a need for assistance that could be met by Zhao Wei, then because of her relationship with Li Si, Zhang San has access to Zhao Wei as part of her own relational network. As a result of transitivity, *guanxi* social networks are characterized by long links and strong webs of intertwining relationships. These all carry responsibility and expectations well beyond those of particular individuals. Therefore, transitivity goes far beyond the American understanding of how relational networks operate. Relational responsibility associated with *guanxi* webs suggests a "social exchange" nature to relationships for the Chinese. In other words, trust is built or broken based on whether the parties involved are able to uphold their responsibilities—and even go beyond what is necessary.

Another aspect of Chinese relationships on which Americans often focus is the importance of ingroup versus outgroup. This distinction is useful for Americans who tend not to make such clear distinctions between those belonging—or not—to the relational network. Generally, Chinese ingroup/outgroup relationships are presented as if there were a single circle of relationships; there are those who are on the inside, to whom rights are afforded and from whom responsibilities are expected.

Figure 1 **Comparing Networks in U.S. and China**

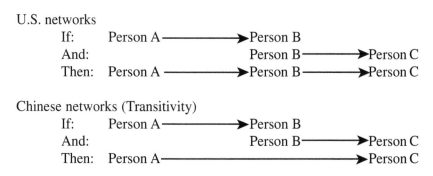

There are those on the outside who are relationally unimportant. But rather than a single circle with inside and outside, Chinese relationships are better depicted using two concentric circles (see Figure 2). The inner circle is the ingroup, where the relationship is certain and secure, such as family and well-established relationships.

Outside of the circles is the outgroup, where there are no expectations for maintaining relational harmony with individuals. But the middle comprises relationships that have the potential for becoming part of the ingroup, but trust has not been sufficiently established nor has time yet proven the relationships to be strong enough to be considered ingroup. By dichotomizing ingroup/outgroup, Americans may perceive that they are either in or out, but in fact, relationships that are neither ingroup nor outgroup require extra effort to give and protect face, to demonstrate a willingness and ability to meet the requirements of transitivity, and to establish trust. Mid-group relationships require a time of testing and establishment that may continue indefinitely, especially for foreigners trying to establish ties in China. Many diplomatic and business alliances between Chinese and Americans fall within this category.

Further complications arise, however, because the establishment of trust operates differently among Chinese and Americans. Historically, Chinese trust primarily ran along lineage lines, not extending to nonfamilial relationships because family was considered more trustworthy. Today, trust extends only to ingroup members. Furthermore, Chinese relationships are based more on contextual factors than on psychological compatibility. In contrast, American relationships tend to be built on trust. In the United States, trust in relationships is developed

Figure 2 **Group Relationships**

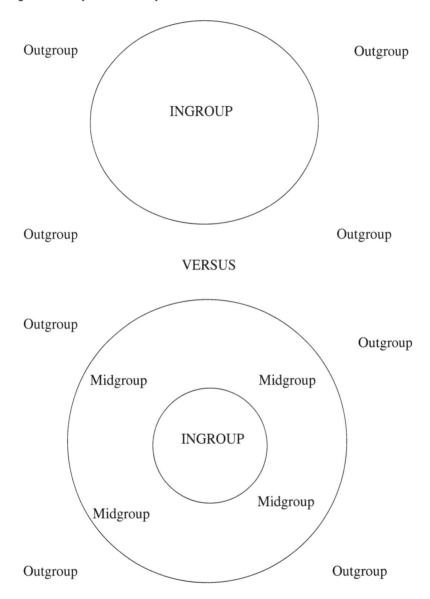

on the basis of perceptions that the other party has integrity and is dependable, benevolent, and competent. These perceptions develop based on sharing and disclosure of information that increases as the relationship strengthens. Sharing and disclosure are used both to establish trust initially and to strengthen trust as the relationship develops.

But these psychological and communication factors do not play as important a role in the establishment and maintenance of relationships in China. Disclosure is important to the extent that it establishes relational compatibility between parties by uncovering network ties such as similar family backgrounds and hometowns, educational linkages, friends who may know one another and so on.

Instead, the establishment of Chinese relationships is more dependent on intermediaries who connect people within the transitive networks. Trust is automatically established between those who are connected because of the existing trust relationship each network member has with the intermediary, so that trust is based more on the structure of relationships than on emotional or psychological factors. Literature for Americans on how to do business with the Chinese often prescribes the need to "make friends" and "build trust" with the Chinese. Yet the role of trust in "making friends" is understood quite differently across the two cultures.

Conclusion

The subtleties of Chinese and American cultures discussed in this chapter have far-reaching implications. Although there is a vast literature on how to negotiate with the Chinese—and despite greater numbers of Americans working in the PRC as well as Chinese coming to the U.S., there are still many subtleties about the two cultures that can result in misunderstanding and conflict. This chapter touches on a few of the basic issues that must be understood by both sides. A better understanding of these cultural subtleties will not rule out disagreement. Yet by going below the surface, both sides should be able to communicate more effectively concerning both agreements and disagreements.

Confucianism, Modernity, and Restoration in Contemporary China

Mark T. Fung

The title of this compendium is *Tigers' Roar,* yet China is more often associated with the dragon. And with the ethereal comes a distant time and place, both past and future. Legend has its own texture and maneuverability in a history of what once was and what could be. To examine China is to examine legend. From epoch to epoch, the nation has engaged in a search for a new ethos—new values and norms peculiar to the Chinese people. Mass introspection was a political and philosophical odyssey that paralleled the rise and fall of dynastic cycles and domestic turbulence. When the Emperor failed in his heavenly mandates to do "good" and provide for the citizenry, a new search ensued; Confucianism in Chinese society has tended to be cyclical, accented with a Sisyphean quality.

This search yielded the usurpation of dynastic order, thus forming a new order—or spawning domestic upheaval. The concept of disorder and chaos is all too familiar to China. When there was internal turmoil, it bred intervention by external forces (*nei luan, wai huan*), to be averted at all costs. But the element of continuity of Chinese society has been Confucianism (in various iterations); it formed the foundations of Chinese political thought. Confucianism remains the unofficial national ethos in China.

Modernization Theory Relevant to China

Modernization theory often knights non-Western nations with the honorific of being Western, of reaching modernity. The gift of modernization theory is its assumption that social mobility increases political development. Classic modernization theory cannot explain why the PRC's economic development occurred and what is to be expected over the next horizon.

Lack of mobility plays a central role in the taxation of China's rural sector: farmers are forced to remain in villages and townships where wages are stagnant. Increased mobility would defuse the mounting social instability in the countryside—a major challenge facing China.

Consider one example of mobility and of how traditional Chinese thinking would assess contemporary conditions. In August 2000 protests erupted in Jiangxi Province, where 20,000 people protested unduly burdensome taxes. Peasants were taxed to over sixty percent of their income. Most peasants are unable to travel beyond the provincial parameters because of the dearth of infrastructure, poor road interconnectivity, and the high costs of such travel. Confucian thought would condone such protests since the rules were unjust and the ruler was not a "superior man" who adhered to the highest moral standards. Central government directives to limit taxes often fall on the deaf ears of local bureaucrats.

Institutional change occurs in an incremental fashion. Incrementalism is one of the overarching political and economic themes in the PRC. And related to incrementalism is Confucianism.

The Predicament of Confucianism

Throughout China's history there have been varied approaches to governance. For instance, the Song dynasty Neo-Confucianists were concerned with the nature of being. The later-Ming dynasty teachings were ontological in their worldview. Hence, the interpretation of Confucianism was integrally linked to the imperial imprimatur. There were lasting tensions inherent in Confucianism. Within the "polarities" of Confucianism, three themes were central to Master Kung's teachings: Self-Cultivation and the Ordering of Society; the Inner and Outer Realms; Knowledge and Action. For it is in the Inner Realm, or the notion of *li,* that hierarchical social orders are evident: ruler to minister;

father to son; older brother to younger brother; husband to wife; friend to friend.

Confucianism has a tensile strength that is its own. One misconception of Confucianism is that it is monolithic. In fact it expands and contracts, ascends and descends, depending upon how Confucian precepts are interpreted at any given time. This permits the rising young elite to shape Confucianism to fit contemporary China's mold. In their purest form, the teachings provide broad prescriptions for societal and familial relationships.

Yet one Confucian verity has remained unchallenged: the role of the bureaucrat. Duty and respect for the ruler was paramount to the underlying Confucian ethic within the ruler-minister rubric.

The last dynasty in China, the Qing, institutionalized these teachings. Considered unworthy Manchus, the Qing were sensitive to being perceived as outsiders. Their attempt to institutionalize Confucianism was intended to show that they were more Chinese than the Han (Chinese) ethnic group. Strict adherence to bureaucracy required an endless supply of men of letters and of rulers who were interested in knowledge. If a ruler was a patron of the arts, the country would experience cultural munificence. If absorbed with finance, the province would "dabble" in currency reform. Foreign intervention during the Qing era precipitated China's gradual social and economic decline. But one fundamental reason for the Qing collapse was that the court failed to attract men of letters.

Joseph R. Levenson (see bibliography) suggests that attempts have been made by China to restore Confucianism into the straitjacket of Chinese society: "The first wave of revolution in the twentieth century had virtually destroyed him [Confucius], and . . . an historical identity. . . . The communists had their own part in the search for time lost, and their own intellectual expedient: bring it back, bring him back, by pushing him back in history."

Modernity was jettisoned for the sake of China's self-preservation. Confucianism will again become the expedient for China's rising young elite. As long-time observer Ezra Vogel notes, the teachings' contribution to social mobility—and hence industrialization in East Asia—is its emphasis on self-cultivation. They will claim ownership of this ideal, as it is untainted by the PRC's immediate past. Young elites want something to call their own, and rightfully so, when they choose to resuscitate Confucianism.

Young Mandarins: The Emergent Elite

The present epoch of post-Deng modernization is more than an edifice of capitalism in socialist veneer. China is undergoing a period of renewal and restoration. Stemming the decline of service to the bureaucracy, even if temporarily, requires renewal or restoration (*chung xing*). During the nascent stages of China's economic development, its leadership relied upon Soviet-trained technocrats who promoted self-reliance in industry and agriculture. Economic reforms during the past two decades heralded engineers and economists as architects of the economy. The next stage requires technologically trained leaders.

As was true during the later Qing period, the young elite no longer serve in the bureaucracy—it is no longer the highest calling. This is China's contemporary dilemma. The rulers can no longer attract men and women of letters. Instead, they are drawn to the Western cosmopolitanism and the financial rewards that Western higher education brings.

The young elite have returned to China motivated by financial gain. This overshadows Confucian notions of public service. In ten to fifteen years, after a period of restoration, the young elite will return to government service, not to seek personal gain (they will have already achieved it) but to reinstate Confucian bureaucratic destiny. They will be accidental Confucianists, the fifth generation of Chinese leaders. The fourth generation, led by Hu Jintao, the current vice president and likely future president, may serve as a custodian during this interregnum period of Chinese reordering of Confucian values. Again, as with previous dynastic cycles, the interpretations of institutional Confucianism will change, and virtues such as the Inner Realm will resurface.

Where will they emerge? Shanghai—halfway between Beijing and Hong Kong—is a blend of dynamism and cosmopolitanism. Shanghai has been an incubator for contemporary political leaders in China (such as President Jiang Zemin and Premier Zhu Rongji). The city has cultivated many rising stars of young entrepreneurs, including Edward Zeng, the cybercafe movement leader. He and others, lured by the panacea of technology, will reassess their contribution to society; their disillusionment will cause the crestfallen young elite to serve in the bureaucracy during China's restorative period from 2000 to 2015.

To understand modernity in China is to grasp the interplay of Confucianism, social and political mobility, and technological and economic progress. Confucian precepts do not demand absolutism, nor are they monolithic. Whereas modernization theory reveals how man can conquer his environment, Confucianism prescribes how to work within the environment. Is it possible to straddle the practice of Confucian verities while objectively accepting modernity? Confucian China is like an artesian well, layered with impermeable strata of history, order, and tension; and as internal hydrostatic pressure builds, it will ultimately give rise to an elite that answers the call of Confucianism.

Bibliography

Almond, Gabriel A., and Sidney Verba [1963] 1989. *The Civic Culture: Political Attitudes and Democracy in Five Nations.* Newbury Park, CA: Sage Publications, Inc.

Amsden, Alice H. 1979. *Modern China* 5, no. 3: 341–379.

Dahl, Robert A. 1971. *Polyarchy: Participation and Opposition.* New Haven: Yale University Press.

Deutsch, Karl W. 1961. *Social Mobilization and Political Development.* New Haven: Yale University Press.

Diamond, Larry. 1999. *Developing Democracy: Toward Consolidation.* Baltimore: Johns Hopkins University Press.

———. 1996. "Is the Third Wave Over?" *Journal of Democracy* 7, no. 3 (July): 20–37.

Eckstein, Harry. 1996. *Culture as a Foundation Concept for the Social Sciences.* Newbury Park, CA: Sage Publications, Inc.

Ford, Steven R. 1981. *The Protestant Ethic and People's China: The Weberian Thesis Reconsidered.* New York: Hemisphere Publishing.

Huntington, Samuel P. 1965. *Political Development and Political Decay.* Princeton: Princeton University Press.

———. 1968. Political Order in Changing Societies. New Haven: Yale University Press.

———. 1971. "The Challenge to Change: Modernization, Development, and Politics." *Comparative Politics* 3(2): 282–322.

———. 1991. *The Third Wave: Democratization in the Late Twentieth Century.* Norman, Oklahoma: University of Oklahoma Press.

———. 1996. *The Clash of Civilizations and the Remaking of World Order.* New York: Simon and Schuster.

Johnson, Chalmers. 1982. *MITI and the Japanese Miracle: The Growth of Industrial Policy, 1925–1975.* Stanford: Stanford University Press.

Laitin, David D. 1978. *Religion, Political Culture, and the Weberian Tradition.* Princeton: Princeton University Press.

Levenson, Joseph R. 1968. *Confucian China and Its Modern Fate: A Trilogy.* Berkeley: University of California Press.

Lipset, Seymour Martin. [1960] 1981. *Political Man: The Social Bases of Politics.* Expanded ed. Baltimore: Johns Hopkins University Press.

———. 1993. "The Social Requisites of Democracy Revisited." *American Sociological Review* 59 (February): 1–22.

O'Brien, Donal Cruise. 1972. "Modernization Theory Revisited: A Review Essay." *Comparative Studies in Society and History* 30: 753–61.

Razzell, Peter. 1977. "The Protestant Ethic and the Spirit of Capitalism: A Natural Scientific Critique." *British Journal of Sociology* 28 No. 1 (March).

Rostow, W.W. 1961. *The Stages of Economic Growth: A Non-Communist Manifesto.* Cambridge: Harvard University Press.

Rustow, Dankwart. 1968. "Modernization and Comparative Politics." *Comparative Politics* 1 (October): 37–51.

Schwartz, Benjamin. 1959. "Some Polarities in Confucian Thought." In *Confucianism and Chinese Civilization*, Arthur F. Wright, ed. Stanford: Stanford University Press.

Shils, Edward. 1960. *The Intellectuals in the Political Development of the New States.* Notre Dame: Notre Dame University Press.

Vogel, Ezra. 1991. *The Four Little Dragons: The Spread of Industrialization in East Asia.* Cambridge: Harvard University Press.

Werlin, Herbert H. 1994. "Politics versus Culture: Which Is Stronger?" *Studies in Comparative International Development* 29(4): 3–24.

Wiarda, Howard J. 1989. "Political Culture and National Development." *The Fletcher Forum of World Affairs* 13, no. 2.

Wright, Mary Clabaugh. 1957. *The Last Stand of Chinese Conservatism: The T'ung-Chih Restoration, 1862–1874.* Stanford: Stanford University.

Cross-National Competence and U.S.-Asia Interdependence: The Explosion of Trans-Pacific Civil-Society Networks

Peter H. Koehn

The arrival of the twenty-first century offers policy-makers, cultural leaders, media, scholars, and the attentive public an opportunity to take a fresh look at the changing context of U.S.-Asia relations.

Three ongoing developments undermine the viability of prevailing twentieth-century perspectives. First, the welfare of local communities in Asia and the United States increasingly involves linked, rather than separate, destinies. Second, non-governmental actors, operating along and across porous nation-state boundaries through civil-society networks and independent micro-political processes, have become key players in international relations. Dense trans-Pacific interactions among non-state actors have arisen in virtually all fields of human endeavor. Third, the worldwide revolution in skills enhancement is dramatically increasing the ability of individuals—acting on their own or through organized groups—to address the challenges of interdependence.

The interaction of these three developments suggests that past patterns of U.S.-Asia relations will be altered in fundamental ways. Emerging actors will pursue *diverse interests* through *alternative processes*. In the wake of this invasion, *new dramas* will command the attention of those occupying the center stage. The imposition or inculcation of hegemonic nation-state or global-capitalist approaches will be diminished by a compelling need for *mutuality and reciprocity* in addressing interdependence challenges.

The direction of prevailing responses to these dramas will be determined largely by the outcome of *collaboration/conflict* among cross-nationally competent professionals and activists, transnational corporations and their institutional allies, and state authorities.

Linked Destinies and Interdependence Dramas

Whether their members embrace it or resent it, the welfare of local communities in Asia and the United States is linked in many ways. Economic roles and individual/community well-being increasingly are shaped by trans-Pacific trade, investment, migration, capital accumulation, currency alignments, and more.

U.S.-Asia interdependence reaches far beyond economic interests. From approaches to health care to mass entertainment, what matters in people's lives depends increasingly on developments outside national borders.

Dependence on distant, less directly controllable visions and decisions heightens the vulnerability of participants. The result is a dramatic rise in the number and scope of problems related to interdependence, challenges that are largely resistant to state influence. Preoccupation with security (armed conflict) and economic issues has overshadowed many of the emerging U.S.-Asia dramas demanding priority. The most pressing of the invasive challenges include environmental protection, energy and natural resource conservation, population, migration pressures, human rights, and provisions for ensuring and improving physical as well as mental health. Cutting across interdependence is the relevance of mutual learning.

Civil-Society Networks

There are clear limits to what nation states, acting on their own or through multilateral institutions, are able to accomplish in addressing interdependence issues. An extensive and diverse array of civil-society actors—including individuals, large-scale and small-scale (international and domestic) non-governmental organizations (NGOs), and transnational social movements—have demonstrated that they can fill key gaps at international, national, and local levels of political action. Non-state actors fill important roles by becoming involved in four influence systems:

- international-agreement shaping
- nation-state policy making and international-agreement implementation
- local/community project initiation and implementation
- value sharing and change.

A single actor (e.g., an NGO), typically part of a transnational civil-society network, often is active in more than one influence system—on one, or both, sides of the Pacific. Whether a specific civil-society actor opts to become involved in a U.S.-Asia interdependence challenge depends on the nature of the issue at stake. Once a non-state actor decides to engage an issue, the focus and geographic locus/loci of its activities are determined by the individual or organization's ability to exert leverage within the activated influence systems.

Some civil-society actors, such as associations of scientists, can either influence agreements requiring bilateral or multilateral negotiation (e.g., stratospheric-ozone depletion) or assist in formulating local problem-solving approaches. Consider project initiation and implementation. The Association of Medical Doctors of Asia (AMDA) is an excellent example of a globally networked, humanitarian, nonpolitical, non-profit NGO—with twenty-seven chapters and fourteen project offices throughout Asia, Africa, and the Americas. It successfully carries out refugee assistance and emergency-care operations throughout the developing world (and in Japan, after the 1995 Kobe earthquake). From a small organization formed in 1984 by dedicated Japanese physicians, AMDA has become one of the largest Asian NGOs. Its network, which functions primarily at the local/community project level, is infused by Asian views and practices—such as its *sogo-fujo* approach (i.e., creating partnerships with local organizations, all based on mutual assistance).

Individuals—across the complete spectrum of political and ideological persuasion—are most prone to affect the personal values of those they come in contact with (e.g., by serving as role models) and are least likely to shape international agreements. Nevertheless, consider the personal "Track II Diplomacy" that Korean-American academic K.A. Namkung used single-handedly in brokering national-security policy between North Korea and the United States in 1993. Leon Sigal summarizes Namkung's exceptional role in the following passage that appeared in the June/September 1997 issue of the Social Science Research Council's *Items* (51, no. 2/3: 35–36):

> In late May 1993, just before high-level talks between the United States and North Korea were to resume in New York, Namkung made his fifth visit to Pyongyang. He met with First Deputy Foreign Minister Kang Sok Ju and other members of the Democratic Republic of Korea (D.P.R.K., or North Korea) negotiating team as they were about to board a plane for New York. . . . From these conversations he concluded that Pyongyang would postpone its withdrawal from the Nuclear Nonproliferation Treaty, but try to delay inspections, pending the conclusion of an agreement in high-level talks with the United States.
>
> Namkung encouraged his Korean interlocutors to remain partially in the treaty. He also surprised them by urging them to try for a joint statement with the United States in the coming round of high-level talks. The North Koreans asked him to suggest communique language that the United States might find acceptable, and Namkung, drawing on the wording of the U.N. Charter, jotted down a few broad principles on a sheet of paper and handed it to the North Koreans. They became the basis of the June 11, 1993, U.S.-D.P.R.K. joint statement, the first ever between the two countries, in which North Korea announced it was suspending its withdrawal from the Nuclear Nonproliferation Treaty in return for high-level talks with the United States.
>
> [In the end, K.A. Namkung had] helped turn the American government around to negotiate an agreement that, if fully implemented, would keep North Korea from nuclear-arming.

The Skills Revolution and Cross-National Competence

Spurred by advances in information technology and means of human mobility, people around the globe are experiencing a skill revolution that is transforming the world in myriad ways. An important—and rapidly expanding—dimension of the skills revolution is the development of cross-national competence. The explosion of interpersonal interactions across nation-state boundaries provides the energy that drives the transformative efforts of transnational civil-society networks. The complexity involved in such interactions highlights the relevance of cross-national competence. Cross-national competence requires mastery of four sets of skills: analytical, emotional, creative/imaginative, and behavioral.

Table 1 illustrates these four dimensions of cross-national competence. The table is based on findings reported by scholars who specialize in cross-cultural psychology, intercultural communication, international business, development management, and international relations. Individuals, organizations, and communities in Asia and the United States possess these skills in varying degrees and in different mixes. Based upon systematic research, each transnational actor could be located on a continuum—one ranging from those defined as cross-nationally proficient to incompetent.

Especially important in this discussion is evidence that greatly expanding numbers of people on both sides of the Pacific are shifting in the direction of cross-national competence. Contributing to this development are permanent and circular migration from East, Southeast, and South Asia to the United States—along with the rise of global electronic networks.

From less than one million in 1965, the number of Asian-Americans now exceeds twelve million, about seventy percent of whom are first-generation immigrants maintaining close ties with family members, friends, and associates in the countries of origin and keeping informed of homeland developments. Many of these immigrants quickly develop analytical, emotional, creative, and behavioral competence in mainstream U.S. society while retaining their country-of-origin skills. Immigrant and U.S.-born Asian-American professionals alike increasingly are inclined to perceive their bicultural heritage as a major asset and to become involved in diverse transnational capacities.

Another important contributing factor to the development of cross-national competence is the experience of studying and living overseas. The implications of study-abroad patterns for U.S.-Asia relations are mixed. While Asian students—particularly from Japan, China, and Malaysia—are among the largest groups of overseas students in the United States, far fewer U.S. students and scholars pursue academic interests, or complete internship assignments, in Asia.

To some extent, the resulting educational and language deficit on the U.S. side is offset by immigrants who elect not to return to their homeland (for example, Chinese students and scholars who left the PRC in the wake of the Tiananmen Incident). Recently, however, most Asian students who study in the United States have not been inclined to stay.

Table 1

Illustrations of Cross-National Competence

Analytical Competence
　　Possession of reasonably complete understanding of the central beliefs, values,
　　　　and practices of counterpart culture(s) and society(ies)—including political
　　　　and ethnic sensitivity
　　Ability to discern effective cross-national transaction strategies and to learn
　　　　from past successes and failures

Emotional Competence
　　Ability to project an interest in, and to gain and reflect sensitivity for, different
　　　　values, traditions, experiences, and challenges (i.e., cross-cultural/cross-
　　　　national empathy)
　　Ability to manage multiple identities

Creative/imaginative Competence
　　Ability to foresee the synergistic potential of diverse cultural perspectives in
　　　　problem solving
　　Ability to design innovative and culturally acceptable approaches

Behavioral Competence
Communicative Facility
　　Fluency in and use of counterpart's spoken/written language
　　Proficiency in and relaxed use of culturally appropriate nonverbal cues and
　　　　codes
　　Ability to listen to and discern different cultural messages; to facilitate mutual
　　　　self-disclosure
Functional Adroitness
　　Ability to relate to counterpart(s) and to develop and maintain positive
　　　　interpersonal relationships
　　Ability to overcome problems and accomplish goals when dealing with
　　　　cross-national challenges

Twenty-first Century Approaches to U.S.-Asia Interdependence Dramas

U.S.-Asia relations are being transformed by growing recognition of linked destinies, the explosion of independent transnational actors and networks, and the global revolution in skills enhancement. The sections below treat some of the important implications arising from these developments for (1) trans-Pacific interest articulation and processing and (2) the ways in which interdependence dramas will be managed in the new century.

Alternative Processes and New Interests

Trans-Pacific non-governmental actors are advancing a diverse set of interests rooted in transnational linkages among "communities" and organizations. The vast majority are shaped and pursued independently of bilateral and multilateral nation-state controls, in forums that avoid public scrutiny. Networking, rather than regulating or diplomatic negotiating, is gaining primacy as a means of dealing with international affairs.

In the economic sphere, U.S.-based multinational corporations, Japanese and Korean firms, and Chinese families, among others, have long demonstrated mastery in network-building and decision-making. Other institutions—universities, scientific and professional associations, labor unions, churches, environmental organizations, local communities, women's associations, activist groups, and so forth—are rapidly following suit.

While nation-state authorities retain varying degrees of influence, the range and scope of civil-society networks renders trans-Pacific decision-making fragmented, complex, and largely self-regulated. Participants in truly transnational networks will work to negate rather than perpetuate U.S. hegemonic tendencies. They will innovate and partner with, rather than subdue or submit to, counterparts from diverse and hybrid cultural backgrounds.

Out of these alternative networks and processes, issues previously kept off the agenda will rise to the forefront of trans-Pacific relations. Most emerging civil-society networks do not place priority on advancing global capitalist interests or on accumulating material wealth. Although they will not disappear, visions of economic aggrandizement will recede in importance. Gradually, as new challenges reach crisis proportions, today's materialist ambitions will be displaced by heightened attention to trans-Pacific dramas involving interdependent environmental and health concerns, natural-resource depletion, human rights and labor exploitation, as well as the growing gap between rich and poor. Simultaneously, cross-national, national, and local decisions on how to address these emerging issues will be shaped by the volatile consequences of porous borders: transnational population movements, struggles over identity as a source of social meaning that transcends citizenship, efforts to reconcile Confucianist traditions with a worldview influenced by accelerated interdependence, and education in and for a networked information age. For instance, at the 1998 Summit, China and the United States agreed to introduce a multiweek program of paired secondary-school student and teacher exchanges. This new initiative, scheduled to commence on a pilot basis in Fall 2001, aims to "develop linkages between schools and communities in the United States and China for the purpose of *mutual* education and the development of student participation in community affairs" [emphasis mine]. According to guidelines issued on 8 June 2000 by the Bureau of Educational and Cultural

Affairs, "each one-to-one school partnership will choose a theme relevant to their communities; students will work together [via internet connectivity and exchanges of three to four weeks in duration] to complete a joint project related to this theme."

Managing Interdependence Challenges in the Twenty-first Century

Success in dealing with future trans-Pacific challenges will require emphasis on approaches that are based on reciprocity and global/local linkages rather than on national self-interest and profit making. Some emerging civil-society actors (e.g., "epistemic communities," or networks of knowledge-based experts in a particular domain) will shape outcomes in the four critical influence systems described above primarily by contributing insights and expertise. For instance, a growing number of organizations for Chinese American scientists and engineers, such as the 1500-member Society of Chinese Bioscientists in America and the 1000-member Chinese-American Chemical Society, are strengthening linkages to China that involve training Mainland scientists in the United States and placing Chinese American experts in positions in Asia as part of an overall effort to "develop more researchers who can contribute scientifically on both sides of the Pacific" (Richard Stone, "The Chinese-American Connection," *Science* 262, no. 5132, 15 October 1993: 350). Others (such as local communities) will establish joint projects or transnational Peace Corps–like programs. Still others (e.g., activist communities) will focus on appealing to emotion and will challenge dominant values and institutions.

All such trans-Pacific and country-specific activities will be infused by knowledge-sharing and mutual learning. Cross-nationally proficient actors from Asia and the United States will play decisive leadership roles within the transnational networks that address the new interdependence challenges. Within civil society networks, these actors will function as the principal decision initiators and facilitators, the "switchers" who connect participants, instead of being relegated to roles as conduits or peripheral consultants for U.S.-based corporations seeking entry to Asian markets or access to Asian resources. As the relevance of cross-national proficiency for solving a broad range of interdependent problems becomes more widely appreciated on both sides of the Pacific, these non-state, foreign-policy-influencing, leadership roles increasingly will be filled by Asian Americans—especially first-generation immigrants—and by graduates from institutions of higher education in the United States who return to Asia.

The recent explosion of Asia-U.S. non-governmental interactions has both contributed to and resulted from expanded awareness of the extent to which the peoples and local communities of Asia and the United States share an interconnected future. As we enter the new century, the trans-Pacific foundation required to cope with potentially contentious challenges inherent in interdependence exists through extensive and vibrant civil-society networks that are active along interconnected political, economic, cultural, and scientific boundaries. Cross-nationally competent actors will contribute unique insights and abilities in a multitude of ways across trans-boundary influence systems; that is, in international-agreement shaping, nation-state domestic-policy making, international-agreement implementation, project initiation and execution, and values sharing/change. These actors' increasingly influential—even decisive—roles will advance Asia-U.S. relations.

In this new environment, will the interests of indispensable, but currently exploited, populations be addressed? Similarly, will the "digital divide" result in the creation of network-dispossessed and electronically "switched off" groups and areas, both in Asia and in the United States? Will the cross-national-competency skills revolution spread much more deeply, encompassing a representative cross-section of populations on both sides of the Pacific? Will trans-Pacific network interconnections be open and available to all people or only to elites? Given the proliferation of transnational networks and the relative absence of cross-cutting cleavages among them, how will priorities be set and conflicts be managed in a linked—but simultaneously fragmented—world?

In year 2001, answers to these crucial questions remain undetermined. Clearly, however, the nature of the trans-Pacific theater has changed. State agents, transnational corporations, and their institutional allies no longer have the center stage to themselves. Cross-nationally competent professionals and activists, acting as individuals and through civil-society networks, also will play a major part in determining the outcome of U.S.-Asia interdependence dramas in the twenty-first century.

Japan's Socio-Cultural Transformation: The Breakdown of the Japanese Dream

Alexei Kral

"There is no good news in Japan anymore," a young Japanese woman with orange-dyed hair told me recently. You know Japan is changing when housewives, teachers, businessmen, and bureaucrats echo frustrations shared by those dyeing their hair orange or blonde.

This Northeast Asian country's most important challenge is defining a "Japanese dream." To understand Japan's future, we must consider the profound socio-cultural transformation prompted by a crumbling Japanese dream. The Japanese dream evolved during the postwar era; its origins were psychological and emotional—not political or economic. Social psychologists have noted that when a group's prestige is threatened, members often seek to restore pride. By rebuilding their economy, the Japanese restored a positive group image, reinforcing it by identifying elements of their economic development and social order as uniquely Japanese. Many Japanese therefore felt beholden to social norms and practices that facilitated Japan's postwar progress—except for the younger generation (as they did not experience the rebuilding process).

The Japanese dream provided a model with core values such as hard work, achievement, persistence, and dedication to performing one's social role. Like the American dream, the Japanese dream did not come true for everyone, nor did every citizen aspire to it. Indeed, today many people are giving up on the dream.

The Japanese Dream as a Socialization Process

The Japanese dream offered a guideline for a person's entire life and began with childhood, outlining various rites of passage. For men, the dream was to study hard as a child, pass high school entrance exams, pass exams to enter a prestigious university, obtain a job in government or a large company—and work selflessly for an employer. Evolution to each stage depended on successful completion of the previous stage.

The process socialized the Japanese people, assuring the continuation of common ideals. The final step would bring material comfort and honor to one's family, but participating in the dream and persisting from one stage to the next was given priority. In essence, the dream demonstrated devotion to one's role.

For women, the dream followed the same path through college graduation. The next step was to marry a man who worked for the government or a large company, and to raise children who would similarly succeed. Women's lives centered on ensuring that their children passed high school and college entrance exams.

The dream provided models for an ideal mother, an ideal student, an ideal father, and an ideal worker—and images were reinforced in daily life at schools, workplaces, in homes, in newspapers, on television, and even in advertising. Today, however, all groups of Japanese are questioning the ideals at each stage.

Entrance Exams and Alienated Young People

A student's mission was to pass aforementioned entrance examinations. Most youth attended "cram schools" to guarantee this mission will be fulfilled—and at home they studied more. A common maxim was, "pass with four, fail with six," meaning students would score high in these exams if they slept only four hours a night and risked failing if they dared sleep longer. Aiming for the future, many students lost their childhood years: it was not unusual for parents to worry about their child's enrollment in the appropriate kindergarten (so as to boost exam success years later).

Today, underlying support for this system is eroding: graduating from

Table 1

The Japanese Dream

Men	Women
1. Study for entrance exams. Attend cram schools.	1. Study for entrance exams. Attend cram schools.
2. Go to a good university.	2. Go to a good university.
3. Get a job with the government or large company.	3. Marry a man who works for the government or a large company.
4. Work selflessly for the employer.	4. Make sure children pass their entrance exams.

a prestigious university does not guarantee a job. Links between businesses and universities—as well as vocational schools—to recruit graduates are disappearing. Some sixty percent of 1998 college graduates did not have jobs lined up upon graduation. As guaranteed rewards vanish, young people are frustrated with a high-pressure education system. However, they are afraid to reject the latter without alternatives. Resulting alienation is manifested in bullying at schools, increasing rates of truancy, and "classroom collapse" (*gakkyuu houkai*), chaos wherein once-docile students refuse to listen to teachers.

Many adults lament youth values, especially as sensational crimes by minors capture news headlines. Critics suggest the educational system's focus on academic achievement neglects young people's social and moral development. Disillusioned Japanese remember that the Aum Shinrikyo cult (which unleashed poisonous gas on the Tokyo subway system in 1995) consisted of graduates from top universities. Newspaper editorials are demanding a new educational system to foster critical thinking.

Some universities established alternatives to the "one-shot" entrance exam and accept applications emphasizing high school activities, but Japanese are taking a cautious approach.

The Workplace and "Lifetime Employment"

The Japanese dream appears to be breaking down more rapidly in the workplace. High unemployment figures cause anxiety, and, as noted else-

Table 2

Corporate Attitudes Regarding Lifetime Employment

	Important	Not essential	Can't say either way	No answer
1990	27.1%	36.4%	25.4%	11.2%
1999	9.9%	45.3%	38.3%	6.5%

where in this book, corporate restructuring is occurring. Lifetime employment was never universal, but perceptions that it was widespread supported the Japanese dream.

Japanese workers confront a frightening prospect: their hard work and voluntary overtime no longer guarantee job security. This removes a primary incentive for participating in the Japanese dream. And working as a bureaucrat—which marked the pinnacle of the Japanese dream—is not as respected as before. The public is frustrated with bureaucratic inertia. Scandals stemming from close relationships between bureaucrats, politicians, and big businessmen have hurt the bureaucrats' image.

"Death from overwork" (*karoushi*) incidents are more common, reminding many that pursuing the Japanese dream can lead to an early grave. Families of businessmen who committed suicide or died from overwork are being compensated, yet, lasting change requires workers to insist that personal lives take precedence over loyalty to employers. (In a November 27, 1996, poll by the newspaper *Asahi Shimbun*, only sixteen percent of the respondents cited work was the most fulfilling part of their life, while forty percent stated families were the leading source of fulfillment.)

Changing Marriage Ideals

Women are revamping their criteria for a good husband. Professor Chikako Ogura of Aichi Shukutoku University observes that Japanese women seek someone who is communicative, cooperates with household chores and childcare, and earns a comfortable income. Clearly, Japanese women now envision marriage as more than a passing step in the Japanese dream. Until recently, women were compared to "Christmas cakes" (a popular delicacy). The best time to get a Christmas cake is on Christmas Eve—a date representing the ideal age for a woman to marry. A woman over twenty-five would be like a Christmas cake after December 25, stale.

Table 3

Percent of Women Never Married

Age	1970	1995
20–24	71.6	86.4
25–29	18.1	48.0
30–34	7.2	19.7
35–39	5.8	10.0

Today, young women put off marriage until their thirties, and continue to live with their parents. Sociologist Masahiro Yamada calls these young women "parasite singles," contributing little to household expenses and using paychecks for expensive entertainment such as overseas trips. These women insist they want to enjoy life because marriage—and family responsibilities—reduces freedom.

Shifting Attitudes Towards Family Roles

By identifying home as a focal point in a woman's life—but merely a stopping-off point for men and children—the Japanese dream discouraged development of close families. According to the dream, a mother's mission is to make the home conducive to the success of her husband and children. Because of cram school routines and other reasons, children are disconnected from family relationships and responsibilities.

A father's role is to provide income, but his life revolves around the workplace. Companies still demand long working hours, often followed by drinking parties with co-workers or clients, then by long commutes. Fathers return home after their children are asleep. The proverb, "a good husband is healthy and out of the house" (*Teishu genki de rusu ga ii*) was in step with the Japanese dream; but today, social critics ask fathers to spend more time with their children. The Ministry of Health and Welfare began a campaign encouraging men to share household responsibilities, and posters featured a famous young musician holding his baby son, declaring "a man who does not help in child rearing cannot be called a father."

These campaigns face obstacles. Many job assignments send men away from home. Families stay behind because the children's education requires remaining in a specific location. Even younger managers are reluctant to refuse these assignments. The "education mother" (*kyoiku mama*) role is critical: mothers still devote their lives to ensuring off-springs' academic success.

New Heroes—and Ideals—in Popular Culture

Popular culture reinforces new values. Television is an especially important avenue of socialization in Japan today. When stressed-out Japanese turn on TVs to escape, many watch heroes and heroines struggling with identical pressures. TV characters approach society in non-conformist ways.

Naomi was a popular 1999 series about a dynamic young teacher who fosters each student's personal development, not merely academic success. In each episode, Naomi disregards social conventions and rules to help troubled students recognize individual strengths. Naomi gains the respect and friendship of her fellow teachers and students, but she outrages administrators, parents—and even the police.

Rules for a Love Marriage (Renai kekkon no ruru, 1999) highlighted a thirty-one-year-old woman's efforts to marry for love. In the final epi-sode, Asako (the heroine) decides to follow her heart, abandoning her fiancé at the wedding altar. The jilted fiancé is a successful yuppie whose life revolves around work. Asako marries a friend who is a country bump-kin and not "cool," but he makes her laugh, likes children, cooks, and does household chores.

Papa, *My Favorite Person in the World* (Sekai de ichiban papa ga suki, 1999) portrayed a middle-aged lawyer raising a headstrong teen-age daughter following the death of his divorced wife. The hero wins his daughter's respect, combining the traits of the traditional stubborn fa-ther with a recent ideal—a parent who is a friend, devoting time to home and family.

Finally, the 1997 hit series *Rhythm and Police* (Odoru Dai Sousa Sen) humorously illustrates the frustrations of young Japanese with the work-place and the bureaucracy. The main character is an idealistic young man, Aoshima, who leaves a computer job to become a policeman. Aoshima wants to help society, taking a common sense approach to problems. Inept superiors—who worry about procedures more than justice—thwart him. In the end the young hero is demoted for disobey-ing the hierarchy. The audience is left with some hope, though, as Aoshima's lone supporter in the National Police Agency retains a senior position and looks out for the ordinary cop.

Table 4

Characteristics of Recent TV Heroes and Heroines

Strong individuals
Remain honest to oneself
Communicate casually and directly
Will challenge authority if necessary
Break social expectations, but contribute to society
Focus on relationships rather than success

Future Challenges for Japan

The Japanese dream is rapidly losing its appeal, but there is no model to replace it. This is not a problem that government officials can solve; economic recovery would not re-inspire the dream. Indeed, changes in contemporary Japan are fueled by several factors, including popular culture, the media, a young generation with a different outlook on life, new employment patterns and new aspirations. Economic affluence underwrote the old dream but led to disconnected families and alienated youth.

Japanese society must change from the bottom-up, identifying new dreams before the present malaise causes further breakdown in interpersonal relations. Abandoning the old dream is painful. Three new factors pose challenges to society. First, rural inhabitants—geographically isolated from institutions and opportunities integral to the Japanese dream—did not share aspects of the previous system. They are not joining urbanites in becoming more assertive and moving towards individual preferences (versus social conventions). Secondly, the "generation gap" is such that older Japanese—dependent on the younger generation—fear their offspring are too individualistic and self-centered to be reliable.

Table 5

Competing Tendencies in Twenty-first Century Japan

The Japanese Dream from 1945–1990s	Japan in the twenty-first century
One dream	Many dreams
Pursuit of success	Pursuit of happiness
Dedication to social roles	Dedication to personal preferences
Education for exams	Education for indivisual development
Marriage for status	Marriage for love
Living to work	Working to live
Disconnected families	Demands for closer families

Thirdly, the breakdown of the Japanese dream makes it easier to accept immigrants. With its rapidly aging population and shrinking birthrate, Japan will have to begin importing labor. Heated debates are inevitable, but behaviors defined as uniquely Japanese are now questioned, so foreign ways appear less threatening.

The pursuit of happiness will overtake the pursuit of success, and personal preferences will gradually replace social roles as primary determinant of behavior. These new orientations will compete with elements of the old dream, creating some tension.

Urbanization in Asia: Prospects for Sustainability

Ooi Giok-Ling

Introduction

To adapt a statement from Charles Dickens's novel *The Tale of Two Cities*, it is the best of times and also perhaps the worst of times to be considering Asian urbanization and its prospects. Before the Asian economic crisis, cities were where all the action was—"the hip, hop, and happening" were found there. This is not surprising considering that cities such as the Bangkok Metropolitan Area in Thailand were generating half the jobs and significant shares of each country's GDP.

The Asian economy was planned around cities, or centered on the expansion of urban areas. Cities in Asia were burgeoning, as rural-urban migration together with the regional and international migration of labor contributed to the large urban populations. Primate cities, several times larger than any of those around them, have always been characteristic of the urbanization process in the region.

The many large metropolises that seemed to be bursting at the seams have led to the term mega-cities, cities with several million people. These included Jakarta and Metro-Manila, each ten million, Shanghai with twelve million and Dakka in Bangladesh with ten million. Cities and their economic outreach had profound impact: employment opportunities brought a work-commuting population from an ever-widening sphere around these urban corridors. Instead of speaking about cities in Asia, it is far more appropriate to talk about extended metropolitan areas, regions extending far beyond the boundaries of the cities. Much of the economic activity and the working population is linked to the cities through business or work relationships.

The forecast before the Asian economic and financial crisis of 1997–98 was that by 2020 thirty-six of the world's 100 largest cities would be in Asia. Half of Asia's cities would have populations of more than fifteen million, while one-third would have populations of more than five million each.

The population projected to be living in these cities is 2.3 billion. Some believe that if population growth was the development issue in the latter part of the twentieth century, the spatial distribution of population will be the greater issue for decades to come.

Urbanization and Development in Asia—Then and Now

Views on the region's development prospects are more sober since the onset of the economic crisis. Visitors have observed the half completed concrete pylons in Bangkok along the highway from the Don Muang Airport, testimony to the financial crisis. These pylons were intended as part of an integrated toll-way and elevated railway system that may never be completed. Some point out that these pylons stretch for many miles on the drive into the smog-shrouded and congested metropolis of Bangkok. In turn the city sits astride the highly polluted mouth of the Chao Phraya River, itself a reminder of the dark side of development in Asia.

Certainly development prospects held out by cities and urbanization in Southeast Asia today in the post-crisis era are much improved compared to the situation as it was in the 1960s. Then, much of the region was emerging from war and colonial rule. In the newly emerging nation-states of Asia, most if not all national governments were faced with the almost insurmountable challenge of shifting their national economies from dependence on trade with the industrialised West to a more equitable spread of development benefits.

Cities in Asia had been the hubs of a colonial economy or service centers for the colonial commercial activities that for decades had been spawned across East and Southeast Asia. Many cities originated during that period and served as administrative and processing points for the trade in agricultural and plantation produce exported outside the region. Lacking the West's industrial base—a factor responsible for the prosperity of its own cities—Asian urban areas were considered "parasitic" and the urbanization process a pseudo-version of that which the industrialised West had experienced.

Efforts by many national governments to spread development resources more equitably between city and countryside were reflected in massive programs launched to bring growth to those geographic areas neglected during colonial rule. A major goal was to discourage the population from migrating to cities in search of economic opportunities in favor of staying in the rural hinterland and supporting the development projects aimed at generating economic vitality. There was great concern among planners that rural-urban migrants would only add to urban poverty, create squatter settlements and bolster the already-huge "informal" sector.

Policies and Prospects

Socialist states such as Vietnam and China actively adopted a de-urbanization strategy by controlling the flow of migrants to cities.

On the other hand, city-states such as Hong Kong and Singapore, as well as the newly industrialising countries of Taiwan and South Korea, took a different path. The route to urbanization was favored in their economic planning. These four focused on cities—and on development projects aimed at leveraging infrastructure already concentrated in large metropolitan areas. None of the four have looked back: their extraordinary successes, as well as the rapidity of growth experienced, was viewed favorably.

The so-called second tier of newly industrializing economies—Malaysia, Thailand, and the Philippines—have been playing catch-up since the 1980s. Then, much of the development reverted to the capital city in each of these countries. When the multinational corporations brought increasing amounts of investment and capital to the region, there was a tendency for siting and locating where infrastructure was concentrated. This meant, of course, in or on the immediate outskirts of cities.

Transitional economies such as those of Indochina, China, and Myanmar do not appear to be deviating from the norm of urban-centred economic growth and development.

Thus, cities in Southeast Asia today are viewed very differently by their national governments than was previously the case. Consider the mega-urban projects underway today: the intelligent city developments in Singapore, the Multi-Media Super-Corridor of Malaysia, the Fort Bonafacio development in Manila, and industrial estate development in Bangkok Metropolitan Area and elsewhere. These massive development projects are responses to globalization. They are a concession that urbanization will drive economic growth and development in the region.

Ironically, the Multi-Media Super-Corridor of Malaysia has been developed on land where oil palm plantations were the source for, and mainstay of, regional development programs in the immediate post-colonial period. This was because of the interest in correcting inequalities in rural-urban distribution of resources.

Studies on these issues focused on the tensions and conflicts arising from the share of development seen in cities compared to the countryside. Based on rapid growth that was urban-based, and on coping with enormous infrastructure needs, most of the governments' development policies reflect an ambivalent attitude towards cities and socio-economic development.

Urbanization as a development process, if managed well, promises to achieve societal goals—many of which have eluded Southeast Asian countries. With large population bases, many cities potentially offer economies of scale. They can thus enable countries to meet the basic needs of housing, health care, and education. The alternative is to attempt to achieve the same goals with geographically diffuse populations, as is typical of rural settlements.

Cities offer the means of introducing sustainability in managing population growth and aid with demands for natural resource protection, particularly in the current era of advanced technological progress.

However, burgeoning urban population growth and the concentration of economic development in the metropolitan areas have led to deteriorating urban environments. In addition, there is a substantial problem of urban poverty, often juxtaposed closely with the luxurious standards of living of the high-income elites. Hence, with the onset of the Asian economic crisis, it was hardly surprising that rioters and looters in Jakarta targeted a shopping mall in an "urban glamour zone" catering to the tastes of global—and local—jet-setters.

With prospects of growth likely to remain concentrated in cities and the process of urbanization set to increase in both pace as well as magnitude, governments must be far more innovative than in the past. There were, and are, opportunities that were often missed before the potentials offered by urban growth were fully recognized. Both the state and market sectors have to be far more inclusive of the urban population—and of civil society—as development agendas are crafted.

Cities have been likened to business corporations; some argue there is a need to regard cities as entities that should be managed as efficiently and effectively as business firms. Cities in Asia must aspire to reach their potential and regard their inhabitants not just as a ready labor force but as citizens who bring to the cities their hopes and dreams for a better life.

The globalization process is not unfamiliar in a region which has known trade and commerce since the beginning of ancient civilizations in China, India as well as across Southeast Asia. Their trade routes gave birth to many cities. Centuries later, colonialization spawned capital cities and ports.

Apart from recovering successfully from the regional economic crisis, Asian cities face many challenges in this millennium—not least among them environmental problems and resource scarcity (including land on which to expand infrastructure and services and waste removal). There is also burgeoning population growth with a rising proportion of populations being accounted for by the elderly. Added to these issues are divisions between the local workforce and expatriates, social divisions caused by multi-ethnic populations, and other problems.

Many Asian cities have shown a resilience that has been impressive in the face of common characteristics such as high densities, large population numbers, and the concentration of economic, social, and cultural activities. In one sense, Asian cities offer the prospect of devising highly sustainable ways of organising human settlements. Given their scale and size, they function surprisingly well in many cases; they have been successful in keeping costs of living lower than in developed countries.

They remain vibrant in every sense. Yet as the different waves of global capital and labor reaching Asia have amply demonstrated, there has yet to be the establishment of strong institutions and good governance. Without these qualities, cities cannot ensure their citizens will benefit from growth—and from attendant progress.

Conclusion

Politics and political ideology marred the progress which cities and urbanization could have achieved in Asia in the closing decades of the last millennium. The metropolitan governments in Asia will have to secure greater financial autonomy and work on improving their political status vis-à-vis their national governments. Not many East and Southeast Asian cities have the independence, politically or financially, to draw up long-term plans. Changes in government can be so frequent. Many metropolitan development plans remain merely blueprints and have never seen the light of day. Nevertheless, several city governments in the region are working either with civil society groups, professionals, or private businesses on programs to improve the urban environment and the citizens' quality-of-life. Before the crisis, large business groups developed some "edge cities." One such area outside Jakarta is managed at a level of efficiency which surpasses that of the metropolitan government.

With the countryside offering fewer prospects for growth, Asian people will continue to move to cities—and in particular to the largest or primate cities. Many will join the urban poor. A major concern is whether there will be any room left for them, given pressures on, and the gradual disappearance of, the so-called squatter settlements. There is rapacious demand by developers for land for up-market office, hotel, and shopping complexes that cater to tourist and global business needs. The poor, as well as the low-skilled migrants moving about the region in search of work, find it increasingly difficult to locate affordable urban accommodation. Keeping land and housing costs affordable for not only the poor but also the middle-class households in city centers—and throughout the entire urban area—will be a major challenge to city governments. Land and land ownership persist as key issue areas in urban development. Dense urban populations were once viewed as major challenges to the efficient and effective management of urbanization and urban growth. The same populations might yet prove the basis for just the strategy needed for Asian economies to grow to a stage offering greater social and economic progress.

Hong Kong and the Pearl River Delta: The Makings of an Asian World City

David Dodwell

During the four years since Hong Kong's return to Chinese sovereignty, interest has remained strong in how the Special Administrative Region (SAR) managed this unprecedented transition. So far, the story has been encouraging: Hong Kong's reputation for flexibility and resilience has been tested as never before—but still stands firmly intact. The unique "one country, two systems" formula that provides the basis for Hong Kong's return to Chinese sovereignty is also starting to be better understood. Above all else, the formula's flexibility—Hong Kong as a part of China while preserving the distinctive characteristics that have underpinned its success—is starting to be appreciated. The fact that the formula has provided stability and resilience even through Asia's worst economic crisis in decades is a remarkable—and underappreciated—achievement.

Inevitably, Hong Kong's reunification with the Mainland spurred interest in the SAR's relationships across China, in particular with the municipalities across the Pearl River Delta (PRD; the SAR's immediate hinterland). Thousands of Hong Kong–invested companies operate across the delta region, yet relationships cover more than economics. They embrace administrative, familial, social, infrastructural, and environmental links that have attracted very little attention. The post-1997 transition has made everyone living on both sides of the Hong Kong–Shenzhen boundary increasingly aware of the increasing interdependence of PRD communities.

During the initial stages of the SAR's transition, most attention in Hong Kong was focused on the "two systems" aspect of the "one country, two systems" formula. This was not surprising, given the need to assuage concerns in the local community that long-held freedoms not be eroded. But as concerns subsided, many inhabitants began to look to future—and fascinating—opportunities arising from Hong Kong's distinct status. Foremost among the research on this issue was a report by the Commission on Strategic Development, prepared over a two-year period by Hong Kong's chief executive, Tung Chee Hwa. Private sector studies, like that of the Business Professionals Federation published in summer 1999, have had a similar focus.

Hong Kong's economy has undergone other massive transformations in the past half-century: from entrepôt to manufacturing hub in the early 1950s (when thousands of Shanghai merchants fled Mainland turmoil); from enclave manufacturer to coordinator of manufacturing assembly across the PRD (following Deng Xiaoping's 1978 "open door" policy). The current phase is that of a "world city" not unlike London or New York. This latter transformation is still in progress and was triggered by numerous factors, like the Asian financial crisis, the global technology revolution, and the SAR's creation and progressive opening of the Mainland's domestic economy.

Locally based analysts conclude that linkages between Hong Kong and the Pearl River Delta—home to some twenty-three million people—are more important than was previously thought. The strengths and weaknesses of the delta economy are components of Hong Kong's own strengths and weaknesses. Hong Kong's competitive future—both as a hub for the Asia-Pacific region and as a competitor in the domestic Chinese market—is linked with the (also competitive) future of its Mainland hinterland. However, a comprehensive review of potential linkages has not been undertaken. And while people in Hong Kong have been preoccupied by the 1997 changes, a similar transformation has been in progress in the Pearl River Delta hinterland.

It is clear that Hong Kong's post-1997 community has begun to stop thinking of itself as "transient." As a result, local quality-of-life issues have come to loom larger, whether these involve the environment, transportation, urbanization or culture and recreation.

Government and business leaders on both sides of the SAR border now focus on the fact that Hong Kong is emerging as a key metropolitan driver for its hinterland region, rather than as a separate enclave economy. They identify both problems and opportunities shared in common—whether it is efficient infrastructure planning and an effective assault on environmental challenges, or the identification of cooperative opportunities and economic synergies.

Just as Hong Kong has been transformed since the late 1970s, so the Pearl River Delta region has seen radical change. From a largely agricultural region at the margins of the Mainland economy—important only for the production of sugar, rice, and other farm products—the Pearl River Delta region became a massive export economy. Investment by Chinese companies in the Special Economic Zones along the coastal regions of Guangdong, combined with investment from Hong Kong (and more recently from Taiwan), brought about a boom in the manufacture of light industrial goods. Tens of thousands of factories were established, providing manufacturing employment for millions of workers. As a result, the province accounts for over forty percent of China's exports.

Over the past decade, as China's own domestic economy has steadily been liberalized, a new potent force for change has emerged: Increasing numbers of PRC-based companies have invested in municipalities south from Guangzhou along the eastern and western banks of the Pearl River. Their focus has been intensively on high-tech enterprises, transforming Shenzhen, Dongguan, Panyu, Shunde, Zhongshan, Zhuhai—and Guangzhou itself—into national leaders in a number of scientific areas. Shenzhen alone is home to more than 1,500 computer component-makers and over 500 software companies. It boasts more than 200 research and development centers. Leading Chinese universities like Qinghua and Beida are using Shenzhen as a base to commercialize academic research in electronics and computer science. In 1998, high-tech industries accounted for more than thirty-five percent of the municipality's industrial output, and one-third of its exports.

The PRD economy is far more diverse than it was two decades ago and plays a central role in national economic development. It is also among the richest regions in China, making it an important domestic market in its own right.

This dramatic transformation of the Pearl River Delta economy is linked with the role across the region of Hong Kong–invested companies. In addition, there is Hong Kong's role as an intermediary in global markets. All this bespeaks immense potential for synergistic development, making exporters across the delta more competitive in world markets. They are now poised to compete in China's domestic market.

Delta Dynamics

By retaining distinctive "one country, two systems" features, Hong Kong continues to offer a low tax regime, a liberal environment for movement of capital, and a venue for the open exchange of information. The SAR therefore provides Mainland enterprises with a platform from which they can perform complimentary roles. Hong Kong's legal system provides international companies with a solid business environment as they build links to the PRC and elsewhere in Asia.

While in most metropolitan regions property and other costs fall gradually from the city center out to farthest suburbs, Hong Kong's boundary with Shenzhen has prevented such a gradual transition. As a result, property prices and wage costs have remained significantly higher in Hong Kong than on the Mainland, where costs remain unusually low by comparison. This encourages leverage of the "one country, two systems" concept, stimulating strong flows of investment into the Delta in land- and labor-intensive activities, and in industries where skills are locally in short supply—as in the high-tech sector.

Companies are forced to focus on high-value-adding, knowledge-intensive activities within Hong Kong, and on building a substantial complimentary PRD presence, stimulating investment and job creation there. Economic benefits are thus brought to the entire region. In short, efficiency and a rational division of labor are encouraged, enhancing competitiveness on both sides of the boundary.

The SAR-PRD represents unique forms of economic interaction. Foremost among these is the effect of physical boundaries on the movement of people and goods. Travel to Hong Kong by Chinese nationals based on the Mainland is significantly restrained, a situation that mitigates against the commuting lifestyle typical of other large metropolitan areas such London or New York. The absence of an integrated infrastructure enabling speedy transport through the delta to Hong Kong means few Hong Kongers are willing, despite their considerable savings (measured in terms of both property prices and rental levels), to settle in neighboring PRD municipalities such as Shunde or Panyu. The limited development of international schools or world-standard hospitals in the delta further discourages Hong Kongers from settling there.

Restraint on immigration from the Mainland creates a dynamic for the future development of the SAR's economy. Other large cities requiring highly specialized and knowledge-intensive workforces do not rely on local populations and educational institutions to meet their needs. It is becoming clear that Hong Kong also needs to examine its Mainland linkages if it is to become a "World City."

Nonetheless, economic forces are fostering solutions. An estimated one-third of the students graduating from Hong Kong's universities take jobs in Chinese (Mainland) enterprises upon graduation. Many will in due course return to work in Hong Kong, but a number will almost certainly settle on the Mainland, buy homes, marry and raise families there. A recent survey in Hong Kong discovered that approximately one million people—over fourteen percent of the population—wish to settle or retire in the PRD.

At the same time, hundreds of thousands of Hong Kong people cross the border every day in what is becoming one of the world's busiest border crossings. From just 8,000 vehicles crossing the boundary every day in 1983, there are today more than 30,000 taking the same trek. This despite the fact that the boundary is not open twenty-four hours a day. By comparison, one hundred and forty thousand vehicles a day cross the George Washington bridge between New Jersey and the city of New York, so there is clearly much room for growth in Hong Kong in this respect.

Future Prospects

If opportunities are appropriately exploited and challenges effectively managed, future scenarios of the shared region are exciting in the extreme. As more Hong Kong residents settle in delta townships—commuting daily to work as would a commuter from Connecticut or New Jersey into New York—and as these commuters mingle with an increasingly well-off middle-class local workforce, there is the prospect of attractive new PRD communities emerging. Their residents will be in the vanguard of groups demanding infrastructure improvements. Perhaps most important of all, they will become a potent force for environmental clean-up in a region that has suffered significant environmental degradation as a result of hectic economic development.

If challenges are managed badly, aspirations for improved prosperity throughout the delta, including within Hong Kong, could be frustrated. Managed well, the region can become one of the most prosperous in the world, a leading global exporter, and a significant contributor to Mainland economic development as the PRC progressively liberalizes in the decades ahead.

Administrators across the region can contribute powerfully to optimal management of these challenges. One way is to give highest priority to building an infrastructure that meets the needs of all inhabitants. The private sector can undoubtedly provide support, but given political and diplomatic sensitivities linked with cross-boundary liaison, it is not well placed to take a lead. This is true no matter how committed private sector executives are to build—or provide funds for—an efficient infrastructure.

These problems could spawn intensive dialogue and cooperation between administrations at many levels. There are some international precedents for such cooperation (such as cooperation between the port authorities of New York and New Jersey). Yet many metropolitan regions worldwide are paying a high economic price for failing to capture cooperative strategies. Sometimes, local jealousies and rivalries have for decades both blocked optimal cooperative approaches to infrastructure building and burdened communities with damaged environments and dysfunctional infrastructures. Deterioration of the PRD's environment is a shared concern, and there is rising awareness that action on one side of the border, if it is to be successful, needs coordinated commitment on the other side. Perhaps this is an excellent platform from which to forge strong and constructive working relationships across the boundary.

An opportunity exists for the Pearl River Delta region to become one of the world's most powerful and dynamic economic communities. Signposts as to how these opportunities can be captured are beginning to emerge. So too are glimpses of what the PRD could look like twenty years from now. Its unique and distinguishing characteristics will be determined by the way administrators, politicians, and businesses wrestle with the challenges outlined above. Businesses, publicly concerned citizens, and government officials on both sides of the boundary must work hand-in-hand to ensure development of a region offering dynamism and a high quality-of-life to its thirty-odd million people. This cooperation will without doubt take time and careful diplomacy, but it is essential if the region is to emerge as one of the world's leading metropolitan economies, and as Asia's "world city."

The Asian Media:
Internet Emergence and
English Language "Comeback"

Edward Neilan

Several trends affect the Asian media. Foremost among them is the fact that through wired and unwired connectivity, East and Southeast Asia's 1.9 billion people have found their voice as never before.

Likening these trends to fingers on a hand, consider the Internet as the forefinger: its implications for individual opportunity, entrepreneurial surge, diversity of expression, and intellectual efficiency are staggering. We are only at the beginning of this exciting era. The index finger is the English-language press: once wearing colonial wardrobe, it has not been—but should be—resuscitated. The ring finger represents the traditional print media—now in flux. Circulation has increased but advertising revenues have declined; newsprint prices are rising. Entrenched interests protect this segment of the Asian media despite the Internet's

Editor's note: The chapter author—a long-renowned figure in Asia-Pacific media circles—passed away shortly after this manuscript was completed. Like many of the contributors to this volume, Ed was a diplomatic *sherpa*—someone who, in a way analogous to the pathfinding function of the renowned Himalayan trekking guides, engaged in critical preliminary negotiations in order to pave the way for the successful triumphs of foreign ministers. Ed Neilan valiantly led our expedition over the peaks and valleys, not in search of Shangri-La, but in search of truth.

challenge. There is the little finger: Press freedom. It has arrived. And as for the thumb—television, radio, cable, multimedia—it is growing, but quality suffers.

Five fingers, one giant fist? Even reduced to five fingers—"What is the sound of one hand clapping?"—the Asian media's potential impact is enormous. As of last year, there were 1,382 print newspapers published in Asia. AOL carries 118 of them. Magazines and radio and TV stations originating in the region provide a dynamic media mix. Their leaders are determined to break away from what they view as Western influence. It won't happen today, but it might. . . .

Asia: Wired and Unwired

The Internet and other "IT" (information technology) aspects of Asia are moving targets; changes occur daily. The old "oil for the lamps of China" predictions were meager compared to exaggerated claims of modern—perhaps well-meaning—Internet hucksters. There were more than 350 million Internet users worldwide last year. North American, European, and Asian markets differ in cost of hookups and equipment. But these basic figures, with non-Asian nations shown for comparison's sake, give an overview of how the Internet and mobile phone world is structured, from an Asian viewpoint.

English-language on-line news services proliferate. Newspapers such as *Dow-Jones,* the *Financial Times* and the *International Herald-Tribune* (IHT) are thriving. Asian cities where English is not the first language have more English-language newspapers than most major American cities. Asian-based competition is tough: In Tokyo the vernacular press is led by *Yomiuri Shimbun*, with a circulation of ten million, and *Asahi Shimbun* with eight million. Three other Japanese-language papers have circulations above four million. Tokyo has five dailies printed in English, including the prestigious *Japan Times* (at 90,000 daily circulation) and the *Mainichi Daily News*. There are weeklies helping the newly arrived locate a language tutor or a bicycle.

Another pair of English-language papers, the *South China Morning Post* in Hong Kong and, in Singapore, the *Straits Times* (each with more than 300,000 daily circulation), are considered the best regional dailies. Both offer attractive on-line editions, creating new opportunities for advertisers to reach upscale English-language audiences keen on stock markets and financial deals. The English-language IHT has nineteen editions worldwide, and circulation has reached 234,000. It had been affiliated with *The Washington Post* and *The New York Times*.

English-language papers strive to boost circulation. The *Asian Wall Street Journal* is increasing its use of graphics. In Seoul, the *Korea Herald* and the *Korea Times* are considering special editions for Pyongyang, North Korea. In Taipei, Taiwan, a third English-language daily—*The Taipei Times*—challenges *The China Post* and *The Taiwan News* (formerly the *China News*). *Taipei Times* is published by the Liberty Times group, close to outgoing President Lee Teng-hui. The new editor-in-chief of the *China News* is Melvin Goo, former Neiman Fellow and ex-news editor of the *Nikkei Weekly* in Tokyo.

Sprucing-up is evident in China's English-language newspaper world. The *China Daily*, established in 1981 and boasting a world-wide circulation of 150,000, added a vivid color logo—red, of course. A recent start-up—the *Shanghai Daily*—used full color in its first issue.

English—the lingua franca of the region's businessmen and of the Internet—is appreciated by all but the Japanese. Faxed-in newsletters, out-of-town newspapers and on-line computer services overcome the gap. It is difficult for expatriates—and others—to ascertain what is news and not merely the product of *kisha* media "club" dis-information.

Tokyo needs a top-flight English-language newspaper to maintain its leadership as a great city. There are contenders—the *Nikkei Weekly,* the *Japan Times* and Mainichi's English language press among them. Yet, "the system" intervenes. English-language newspapers of Japan face a fundamental disadvantage: backers do not commit the funds necessary for personnel, advertising, and circulation. Listen to the advertising gurus at Dentsu or Hakihodo and you discover they regard the English-language market as insignificant. Further, they don't want to divert any of that golden stream of commissions and profits away from the multi-million circulation papers. You can't effectively publish by doing things "the Japanese way," including a lack of enterprise and flair, a failure to utilize the talents of qualified native speakers in management, poor promotion, and a fear of criticizing Japan. Also, distribution systems force English-language newspapers to rely solely on street sales at railway station kiosks and hotels—at higher costs than for their Japanese-language rivals.

Tokyo's reputation as Asia's news capital—with all of its shortcomings in that uneasy role—was enhanced after the handover of Hong Kong to Chinese sovereignty in 1997. Asians want to know about trends in Japan and would pay to read about them from knowledgeable sources.

The rise of a vibrant English-language press would do much to harness other forces which, when put together, would result in a potent media "fist" that complements the "five fingers" listed above.

On-Line Competes with Print

The Internet and e-commerce are covered elsewhere in this book. As regards the print media, the Internet will not replace traditional newspapers but augment them. Many Websites created by newspapers are not current. This may account for the fact that there is no significant migration of advertising dollars from traditional to on-line papers. Newspapers can rest easy. And a mere fifteen percent of newspapers with Websites are making a profit. Yet, next year, as many as 400 million people will be on-line: dailies must undergo a metamorphosis to hang on to the reader.

As societies mature politically—and differentiate reality from hype—unverifiable facts cast doubt on on-lines' authenticity. Printed papers have an advantage in that their credibility is supported by their history, and there are complete names, affiliations, and addresses accompanying letters to the editor. When necessary, these are checked for authenticity. Letters to editors appearing on-line need not meet the same requirement. Anyone can set up a false e-mail address to attack a person or policy.

Newspapers face challenges. Japanese novelist Natsuo Sekikawa says they must "realize that a uniform readership has not existed since the 1970s. Newspapers called for diversity in society, but now they find themselves troubled by that same diversity." Indonesia's leading newspaper publisher, Jacob Oetama of the *Kompas Daily,* insists that on-line's instantaneous delivery, simplicity and interactivity all pose threats to print. In addition, says Oetama, established dailies should "use our databases to supplement the content of news Websites," adding that "the major enemy of the press is not muzzling, but the soaring price of paper."

"The East Was Read—Not Red"

The *People's Daily* is one of 2,000 newspapers in the People's Republic of China (PRC). All Chinese newspapers are owned by the Party, the government or the military. Government guidelines for "approved" Internet news will clarify directions in the "Great Firewall of China"; the PRC has been a domestic "Intranet" partially isolated from the world. "Present leaders are figuring out how to 'open the door' but 'keep the flies out,'" says Duncan Clark of BDA Consulting in Beijing. "They want the economic benefits while filtering out harmful cultural, social and political influences."

How is Hong Kong's free-wheeling press faring? A senior Chinese official in October 2000 urged Hong Kong's press to be selective when reporting on Taiwanese independence and not to spread separatist ideas despite Beijing's promise that the city-state's press freedoms would remain intact. The Hong Kong media continue aggressively to report on issues such as Taiwan and corruption in China.

Pressures on the Asian press come from other sources. Malaysian Prime Minister Mahathir Mohamad urged Muslim nations to share news with each other rather than depend on "corrupt" Western news organizations. Mahathir, a vociferous critic of the West, says the global media discriminates against Muslims, linking terrorism to Islam.

Cable Splicing

TV programming in the region ranges from the informative and entertaining to the meaningless. Cable television (CATV) in Taiwan emerged as an underground medium during the days of heavy government censorship. Media observers predicted that CATV would become a strong competitor to electronic and print media, bringing the island more information and programming. Within twenty years, CATV subscription rates reached seventy to eighty percent, the highest in Asia. Yet market concentration is a problem: "the big boys" are gaining control and threatening CATV's independence.

"All the News That Fits"

Many media outlets are not the core business activity of their major shareholder but are adjuncts serving the business empire. If not part of a conglomerate then they are invariably controlled by a single shareholder, posing risks for editorial independence.

In Malaysia, as Michael Backman wrote in *Asia Inc.* (June 2000), English-language dailies—the *New Straits Times,* the *Business Times,* the *Malay Mail*—as well as the country's most prominent private television channel, TV3, are ultimately controlled by the Malaysian Resources Group (MRG). The MRG encompasses infrastructure development, engineering, power generation and property. In the timber-rich Malaysian state of Sarawak, Ting Pek Khiing, one of the biggest loggers in Sarawak, owns the *Borneo Post,* the *See Hua Daily News* and the *Sinhua Evening News.* Abdul Rahman Yaacob, a local politician with logging interests, owns the *Sarawak Tribune.* This may create conflict-of-interest scenarios.

"In many parts of Asia . . . local journalists are remarkably poorly paid," notes Backman. In Indonesia many receive less than $300 a month and are susceptible to bribes. A non-corrupt judiciary, independent auditors, and enforceable bankruptcy laws are all-important for economic prosperity. So too is an independent and well-resourced local business media.

Asian Media Strengths

The "East-West news flow" problem, hyped by the "Western dominance" and the aforementioned "English-language" syndromes, means there are more Washington, New York, United Nations, and London datelines than Tokyo, Beijing, and Singapore carried by the world's media. Were it not for its own story of economic backsliding and judicial interpretation clashes with Beijing, the Hong Kong dateline would be scarcely seen. Bangkok and other regional centers are more appropriate bases than Hong Kong for pundits delivering Asian perspectives on the world.

Tokyo has more foreign correspondents than any city in Asia—832, including 334 Americans, from 66 news organizations. Britain and Korea post fifty-two correspondents each in the Japanese capital.

The Japanese press model will compete with the Western model in terms of freedom and openness. Unlike this book's editor and many chapter authors, I challenge the "Asian values" ideal and its success.

There are other comparisons: the Japanese press has strong foreign coverage; major dailies have as many correspondents abroad as do *The New York Times* and *The Los Angeles Times.* While Western writers provide more analysis, their Japanese counterparts offer straight reporting. After the Hong Kong handover, foreign press coverage from the city-state withered; *The Times* of London withdrew its correspondent. But the Japanese press corps maintained intensive coverage, and their China coverage is outstanding in all aspects except analysis.

Multi-faceted media battles will continue in East and Southeast Asia. The bottom line: credibility is the life-blood of any newspaper. Like broadcasters, reporters must accept the commercial and legal basis behind credibility; if reporters are trustworthy, we build loyalty—in print or on-line. To bind our readers to us, we are obliged to remain reliable.

Part VIII

Dragons, Tigers and Would-Be Tigers

Reading Japan's Political-Economic Tea Leaves

Richard Katz

Five scenarios contend for the most accurate portrait of Japan's future:

1. *Continuing Decline.* Japan will continue to decline, suffering stagnancy and perhaps even declining living standards.
2. *Macroeconomic Cure.* As a mature country, Japan cannot recover past growth levels but can perform well after macroeconomic mismanagement and banking problems are corrected.
3. *Muddling Through.* While Japan could benefit from structural reform, many vested interests would be hurt. Hence, Japan will "muddle through," growing at suboptimal rates with slow—but acceptable— improvement in living standards.
4. *Early Revival.* Structural reform is occurring, and revival is likely within a few years.
5. *Structural Reform.* Japan will have to reform because the political economy cannot survive with low growth. Once Japan reforms, it will again become vibrant. However, political-social obstacles mean reform will take a decade. Critical components of reform include openness to imports and foreign direct investment (FDI).

Scenario number five is the most likely outcome, with "muddling through" a distant second.

Scenario one reflects *shigata ga nai* ("it can't be helped") fatalism. Some people insist Japan's culture and psyche is suited to the age of mass production, but not the more entrepreneurial Information Age. In reality, Japan's problems lie in outdated institutions and practices—not in its psyche or culture. The Japanese have demonstrated creative and entrepreneurial talents. Moreover, enormous changes were made in the past and can be made again once consensus is reached.

Nor does the macroeconomic scenario hold up. Ten years after the collapse of the 1980s "bubble," the country still struggles to achieve durable self-sustaining recovery. This, despite budget deficits approaching ten percent of GDP and zero interest rates. Without reform, zigzag growth seems probable. During 1992–2000, Japan's growth averaged one percent. The coming decade could prove as dismal. The Organization for Economic Cooperation and Development (OECD) suggests potential growth (i.e., growth at full capacity) will be only 1.2 percent a year during 2000–2005. The Bank of Japan puts potential growth at one percent.[1] Japan needs better macroeconomic management, but more fundamental issues remain.

The "early revival" scenario is excessively optimistic and underestimates resistance to reform. The factors posing obstacles to growth are pillars of Japan's political system and will not be overturned easily. As of the time of this writing (August 2001), many analysts hailed the arrival of Junichiro Koizumi to the Prime Ministership as the harbinger of reform. Yet, similar enthusiasm greeted Ryutaro Hashimoto back in 1996. No one doubts Koizumi's sincerity or enthusiasm. But it is highly unlikely that the ruling Liberal Democratic Party (LDP) can be the vehicle for reform, no matter who stands at its head. Recall the former Soviet Union, where Mikhail Gorbachev ruled around the Soviet Communist Party, not through it. The LDP electoral and financial base is deeply divided between those who would benefit from reform and those who would be hurt by reform. If the LDP genuinely tried to reform itself and Japan, it would tear itself apart. Indeed, Koizumi's ascension may be the prelude to another LDP split.

The process that put Koizumi in power may end up being more important than whatever Koizumi himself accomplishes. He rose via a grassroots revolt of the LDP machine, and he won huge support in the July 2001 upper house elections due to his maverick image and call for "no pain, no gain" reform. No longer can anyone say the Japanese people are satisfied with "muddling through." They want bold reform—even if they are not yet sure what it looks like.

Neither of the polar views—"Japan is changing overnight" and "nothing is changing"—capture the actual situation: a long drawn-out battle between reformers and the resistance.

The Political Instability of "Muddling Through"

Though Japan's leaders prefer to "muddle through," their capacity to do so is diminishing. The motivation for "muddling through" is to satisfy the vested interests in order to keep the ruling LDP in power. Corporate collusion, protective regulations, and high prices serve as a covert social safety net because the nation has no solid governmental safety net. By shoring up moribund firms and industries, these practices sustain millions of "make work" jobs that would be eliminated in a competitive environment. They provide disguised income transfer from efficient sectors to inefficient ones: Toyota pays high prices for cement, glass, steel, electricity, and wages. Its employees must pay equally high costs for food and housing. Many of those who provide the money and votes for the LDP rely on such practices.

Yet, what proponents of "muddling through" ignore is that failure to reform is destabilizing—economically and politically. The nation's institutions break down without a certain minimal level of real and nominal growth. High corporate debt, lifetime employment, and seniority wages are impossible burdens when sales stagnate. Income transfer through high prices collapses in an era of deflation.[2] Ultra-low interest rates used to keep banks afloat bankrupt life insurance firms, while decimating retirees' income from savings and annuities. The latter results in anemic consumer spending.

Two decades ago, Japan had twenty workers to support each retiree; today, it's down to five; by 2020, it will be approximately two. Without a growing tax base and better returns to institutional investors, the burden is unsupportable. Japan has tried raising the consumption tax, causing the LDP to lose two Upper House elections (1989 and 1998) and triggering the 1997–98 recession. Faster growth and improved productivity are critical.

LDP leaders talk about reform and push through minor changes. Then most LDP Diet members form a caucus to roll back even mild reforms.[3] The reality of reform falls far short of its advertisements. Conflicts of interests among the LDP's base are inevitable: young versus old, urban versus rural, salaryman versus "mom and pop" retailers, and so forth. The LDP's ability to run a one-party state via a "catch-all coalition" is vanishing. The LDP receives less than forty percent of the vote; only ever-shifting alliances with assorted minority parties keep it in power. The LDP will split as it did in 1993. There will probably be several episodes of political realignment. The death throes of single-party rule will continue for years.

Regardless of how well-entrenched regimes are, once they lose their *raison d'etre*, they eventually lose their *etre*. Ultimately, Japan's economic crisis is one of governance—in both companies and government. It cannot be cured without reforming governance.

It is said that Japan's conservative citizens cannot accept major changes. But when failure to change means losing what one has, then, paradoxically, radical reform is conservative. It's the only means of retaining the status quo.

Japan's Deformed Dual Economy

What are Japan's structural flaws and what can be done to revive growth?

The country faces both supply-side obstacles, and demand-side obstacles. The former is dwindling productivity growth that limits long-term GDP growth. The latter is suppressed household income and consumer spending. The result: Japan cannot operate at full capacity without massive budget deficits and excessively low interest rates.

The heart of the supply-side problem is a "dual economy" unique to Japan. There are really two Japan's. The bright side is seen in exporting industries where "superpowers"—autos, TVs, computer chips, machine tools—got their start through initial governmental import protection and/ or subsidy. However, because they had to meet global standards of competition, they learned to compete on the basis of genuine efficiency.

By contrast, the domestic sector was shielded from imports, foreign direct investment (FDI) and fierce domestic competition. Officially sanctioned cartels (some of which still exist); regulations protecting the inefficient; illegal—but widespread—corporate collusion, bid-rigging ("dango"), and boycotts of corporate mavericks, all combine to allow the inefficient to survive. In fact, low imports and FDI levels act as a "bodyguard" for anti-competitive practices. The result is gross inefficiency. Productivity in food processing is only one-third as high as in the United States. Yet more people work in food processing than in auto and steel combined.

Figure 1 **More Exports and Imports Mean Higher Productivity**

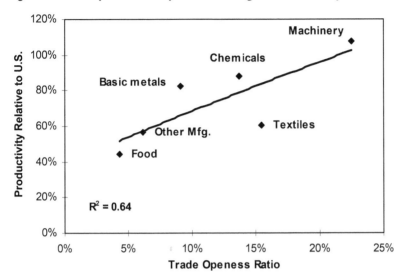

Source: EPA (1995a), van Ark and Pilat (1993).

Note: The data is for Japan in 1987. Trade Openness = Exports as % of Output, plus Imports as % of Consumption. Productivity = Total Factor Productivity (productivity of capital plus labor) of each industry relative to the U.S. level. $R^2 = 0.64$ means that 64% of the difference in each sector's relative productivity can be explained by the trade openness ratio.

The dual economy worked as long as efficient sectors subsidized the inefficient. By the 1980s, the burden became increasingly unsupportable. Finding it easier to flee Japan than to reform Japan, the country's exporters moved overseas. Japan is approaching a state where it produces more cars and consumer electronics abroad than at home. As this "hollowing out" proceeded, Japan's overall productivity growth slowed to the pace of the least efficient.

Economic Anorexia

Making matters worse, Japan has trouble sustaining full capacity without the artificial life support of big trade surpluses and never-ending doses of macroeconomic stimulus. The cartelization that creates inefficiency also led to "economic anorexia"—a chronic inability of private demand to consume what Japan produces.[4]

As economies mature, they move from investment-led demand to

Figure 2 **Falling Real Income Means Weak Consumer Demand**

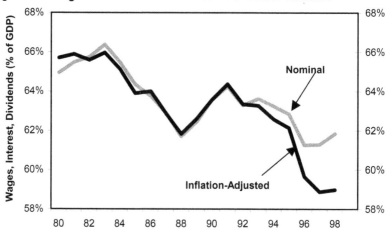

Source: Economic Planning Agency

consumer-led demand. Not Japan. The notorious high prices resulting from monopolistic practices suppressed real consumer income. Once high prices are taken into account, total household income—wages, interest, and dividends—has actually fallen as a share of gross domestic product (GDP) since 1980. Families spend twenty percent of their income for food, compared to ten percent in the United States. Think of the purchasing power liberated for new houses and appliances if food prices could be reduced (via competitive pressures from imports and from efficient foreign producers' operations).

Japan retains practices that made sense in the high-growth era but which are counterproductive today. Japan's miraculous ten percent growth rates during 1955–73 were driven by corporate investment which required equally high savings, some of which came from households. But most came from increased business savings. As in many Newly Industrializing Countries (NICs), the household share of national income declined while the corporate profit share increased. With dividends and interest rates kept low, these newfound profits were retained by firms and reinvested. This was still a good deal for wage earners, who received a smaller share of a pie that nonetheless grew fast: real consumption per person tripled in only eighteen years.

During that era, investment was so high corporations not only used their own internal savings but all that households saved as well. Saving withdraws purchasing power from the economy, investment plows it back in. As long as the two balance, there is no anorexia.

When Japan matured in the mid-1970s, growth slowed and the situation changed. There was less need to expand capacity. Corporate investment in plant and equipment, land and inventories fell sharply from twenty-four percent of nominal GDP in 1960–73 to fifteen percent after 1975 (except during the "bubble"). Had personal consumption risen to take up the slack, all would have been well. This would have required a rebound in the household share of national income, as occurs in maturing economies. Yet in Japan the household share kept falling.

Japan lacked market forces strong enough to force corporations to return their excess cash flow (i.e. business savings) to saver/investors in the form of higher interest and dividends, and to workers in the form of higher wages. Firms took in as much cash flow as in the past but failed to plow it back into the economy via investment. Thus the "paradox of thrift," too much savings equals too little spending. But the problem is not excess household savings caused by an ascetic culture; it's excess business savings caused by a cartelized economy.

After 1973, Japan's firms no longer had enough productive investment outlets to absorb their savings. Nippon Steel built amusement parks and flower shops. Others invested in fruitless property ventures from Tokyo to Thailand. Budget deficits and trade surpluses rose to provide additional demand. In the mid-1980s, some advocated a shift to a modern consumer-led economy. But this required busting up cartels and ending collusion. Instead, Tokyo applied monetary steroids to stimulate unproductive private investment as disguised public works. The inadvertent side effect was the "bubble."

The legacy: a mountain of excess physical capacity and bad debts. Like a patient who abuses antibiotics, Japan has found that past cures—bigger budget deficits, higher trade surpluses, and lower interest rates—have lost their potency. The bubble and the resulting banking crisis are not the cause of Japan's travails but the symptoms.

Globalization: Reform's Best Ally

Globalization could help prompt reform. Across Asia, imports and FDI have proven to be indispensable allies of reform. The pair act as battering rams against oligopolies and the political arrangements that protect them. That is why South Korean President Kim Dae Jung speaks of using FDI to "lock in" long-term reforms. The pace of reform in Korea will probably be faster than that in Japan.[5]

Figure 3 **Sectors Increasing Trade Improve the Most**

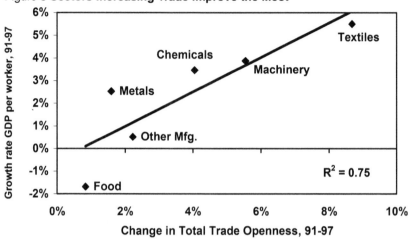

Source: Economic Planning Agency
Note: In top panel, total trade equals that industry's exports plus imports divided by its output. In the bottom panel, import share equals imports divided by consumption. For explanation of R-squared, see note for Figure 1.

To overcome the "dual economy" and "anorexia," Japan must overcome relative insulation from global competitive forces. Japan is virtually the only major industrial country whose ratio of trade (exports plus imports) to GDP is no higher today than it was four decades ago (about 20 percent). It has an exceptionally low share of imports that compete with domestic output. Amounts of inward FDI have been very low.

Even small increases in competing imports and FDI have powerful ripple effects. During the 1990s, sectors (such as textiles) where imports increased had the biggest increases in labor productivity.[6]

Foreign players outside the cozy club often change Japanese insiders' operations. Consider the chain reaction triggered by reforms in Japan's Large-Scale Retail Store Law. Before reform, small retailers could block the opening of larger stores—domestic or foreign—to prevent "excess competition." Toys "R" Us was not allowed to open in Japan. After the law changed it become Japan's largest toy retailer. (Before it arrived, almost eighty percent of toy retailers sold toys at or above manufacturers suggested list prices. By 1994, only thirty percent did so.[7]) The activities of foreign firms formed the tip of a much larger Japanese iceberg. During the 1990s, discounters like Daiei, Jusco, and Ito-Yokado used the reform to invest extensively. The result was a shakeup in an incredibly inefficient distribution system, including removal of whole layers of middlemen. [8]

Until recently, reformers failed to see imports and FDI as allies. That is changing. METI (Ministry of Economy, Trade, and Industry) argues that bilateral free trade agreements with countries such as Singapore and South Korea could put pressure on Japan's less competitive service industries, such as port operations and telecommunications. Moreover, METI has now embraced the concept that increasing FDI will hasten the pace of structural reform at home.[9]

A few isolated sectors have seen the impact of imports. FDI—including buyouts of major firms—has progressed more quickly. It reached $21 billion in 2000. Foreign participation is growing in sectors that can cause systemic ripple effects throughout the economy: finance, automobiles, retail, and telecommunications. If foreign investors demonstrate turnarounds at individual firms (e.g. the apparent success at Nissan) or change ways that domestic players operate, economy-wide ramifications will increase.

The Grand *Nemawashi*

In Japanese firms and agencies, the period of consensus-building necessary to reach major decisions is called *nemawashi,* informal talk that precedes formal overtures. Today, Japan is in the stage of grand national *nemawashi.*

The old order is tumbling but there is not yet a new order to replace it. Incremental change is hard to achieve because so many parts of the system are interdependent. Changing one part threatens to bring down the whole house of cards. (For example, bank reform threatens the lifetime employment system.)

Besides, as one part of the system reforms, the politicians intervene to protect the inefficient. For example, as banks cut off their less creditworthy customers, the government provides these borrowers with credit guarantees. So far, these direct and indirect guarantees add up to nearly 50 trillion yen (US$460 billion), or ten percent of GDP. Thus, without political change, economic reform seems well nigh impossible.

The most likely scenario is long drawn-out tumultuous "trench warfare" between reform and resistance. There will be episodes of political party realignment; several false dawns of corporate restructuring and economic rebound. But, in the end, there will be a new Japan—one more vibrant, less predictable, and more open to the rest of the world.

Notes

1. As Japan moves from under capacity toward full capacity, its growth can be higher than the long-term potential. *OECD Economic Outlook*, May, 2000. Paris: OECD, p. 60; *Nihon Keizai Shimbun*. "BOJ Pegs Potential Econ Growth At Measly 1 percent." October 28, 2000.

2. "Unsustainable: Dual Economy Continues to Fray," *The Oriental Economist Report*, May, 2000, p. 8.

3. A leading LDP Diet member, Kabun Muto, formed an anti-deregulation caucus in early 2000 which comprised the majority of the LDP's Diet delegation. Yoshiro Mori was a member until he became Prime Minister following Prime Minister Keizo Obuchi's sudden death.

4. "Anorexia Index Worsens," *The Oriental Economist Report*, October, 2000, p. 3. Richard Katz, "Economic Anorexia: Japan's Real Demand Problem," *Challenge*, vol. 42, no. 2 (March-April 1999).

5. Jeffery Sachs and Andrew Warner, *Economic Reform and the Process of Global Integration*. Reprint No. 2002. Cambridge, MA: National Bureau of Economic Research, 1994, p. 2; "Korea's Back, but Where's Japan," *The Oriental Economist Report* January, 2000, pp. 1–3.

6. "1990s: Dual Economy Worsens," *The Oriental Economist Report,*November, 2000, p. 4.

7. While there is much concern with Japan's price deflation these days, there is a world of difference between falling prices caused by weak demand and price cuts forced by more competition. The former reflects weak demand; the latter will induce more demand. In terms of the common supply-demand curves of economics, the former reflects a falling demand curve, whereas the latter reflects a falling supply curve.

8. My thanks to Ken Okamura, chief equity strategist at the Tokyo office of Dresdner Kleinwort Benson, for alerting me to this trend.

9. Ministry of International Trade and Industry, *White Paper on International Trade, 2000*, chapter 3; State Department, "Summary Report on April 25, 2001 Seminar on Japan's Changing FDI and Corporate Environment," at http://www.state.gov/p/eap/rls/index.cfm?docid=4049.

China's Human
Resource Riddle

D. R. Zhou

At the dawn of the new century all nations find themselves in a far more competitive environment than was true even decades ago. At the roots of competitiveness are natural resources, financial capital and other economic strengths, science and technology, and military power. The People's Republic of China (PRC) has not reached the forefront in these arenas, but she stands apart from all other nations in one respect: her huge population is nearly 1.3 billion.

The human resource dilemma faced by all industrializing nations is a daunting challenge. Without sound human resource policies, a large population base detracts from socio-economic goals. When the PRC's heralded economic reforms began in 1978, housing and jobs remained obstacles to growth. People either contribute to, or take from, a society; "value-added" concepts apply to people as well as to infrastructure, machinery, and other economic inputs.

Human resources are derived from well-educated human beings fully utilizing knowledge and skills. Machines and land have been eclipsed. In an age dominated by semiconductors, ever-expanding telecommunications, information networks, and automation, so-called "knowledge-based economies" (KBEs) enhance production, providing new and *infinite* services that become the cornerstone of wealth.

How can human resource potential in this most populous of all nations be increased? When the economy reached "lift-off" stage in the early 1980s, some fifty to seventy million young men and women, armed with only primary and secondary levels of education, resided in far-flung rural areas. They moved into coastal cities and towns; rules governing mobility and membership in labor organizations were loosened, permitting massive domestic migration. This "army" was cheap labor for the PRC's manufacturing and export engines, which subsequently spawned a vast domestic construction industry. In an historic economic revolution, more than 120 million members of the so-called "floating population" would arrive at eastern and southeastern the cities. I saw this phenomenon in Shanghai and elsewhere in the People's Republic. Money earned by these once-penniless migrants was transmitted back to rural China. It has been one of history's most remarkable transformations—and a success story for human capital.

The PRC's new challenge is to transform more of its population resource into *human resource*. The term *population* stresses the number of people and their muscle power while *human* signifies the full potential of knowledge and skills. Relevant comments can be found in *The Future of Capitalism—How Today's Economic Forces Shape Tomorrow's World*, written in 1996 by the widely respected MIT economist Lester C. Thurow:

> The World Bank has recently started estimating productive wealth per capita. Large, lightly populated but still well-educated countries such as Australia (US$835,000 wealth per-capita) and Canada ($704,000 per person) have the most productive wealth. . . . In these countries land and natural resources account for most of total productive wealth and human skills account for only about 20 percent of total wealth. In contrast, in a country like Japan (fifth on the list with $565,000 per person), more than 80 percent of productive wealth is held in the form of human skills and knowledge. The United States (twelfth on the World Bank's list with $421,000 per capita) falls in between. Sixty percent of its wealth is human capital (pp. 288–289).

Roots of China's Human Resources Quest

The world has returned, "full circle" to the Renaissance view that human beings (and their power) should be elevated. This is true in the PRC. Human development and the respect for knowledge were always part of China's tradition. Education enjoyed priority status despite imperial mandates and the at-times relentless social control imposed by rulers. Six hundred years ago, China fell behind in global competition because of the Northern Song dynasty's fascination with the Li School of "orthodox" Confucianism. Freedom and creativity were stifled, with absolute power being consolidated in a ruling class that showed little respect for human rights and human initiatives. Centuries later, the Qing dynasty's ruling Manchurians—then a minority in Northeast China—suppressed the educated Hans, although that group constituted more than ninety-five percent of the population. The deterioration of the Qing Dynasty ensued, leading to national humiliation of the Chinese since the 1840s.

Some forces had not forgotten the meaning of human resources. The May Fourth movement of 1919 was a national campaign for spiritual and ideological emancipation, emphasizing science and modernization China abroad. The resulting human resources aided the founding of a New China in 1949. The 1949–66 period witnessed positive changes. Education was generously provided for; tuition for primary and secondary schools was virtually free. Daycare centers, set up universally in state-run enterprises, helped mother-workers by freeing their hands to perform meaningful labor. The children of workers and peasants were preferred candidates for higher education. A cornerstone for modernization was created in the humanities, science, engineering, education, and other fields. The government could unabashedly claim credit.

In 1966 those educated people were subjected to senseless persecution. Paranoia took hold: the "intellectuals," a misnomer for educated people, were considered a threat to the government and to the revolutionary cause. Intellectuals were cast as allies of "Chinese and foreign reactionary forces," supposedly endangering masses of Chinese workers and peasants. All this culminated in the perverse attitudes of the Cultural Revolution. The tragedy was that one faction of government destroyed the human resources which others in government had painstakingly developed.

One of many great achievements of Deng Xiaoping was the reopening of colleges and universities and the institution of merit-driven college entrance examinations for undergraduate and graduate admissions. Many took advantage of these opportunities. A recent survey by the Ministry of Education indicates that these people form the cornerstone of Chinese human resources, forging the PRC's historic socio-economic achievements.

Market-orientated economic development is in the foreground of the quest for enhanced human capital. Surveys reveal that the number one priority on the list of spending and saving for Chinese families is education; those parents denied opportunities to continue with school during the Cultural Revolution tell touching stories today of self-sacrifice in order to provide for their children's education.

In the late 1990s the Chinese government realized that education could also be an "industry" to provide jobs, spawn a new type of consumption, and induce spending. The state encouraged education, setting aside large sums of money for education, especially for higher education. For example, eight major universities have been promised three-year grants (from Beijing and from local state agencies) that range from 1.2 to 1.8 billion yuan, or US$150 million to US$225 million. Technical training schools and other institutions of learning have also been given more government support. The government budget for education in 1998 was 294.9 billion yuan (US$36 billion). It was announced that same year one percent of the total national budget will automatically be added to support education in the PRC. Private philanthropy is also being used.

A nationwide zeal for educational attainment is evident. For example, Shanghai was the first city to provide a certificate-issuing program for training in computer and English open to people of all ages. So-called "English corners" are sections in parks and other public places which provide venues for the local population to chat with visiting English speakers. Many Chinese realize tourism and other businesses depend on some understanding of English. The same corner chats and impromptu conversations can be found in other cities. Other skills—from cooking to music to computer system management to apparel design—are highly valued in the new, always-changing China.

Increases in college enrollment are striking. With 2.8 million enrolled in college, anticipated increases could match, or rise above, the thirty-three percent level (1999 compared to 1998). Nationally, eleven percent of the target (college-aged) group are enrolled at a campus, double what is was ten years ago. Some Chinese educators believe at least twenty percent is needed to achieve goals in human resource potential. Bright young minds, they reason, must be provided with a database and knowledge to take part in China's KBE.

Four years ago in Shanghai, only one in four high school graduates each year could earn placement at a community college or in a four-year institution. Today it is more than seventy-five percent, bringing the total number to 82,000 in 2000. In affluent Guangdong Province, the college student population totals 137,000. This represents an increase of thirty-six percent over 1999. During that year more than two-thirds of high school graduates went on to a higher level of education.

The private sector plays an important role in this process. Retired professors, administrators and engineers are now permitted to open non-state–controlled degree-issuing institutions. These new colleges function on market-oriented principles. Hopefully they will emerge as competitors to state-supported and managed institutions.

The PRC has also opened its education market to the outside world. Last year more than sixty foreign campuses from the West and Japan conducted "road shows" in hopes of attracting Chinese students. Chinese parents spend more than one billion yuan (US$150 million) to send their children abroad. Some of these students will stay overseas, but China will benefit from the economic and science/technological exchanges spawned by these students. At the same time human resource flows will increase through processes related to economic globalization. New student loan programs implemented by state banks provide favorable interest rates, further providing incentives to acquire degrees.

All serious analysts give credit to the society's achievements, to enlightened officials and to the people's entrepreneurship. However, compared with levels in other countries, China's educational growth is insufficient. College enrollment (among the target age group) in Singapore is thirty-five percent, in Japan, fifty-six percent, and in South Korea, seventy-five percent. Four years ago, the international average of enrollment among college-aged youth was sixteen percent. The developed nations had an average of sixty percent—five times higher than the PRC's level.

How all this impacts specific regions of China is apparent. Shanghai hopes to become an Asian center for high-tech, manufacturing, trade and finance. Yet only 3.5 percent of its total population of 13.5 million holds college degrees. Among workers in finance, real estate, and commerce/trade, the rate is much lower: one percent, compared to Hong Kong's eight percent, Singapore's eleven percent, and New York City's fifteen percent. In addition, there are fundamental weaknesses in the educational system. Unless these are adequately addressed, it is unlikely China can develop human resources. The PRC's future competitive edge will thus be jeopardized, falling short of expectations. The issues that should be resolved are:

• Mobility: The relative stability in traditional Chinese society rested on near zero population mobility, despite the fact that each significant population mobility era promoted national economic development. Between 1949 and the early 1980s, mobility was discouraged. There was a near-total ban on rural migration to towns and cities.

Today there is a national policy to develop the still poor central and western provinces. Geographic mobility is important, but so is mobility between government-sponsored institutions to business and academic institutions. Social and institutional obstacles should be removed to allow knowledge workers to move between enterprises (especially from the state sector to the non-state sector). Equally critical is mobility of the educated *knowledge* workers in addition to *manual* workers with minimum education.

Better utilization of human capital potential is possible with an accelerated phase-out of the *danwei* (literally, "work unit") system. This places all institutions—government agencies, schools, hospitals, businesses, factories—under government control "from cradle to grave." The flow of human capital in a free-market environment creates not only wealth and potential for additional wealth. In the Information Age, potential for accumulating wealth has gone hand-in-hand with mobility of a highly educated class with knowledge and skills.

• Recognition of the value of knowledge and skills: The open market is the most effective means of reflecting values of useful skills and of rewarding useful knowledge.

Still lingering in the PRC are egalitarian views: what is important is a person's contribution—no matter how small or inconsequential—to the revolutionary cause (regardless of how well one performs at the job). As a result, knowledge, skills, and improved performance are not equitably rewarded. Meanwhile, wealth accumulation achieved through non-market means (such as through corruption, nepotism, and legal loopholes) tends to retard effective use of human capital.

In general, the Chinese work force is underpaid. Related to this is the fact that workforce productivity is low. Human resources are best utilized by paying for value. In China's case, an increase of thirty to fifty percent of salaries and wages (for most occupations) is required to transform *population resources* into *human resources.* Then, national output will rise.

• A new paradigm: A basic element in developing human resources is the establishment of respect for each human being, extending to civil, labor, and consumers' rights.

Efforts must continue to provide all the citizens of the PRC with equal opportunities at the starting gate. Historically, people were infatuated with machine-crazed fetishes; and in later years, with financial power. Today, many remain convinced that technology plus financial capital are all that are needed for high levels of personal achievement and positive socio-economic goals. But in the post-industrial and KBE era—one wherein knowledge and skills will experience a quantum jump—this new paradigm of human capital must be appreciated.

Urbanization and accompanying problems—infrastructure inadequacy, crimes, and population congestion—have caught the attention of Chinese policy-makers. The flow of rural labor to the coastal cities is no longer encouraged, and smaller towns are being created to absorb the exodus created by farmers trekking to urban areas. Integration of a rural population's characteristics with those of the urban environment requires a transitional process. Schools have been established where rural "immigrants" might acquire the skills needed to become citizens in urban settings—and citizens with sufficient schooling to cope amidst new demands and pressures.

Challenges Remain

The upgrading of knowledge and skills is therefore contributing to urban economic output, which is vital for China's future, and also for entrepreneurship in migrants' home villages. Although government funds are limited for extensive training programs, market mechanisms—paying for education/training today with the expectation of future rewards—is working. Tens of thousands of employment centers throughout the Chinese Mainland offer those seeking better-paying jobs a new message: age or gender might result in discrimination, but skills and experience will count for more in the new Chinese society.

Other challenges confront China. Modern technology implies labor-saving devices and automation, which in turn affects efforts to create jobs on a large scale. Enough employment opportunities must be generated to meet the demands caused by population growth. At the same time, the "graying" of the population threatens the PRC's "pay as you go" social security system. According to one study, those sixty or older in Shanghai number 2.4 million (eighteen percent of all the city's residents). Other parts of China contain similarly large numbers of elderly citizens. The PRC's senior citizens must be considered, as the nation's population as a whole must be, not as social burdens but as a valuable human resource.

Human creativity and entrepreneurship always generate more jobs, new products, and services. Superior medical systems, enhanced education networks, and other advancements prepare the aging and the aged for longer working lives—and for an enriched quality of life. This, plus a civil society and a responsive government help to guarantee social harmony. All this begins at the bottom, at the community level, and works its way to the upper levels of the society. The city of Shanghai, for its part, is delegating a number of powers to democratically elected residents' committees and—in a mirror image of the Chinese village elections held in other parts of the PRC—helping to build a new social structure.

Management of human resource issues in China is complicated, of course. The Chinese approach has been another huge experiment in human affairs. The approach this time is no longer regimented or Utopian, but it should incorporate progressive views of civil society and more a more liberal respect for human nature.

Few deny that the PRC has achieved much through economic development: national output quadrupled in two decades. The PRC will, hopefully, become a major player in the world arena in the twenty-first century, using its geopolitical and geoeconomic base. If its vast human resources are properly utilized, the PRC will reach that goal.

China: Location of the Next Asian Economic Crisis?

Dean Cheng

The Asian economic crisis of 1997–98 left the People's Republic of China (PRC) relatively unscathed. Even as its neighbors watched their stock markets plummet and their currencies depreciate, the PRC succeeded in maintaining its economy on a relatively even keel. However, structural deficiencies have the potential of choking continued Chinese growth. That, in turn, would affect the entire region's economy, not to mention Chinese political stability, and would have implications for East Asian security.

Beijing never had to engage in the sort of extensive, short-term external borrowing that characterized much of Southeast Asia's and South Korea's behavior prior to the 1997–98 economic crisis. Other countries were vulnerable when the flow of foreign capital reversed. And foreign investment in the PRC is primarily foreign direct investment (FDI: factories, assembly plants, or joint ventures) in enterprises involving Chinese partners, rather than in securities. FDI is US$42 billion of the total $56 billion foreign investment pie in the PRC. Consequently, once regional panic struck there was little ability to shift holdings out of the PRC. In addition, the renminbi (RMB) is not a freely convertible currency; China's closed capital account restricts foreign borrowing by Chinese entities, and limits capital movement by both foreigners and Chinese citizens.

Pending Pitfalls

Most observers agree that the PRC economy must grow at an annual rate of at least seven to eight percent, in order to handle the steady influx of new job-seekers. In 1998, GDP growth fell below eight percent for the first time since 1990.

Future downturns in GDP are possible. The interplay of the state-owned enterprise system (SOEs) and the banking system may explain why. The SOEs are among some of the most inefficient industries in the PRC. Failure to implement reform has meant a steady decline in the rate of return on assets and a corresponding increase in the leveraging of firms. Economic reform of the SOEs, unfortunately, has been slow. The SOEs are major employers, encompassing some two-thirds of the urban work force, and rationalizing their operations would inevitably generate massive unemployment—which in turn undermines legitimacy of the Communist Party.

The SOEs are the anchors of the social safety net, in terms of pensions, workers' canteens, day-care, schools, and so forth. Consequently, the number of actual bankruptcies and closures has averaged only 550 per year since 1996 (Overholt 2000. p. 19) To forestall social and political unrest arising from closing or selling off the state-owned enterprises, the Chinese government has sought to reform them—while maintaining them on de facto life support.

This has been accomplished through extensive loans. The Chinese State Statistic Bureau estimated that SOEs rely on bank loans for over ninety percent of their daily working capital. At the same time, most enterprise liabilities consist of debt to banks. These loans serve as transfer payments from depositors to the enterprises, transferring both cash and services to the employees. There is little prospect of such loans being repaid by the borrowing institutions, and they are categorized as non-performing loans. Some forty percent of loans extended by the four state banks in 1998 were non-performing (compared with official estimates of twenty-five percent).

Indeed, the banking system has required two infusions of capital. The first, of approximately 270 billion RMB (US$34 billion) in 1998, was supposed to allow Chinese banks to meet the international minimum of an eight percent ratio of capital to assets (Overholt 2000) The second is estimated to cost some 1.2 trillion RMB, or $150 billion. This would cover barely half of the outstanding bad loans (Gilley 2000). Total non-performing loans may be as high as US$240 billion. China's banks *are* unhealthy. (This is similar to the situation throughout East Asia, where inadequately supervised and capitalized banks made loans to poorly governed firms without due diligence requirements.) It is worrisome that loan-recovery companies are to "eschew hard-nosed tactics" in the course of their efforts (Gilley 2000). Without substantial reform, additional non-performing loans will increase.

One significant fear is that a crisis of confidence might occur, leading in turn to liquidity problems as depositors withdraw savings (Lardy 2000, p. 61).[1] Given the high percentage of non-performing loans, the resultant liquidity crisis would rapidly produce massive instability. A plus: Chinese banks are not driven by the need to be profitable (although this is changing as the banks are reorganized). The central government, in the short-term, can order banks to extend loans. Nor are they likely to fail, since the central government continues to have a hand in their operation.

Long-Term Problems

More worrisome: power, transportation, and energy networks suffer from major shortcomings affecting economic expansion. It is the *synergy* among these networks and their deficiencies that threaten long-term economic expansion.

Consider power. The PRC requires massive increases in the amount of electrical power generated. In Guangdong Province alone, for example, electricity demand is expected to grow from 78.8 terawatt-hours (TWh)[2] in 1995 to 255.5 TWh by 2015 (Battelle 1998, p. 28). By contrast, all of Belgium currently only generates 78 TWh (U.S. Department of Energy, Energy Information Administration website, http://www.eia.doe.gov). The Yangtze River Delta and other important industrial regions suffer from acute power shortages. (Some forty million households, one-quarter of the Chinese population, are without electricity.)

China is the second largest generator of power in the world, with an installed power generating capacity of approximately 300 million kilowatts. The PRC reached 100 million kilowatts in installed capacity in 1987, doubled that by 1995, and added another 100 million in the subsequent five years (Zhao Shaoqin 2000). China's power sector is expected to have the largest growth of any nation, and the World Bank estimates that by 2020 the PRC will have the world's largest power sector.

Power shortages have cost the economy as much as 100 billion RMB ("ICEU" 1999, chap. 9). In the absence of a national power grid, new plants are often of only limited utility. The PRC seeks to establish a national joint power supply network, which will entail establishing power networks in the north, central/western, and southern regions. Then these must be linked. Indeed, "un-unified grids of the several regional power networks make it impossible to trade electricity over long distances across the borders of the power networks" (ibid.). There is a steady effort to integrate the twelve regional grids and to construct major transmission lines, facilitating the creation of a nationwide network: Shanxi and Inner Mongolia to Beijing, Tianjin, and Hebei; Guizhou and Yunnan (and the hydropower potential therein) to Guangdong; and Hubei to Shanghai (Zhao Shaoqin 2000). Chinese demand for power requires the movement of energy resources, mainly coal, to local power plants, a process relying on transportation assets.

Transportation

The PRC's rate of utilization of rail haulage, especially for freight, is one of the highest in the world ("ICEU" 1999, Chap. 9). In 1999 the rail lines moved 976 million passengers and 1.57 billion tons of freight (Deng 2000; Xia 2000). Highways alleviate some pressures, but a State Council transportation report concluded that railways still account for the bulk of long-distance haulage, with typical cargos moving 800 kilometers (km). Much of the problem is due to the physical layout of the Chinese transportation network. The primary rail lines are all north-south, reflecting the centers of previous Chinese economic development, that is, Manchuria and the coastal regions. By contrast, China's east-west networks are far more limited. Ongoing projects hope to build 5,340 km of new railways while electrifying 4,400 km of existing railway (Yang 2000).

Energy

Chinese coal prices are among the lowest in the world, and—despite inefficiency and polluting characteristics—these low costs enable SOEs in chemicals, steel, and cement to stay in business. From 1979 to 1994, Chinese energy use doubled, and energy consumption will triple from 1994 to 2014 (Loose and McCreary 1996). Coal—the major source—is expensive to move and to store, yet i t accounts for most railway freight in the

PRC. Oil, by contrast, accounts for only some five percent of railway freight haulage. Coal transport capacity cannot keep up with demand.

The combination of reliance on coal and insufficient transportation assets leads to a disjunction: the PRC cannot produce the energy resources necessary to power its economic expansion—and lacks the ability to move those resources to where they are most needed. Demand is greatest in those provinces that are either economically booming (primarily along the coast) or are densely populated (primarily in the interior, southern region).

China has resorted to building power stations at major coal mines to minimize the distance and thereby the transportation resources required to transport fuel. Given the absence of a national power grid, however, these inland generating stations can do little more than provide power for local industries. The 1999–2000 economic slackening alleviated some pressure. What is unclear is whether, once the economy recovers, energy demand and consumption will rise.

Mediating Measures

Beijing is attempting solutions, but each one offers other potential problems. Much of China's power generation capacity remains tied to older and smaller plants, which are inefficient and divert scarce transportation resources to keep them supplied. Some nineteen GW of current Chinese power are derived from plants over forty years old ("ICEU" 1999, chap. 9). Moreover, only fifteen Chinese thermal plants (which produce three-quarters of China's electricity) are over one GW in capacity. These smaller plants are often equipped with low- and medium-pressure turbines, reducing efficiency.

The PRC does not manufacture advanced turbines, and 600- or 900-MW systems are imported (Loose and McCreary 1996). Consequently, development of more efficient—and larger—plants depends on access to foreign turbine technology.

Another measure has been to improve the energy efficiency of Chinese industry. China will upgrade seventy percent of all high-consumption electric motors as well as industrial boilers, improving energy efficiency. There are limits, however, on how much energy conservation can be realistically expected. Transportation infrastructure is at fault. Inefficient fertilizer plants dispersed throughout the rural hinterlands rely on coal rather than natural gas as feedstock. Many are operating despite high costs because the more efficient facilities are incapable of moving their products to customers on a reliable basis. The requirement for timely deliveries outweighs higher production costs or energy inefficiencies.

Economic slowdown provided an opportunity for improving energy efficiency with minimal impact. According to testimony at a World Bank conference, demand growth fell to the point of "raising concerns about over-capacity and future development of the [power] sector." And use of coal as final fuel (i.e., used directly) declined, while higher-quality coal is used. Mines in the west and central northern regions (including Shanxi and Shaanxi, sources of very high quality coal) are increasingly used as sources.

However, these positive trends place strains on transport systems: the mines closest to consumers (in the south) are the ones closed down. The average distance per load of coal will now double relative to the 1990s, due to these closures ("ICEU" 1999, chap. 9). Chinese substitution of oil for coal will alleviate only part of the energy-transportation problem. The country has few oil-burning power plants and constructed no oil-burning power plants from 1985–95 in order to save petroleum for export purposes. To fully exploit the increased energy efficiency of oil, the PRC must either convert coal-firing plants to oil or natural gas, or build new oil or gas plants. Both steps take time.

Furthermore, China's existing oil deposits (such as the Daqing fields in the north) are located close to China's old industrial centers in Manchuria. New oil finds, however, are predominantly in the northwest, particularly across the Tarim Basin. Transportation infrastructure there is poor, making construction of refineries and transportation of oil difficult. A 1,000–km pipeline from Xinjiang to Sichuan will cost five million RMB per km of pipeline (Loose and McCreary 1996, p. 33). Rail links between eastern and western China are sparse. Double-tracking the main Lanzhou-Urumqi line will significantly increase capacity, but railway construction to the west—like pipeline construction—will be very expensive. Yet, the Chinese have—out of necessity—committed significant resources to building dedicated coal-hauling railroads. Additional steps such as coal washing would increase transportation efficiency by moving consumable fuel only, abandoning ash and wastes. These plans have, for a variety of reasons, not produced desired results. Coal washing requires significant amounts of water, and northern China faces water shortages.

Moreover, economic growth will not only generate additional demands from industry but also from households as their standard of living improves. Chinese families have marked increased prosperity with a steady growth in power-demanding goods, beginning with electric fans and moving on to refrigerators, color televisions, and VCRs, and now computers. In the period 1991–95 alone, Chinese electricity consumption increased by ten percent annually, while per capita electricity use rose by 8.7 percent in the same period (Battelle Memorial Institute 1998, p. 25). Rising living standards increase electric consumption. Economic growth at three percent—half of what planners believe necessary for social and political stability—boosts coal use by forty to fifty percent.

Prospects for Improvement

Mediating measures are insufficient to solve the energy-power-transportation conundrum. Massive infrastructure development, as well as major reforms of the various players, including industrial consumers, producers, etc., is required. Costs will be US$222–400 billion for the next fourteen years, or between 6.4 percent and 11 percent of anticipated GDP (Loose and McCreary 1996, p. 36). Will there be sufficient capital to fund this growth?

The link to failed SOE reform is clear. The SOEs are notoriously inefficient: steel and iron industries are thirty-five percent more energy-intensive than comparable industries in the United States. Raising prices for energy—especially coal—to world levels would cripple the energy-inefficient behemoths. Keeping prices low, while achieving political ends (through preserving SOEs and minimizing unemployment), has deformed the nation's energy market.

Indeed, the failure to effect greater reforms is already affecting the available resources for investment and restructuring. What would be required to minimize the pain of SOE reform is continued growth in the non-state sector. Jobs and capital thus realized would replace those lost through SOE closures. Unfortunately, the capital required to sustain such efforts are drained off by non-productive state-owned firms. A weak stock exchange and bond market cannot provide non-banking resources for private investment.

In order to maintain growth, Beijing has engaged in extensive bond-financed deficit spending for much of 1998 and 1999 (Clifford and Engardio 2000, p. 258). Much of this spending involved infrastructure projects, both to forestall potential unrest as well as to resolve aforementioned dilemmas. The PRC government issued 100 billion RMB (US$12 billion) of bonds in 1998, and another 60 billion RMB (US$7.2 billion) in 1999, for highway, water supply, and other infrastructure projects (Sinton and Gridley 2000). There are limits on pump-priming's effectiveness, and there is concern regarding potential inflationary effects.

Consequently, the PRC relies on FDI. China's vulnerability to a reduction in FDI is unclear. The PRC has a current-account surplus suggesting Beijing is exporting capital (through central bank purchases of foreign exchange assets and other instruments, such as U.S. Treasury bills). At least on paper, the PRC could, therefore, choose to sell off assets to make up shortfalls in foreign investment. A decline in FDI, however, would affect the non-state sector disproportionately. Recent data show FDI has declined.

As Chinese competitiveness declines—and if internal economic growth slows—sources for new jobs are in doubt. A PRC that cannot maintain steady growth will be one that is more likely to be wracked by internal instability. That, in turn, raises significant questions about the ability of the PRC to act, as it would prefer, as a major political pole, or, as some Americans fear, as a near-peer competitor.

Conclusions

China's period of unending economic growth may be drawing to a close. PRC reforms, while impressive, created significant internal contradictions that will take time to be resolved. If the Chinese fail to resolve these overlapping problems, it is likely the government's hold on power will be questioned; internal stability may be challenged.

Tensions along geographic lines are possible: China's economic growth has been heavily concentrated in the southeast and along the coast, with other enclaves thriving along navigable rivers. However, the Chinese Northeast (encompassing Manchuria), West, and South have so far enjoyed far less economic development. Current economic plans focus on the western regions, both to exploit the vast resources (including oil), and to dampen the civil unrest in predominantly Muslim regions.

A PRC whose economic circumstances are at risk is far less likely to be able to undertake expansionism outside China's borders. A stagnating economy cannot support the acquisition of aircraft carriers or a modern space-based reconnaissance infrastructure. On the other hand, a PRC with a faltering economy may pursue the "Galtieri option" of pursuing foreign adventurism to distract its populace. The need for foreign distractions, and the attendant opportunity to stoke nationalism, however, may create a runaway situation, since such sentiments are far more easily fanned than doused. A Beijing government—internally weakened—would be less likely to negotiate with Taiwan or even exercise flexibility in dealing with Taipei. At the same time, Taiwan is less likely to explore reunification with an economically weakened China. The situation would therefore be ripe for confrontation, with dire consequences for all.

Notes

The author wishes to thank Marcelo Cosma, Ralph Hallenbeck, and Richard Larach for their comments.

1. Dr. Nicholas Lardy of the Brookings Institution suggests that such a move might be triggered if there were a threat of a major devaluation of the renminbi, or a significant slowing of the Chinese economy that affected the Chinese banking system.

2. A terawatt hour is equal to one billion kilowatt hours.

Bibliography

Baring Securities, *Macro Monitor,* March-April, 1995.

Battelle Memorial Institute. *China's Electric Power Options: An Analysis of Economic and Environmental Costs.* Columbus, Ohio: Battelle Memorial Institute, June 1998.

Bottelier, Pieter. "How Stable Is China?" In *Is China Unstable*, ed. David Shambaugh. Armonk, NY: M.E. Sharpe, 2000.

"China's Oil Imports Rise Possible Boon for US." *Oil & Gas Journal.* June 7, 1999: 24.

"China's Petroleum Products Demand to Double by 2010." *Oil & Gas Journal.* June 7, 1999: 26.

Clifford, Mark, and Pete Engardio. *Meltdown.* Paramus, NJ: Prentice-Hall Press, 2000.

Deng, Zhaigao. *China Daily* February 25, 2000; in *FBIS-CHI* February 25, 2000.

———. "New China State Council Transportation Research Report." *Zhongguo jingji shibao.* February 15, 2000; in *China Online.*

Fernald, John G., and Oliver Babson, "Why Has China Survived the Asian Crisis So Well?" International Finance Discussion Paper #633. Board of Governors of the Federal Reserve System, Washington, DC: Government Printing Office, February 1999.

Gilley, Bruce. "Moment of Truth." *Far Eastern Economic Review.* June 15, 2000, 59.

Goldstein, Morris. "The Asian Financial Crisis," International Institute for Economics Policy Brief 98–1. Washington, DC: IIE, 1998.

Huang, Yasheng. "China and Asian Financial Crisis." In *Two Years of Asian Economic Crisis: What Next?* ed. Alexei Kral. Washington, DC: Woodrow Wilson Center, 1999.

"ICEU, Energy Policy and Structure in the People's Republic of China." Internet Publication, 1999.

Ishiguro, Masayasu, and Takamasa Akiyama. *Energy Demand in Five Major Asian Developing Countries: Structure and Prospects.* World Bank Discussion Papers #277. Washington, DC: World Bank, 1995.

Kamin, Steven. "The Current International Financial Crisis: How Much Is New?" International Finance Discussion Papers #636. Board of Governors of the Federal Reserve System, Washington, DC: Government Printing Office, June 1999.

Lardy, Nicholas. "The Imperative of Financial Reform." *Orbis* 43, no. 2 (Spring 1999).

———. "Sources of Macroeconomic Instability in China." In *Is China Unstable,* ed. David Shambaugh. Armonk, NY: M.E. Sharpe, 2000.

Lawrence, Susan. "Little New Year Cheer." *Far Eastern Economic Review.* January 13, 2000: 73.

Long, Guoqiang. "China: Two years After the Asian Financial Crisis." In *Two Years of Asian Economic Crisis: What Next?* ed. Alexei Kral.

Loose, Verne, and Iain McCreary. *China Energy: A Forecast to 2015.* 1996.

Noland, Marcus. "Prospects for Northeast Asia in the 21st Century." Paper presented to the Northeast Asia Economic Relations Symposium, Toyama, Japan, October 13, 1999.

Oksenberg, Michel C., Micahel Swaine and Daniel C. Lynch. "The Chinese Future." In *The China Reader: The Reform Era,* ed. Orville Schell and David Shambaugh. New York: Vintage Books, 1999.

Overholt, William. "China's Economic Squeeze," *Orbis* 44, no. 1 (Winter 2000).

"Railway Construction and China's Economic Growth." China Online.

Restall, Hugo. "Is China Headed for a Crash?" *Asian Wall Street Journal.* September 2, 1999.

Saywell, Trish. "On the Edge." *Far Eastern Economic Review.* February 25, 1999, 47.

Sinton, Jonathan E., and David Gridley, "What Goes Up: Recent Trends in China's Energy Consumption." LBL-44283. February 25, 2000.

World Bank Group. "The World Bank and China." *China Country Brief.* www.worldbank.org/html/extdr/offrep/eap/china.html.

Xia, Lirong. "Railway Industry: turning from Deficit to Profit." *Beijing Review.* March 13, 2000; in *FBIS-CHI,* March 16, 2000.

Xinhua. May 24, 2000 (08:50 GMT); in *FBIS-CHI,* May 24, 2000.

Yang, Fan. "Western Region Will Issue Lottery Tickets to Accumulate Funds for Capital Construction." *Wen Wei Po* (Hong Kong). February 17, 2000, A-1; in *FBIS-CHI,* February 17, 2000.

Zhang, Chenghui, with Qingtai Cheng and Zhiqiang Lu. "Capital Markets and China's Strategic Economic Restructuring." *Zhongguo Jinji Shibao* (Beijing). June 15, 2000; in *FBIS-CHI,* June 15, 2000.

Zhao, Jianping. "Private Power Development in China: The 1000–Mile Journey." In *The Private Sector and Power Generation in China.* World Bank Discussion Paper #406. Washington, DC: World Bank, 2000.

Zhao, Shaoqin. "PRC State Power Corporation Says Power Industry Growing Rapidly." *China Daily* (Beijing). April 26, 2000; in *FBIS-CHI,* April 26, 2000.

Zhiling, Huang. "Railways To Put Southwest on Track, Part I." *China Daily,* December 23, 1993; in *FBIS-CHI*-93–249, December 30, 1993.

The Chinese Middle Class and the World Economy

Ming Zhang

As the People's Republic of China (PRC) rises to the status of economic power, the West is paying attention and monitoring China's activities with respect to a variety of political issues. Yet, few have offered accounts regarding an equally important issue: the emerging Chinese middle class.

What has produced the middle class in this most populous of all nations? What does this new class mean for the rest of the world, and for the world economy in particular?

The Historical Background of the Chinese Middle Class

The soil in which the embryo of this Chinese middle class was planted was that of the heralded domestic economic reforms initiated in 1978. Since then the socio-economic transformation witnessed in the PRC has been profound, and perhaps represents the most important transformation in the nation's five thousand–year history. From 1978 to 1998 China's gross domestic product (GDP) increased more than twenty-fold from 362.4 billion Chinese yuan (US$43.7 billion) to 7,955.3 billion Chinese yuan ($958.5 billion; all dollar and yuan amounts in this chapter are as of 2001).This is an annual increase of 9.7 percent. At the same time, the production structure of the economy underwent a significant shift. The percentage of agricultural output in GDP dropped from twenty-eight percent to eighteen percent, with industry increasing from forty-eight to forty-nine percent and services from twenty-four percent to thirty-three percent.

The percentage of employees in each of these three sectors also changed markedly. From 1978 to 1998, peasants dropped from seventy-one percent to fifty percent, industrial workers increased from seventeen percent to nearly twenty-four percent, and those earning their paychecks from service industries increased from twelve percent to nearly twenty-seven percent. In 1998, the average Chinese consumption rate was 3,094 Chinese yuan (US$372.8) per capita. This represented four times the level seen in 1978.

Equally significant is the fact that between 1978 and 1999, newly established towns—those areas comprised of more than eighty percent non-agricultural population—increased ninefold, from 2,100 to 19,756. China's urban share of population increased from twenty percent in 1980 to 30 percent in 1995, and will reach more than forty percent in 2010. From the year 2000 to 2020, twelve million rural residents will move to urban areas.

China's domestic reforms and social transformation have plowed the seedbed for a new social class. What has fertilized the growth of the Chinese middle class is globalization, which is not only the flow of capital and goods but also the move of information, values, and people. As readers know, China's trade with the rest of the world has skyrocketed, foreign investment has penetrated into every sector of Chinese economy, and the advanced Western technology introduced during these past two decades has facilitated China's modernization.

To appreciate the influence of globalization, consider that by the end of the twentieth century China was the tenth largest trading nation in the world. During this period, foreign-funded enterprises accounted for fifty percent of all Chinese trade, and twenty million Chinese citizens worked in the foreign-funded enterprises. This number represents fully one-tenth of all urban workers in the nation's total labor pool.

The globalization driven by multinationals did not have only physical effects. The multinational corporations (MNCs) have set an example of modern corporate citizenship. They contributed to the establishment of ethical norms and codes of conduct throughout the PRC. They helped to build the rule of law by making Chinese firms aware of the importance of property rights protection and by teaching China's indigenous companies the legal drafting process. MNCs applied their own environmental measures in China and adopted higher environmental control standards than are required by Chinese regulations. Critical to the country's basic and sustainable national development, they established collaborative programs with Chinese counterparts to foster research and development in a wide range of business and technological fields. These projects nurtured the growth of China's next generation of skilled managers, engineers, and front line workers.

To a large extent, multinationals have provided better products and higher quality services. More importantly, they have prepared Chinese labor and resources to compete in the international market and system.

The Image of the Chinese Middle Class

After some twenty years of working, learning, and experiencing the triumphs and hardships of life, the Chinese middle class has emerged—perhaps self-consciously—on the world stage.

Who are they, and what do they think?

The vast Chinese middle class comprises ten percent of urban families, or some sixty million people, as of the end of the last century. These middle-class families actually are the upper-level income bracket in China, with a minimum 30,000 Chinese yuan (US$3,614) a year in family income. Some members earn as much as 100,000 Chinese yuan ($12,048) or more. With this level of income, they invest, travel, and purchase goods and consumer items to support and improve a middle-class quality-of-life.

The middle class is a social group that participates in modern industries and operations. They are intellectuals (educators, researchers, scientists), professionals (lawyers, medical specialists, financial experts), entrepreneurs (business owners, managers, industrialists), or personnel engaged in new economies such as information technology (IT). Members of the expanding middle class live exclusively in urban areas because of the current uneven economic development in China, with metropolitan areas proving to be the most vibrant, opportunity-laden, and dynamic. With the rapid urbanization of the country, the numbers of middle-class Chinese—and their percentage as a share of the entire population—has been growing.

The Chinese middle class has established its own set of social values. As individual wealth increases, men and women tend to invest for continued education. Learning science and technology is of particular interest. During this process the man or woman develops and sustains a higher-quality family life and, more importantly, saves for the next generation. Some eighty percent of the members of this group would make heavy sacrifices to provide for their children's education.

Table 1

Economic and Social Transformation in China, 1978–1998

	1978	1998
Economic change	GDP US$43.7 billion	GDP US$958.5 billion
	28 percent agriculture	18 percent agriculture
	48 percent industry	49 percent industry
	24 percent service	33 percent service

What factors are considered essential for a good life? When surveyed by the *Far Eastern Economic Review* in 1998, over ninety percent of affluent Chinese listed a happy marriage or romantic relationship at the top of the list, followed by health, job security, and a private residence. When responding to what values were critical for business success, near ninety percent in the survey chose hard work. Some seventy percent chose creativity, and approximately thirty percent chose an orderly society. Over fifty percent agreed that economic prosperity takes precedence over political liberalization, whereas thirty percent expressed the belief that both are equally important.

When asked how they believed China's economic situation could be improved, seventy-four percent of these affluent Chinese stated anti-corruption laws should be enhanced. Some sixty percent opted for more foreign investment as a solution; fifty-five percent stated fewer government expenditures would be helpful; and forty-five percent favored a reduction in taxes to keep economic growth on track, or to stimulate it further.

The young Chinese middle class has been on the scene for only two decades. It has no clear image of itself, no strong sense of self-identity or self-consciousness as a new social class. As one of its own members observed, they are the parents of this new class, but not its children. They inherited neither the educational opportunities nor the traditions of the middle class. In order to sustain the present and nurture the future of the middle class, they have a mission to accept and to complete.

The Perceptions of the MNCs

The Chinese middle class has forged and will continue to forge close links with the world economy, and with multinationals especially. The first link comes from the fact that the middle class represents the consumers of the products and services of the MNCs. For example, the increasing demand for air travel by middle class businesses and families in China has opened a large market for Boeing passenger aircraft. Similarly, the emerging e-commerce in China provides United Parcel Services (UPS) an opportunity to cooperate with Chinese online companies to serve the needs of the urban middle class.

The second area where the Chinese middle class interacts with MNCs is in the fields encompassed by science and technology (S&T). China has gradually opened S&T projects and R&D bases to multinational participation. Foreign individuals and corporations can directly collaborate with Chinese research institutions, universities, and enterprises.

Third, Chinese students who studied overseas and returned home as professionals have created another channel for multinationals to connect with the Chinese middle class. Those Tokyo-, Paris-, and Boston-educated Chinese bring home corporate culture and set up new businesses which in turn work and compete with the MNCs.

Finally, Chinese middle class members, especially those private business owners or those in charge of state economy, have increasingly engaged in world markets. They wish to set a foot in the world market for their products or services; as a result, they trade, cooperate, and compete with MNCs.

It is important for multinational corporations to understand those links between the Chinese middle class and themselves. More important, the MNCs need to appreciate the mentality of the middle class because it may forecast the future relationship between the two.

Although the Chinese middle class is not yet a mature social force, its elite members have formed their views of MNCs. They have assessed multinationals from economic, technological, and political perspectives:

- Multinational corporations have changed the content of economic relations among nations and deepened the international division of labor. As trade relations within the MNCs have become increasingly active, the international division of labor has taken place through the format of an intra-enterprise division of labor across nations.
- In the year 2000, one-third of all world trade consisted of trade within the MNCs. Another one-third of all global trade was between multinationals and other traders. In the past, domestic distribution of resources was handled mostly by market-based mechanisms within countries. Today, MNCs have emerged as significant players in this important process.

In terms of technology transfer, the Chinese middle-class elite generally envisions the advent of MNCs as a positive phenomenon despite the competitive relationship (with the very same multinationals) China must face as a result. As China joins the World Trade Organization (WTO) around 2005, the MNCs and their subsidiaries will become further entrenched in the expanding Chinese domestic market. China will also have their own MNCs when its companies explore oil fields, operate ocean shipping, and conduct other businesses overseas.

The European Union, the United States, and Japan remain the key centers of the critical flows of technology across borders. Because developed countries dominate the field of science and technology, developing countries will continue to be in a negative position in sharing the fruits of international science and technology.

In order to solve this dilemma and to help assure a favorable position in receiving technology inputs from advanced MNCs, China must strengthen its own science and technology capabilities. It must, in addition, enhance its own capability to create and absorb technology.

As viewed by the Chinese middle class, the position of a country in this newly spawned MNC-centered environment is not fixed. It is in constant change. Through its own adjustment, China can come up with a new form of comparative advantage. To accomplish this, it needs to improve the environment for foreign investment, strengthen basic infrastructure and financial systems, carry out reforms in the rule of law, develop human capital, and establish more sophisticated high-tech R&D institutions.

With regard to political issues that are linked to multinational activities, a few influential Chinese elite express much concern and caution although they do not advocate boycotts against globalization and MNCs. Some observers point out that Western democracy depends upon a forceful monopoly of the world's limited resources. Whereas the people in developed countries enjoy material and spiritual life, the same countries launched uncivilized warfare against developing countries.

Some leading intellectuals in China warn that globalization is a historical process; only when a national state masters its own political life is its economic achievement in the global arena meaningful and accessible.

These intellectuals face a quandary. They believe that the multinationals' goal is to take advantage of their economic and technological power as a means of maximizing their net profits. Yet, they remain aware that host countries in the developing world wish to import advanced technology and management from the multinationals in order to promote economic growth and raise domestic living standards. It is difficult to reconcile this difference, at least in the near term. Friction and conflict have characterized the relationship between multinationals and sovereign states, and MNCs have challenged the nation-state in many ways.

First, the MNCs tend to restrain and reduce government capabilities. As a large economic holding/sharing is in the multinationals' hands, foreign firms will become barriers of governmental adjustments of the national economy. As MNCs penetrate into, merge with, or purchase competitive elements of the domestic economic sectors, they restrain and reduce the government's ability to protect the domestic economy. As foreign trade becomes multinational trade, governments also lose the capability to manage and protect their countries' foreign trade.

Second, multinationals' political activities further infringe upon national sovereignty. Through cooperation with the same business of a hosting country, with certain government departments, and with economic, financial, as well as legal groups, the MNCs directly or indirectly play a role in the national decision-making of a hosting country. Since multinational power expansion challenges sovereignty, a sovereign state necessarily will react to the multinationals' actions, possibly by changing policy regarding MNC direct investment.

Third, the conflict between MNCs and sovereign states does not mean the former will replace the latter so that the latter will lose its sovereignty. Instead, a sovereign state is challenged to function at a higher level, to more responsibly handle domestic affairs and let state sovereignty transcend national boundaries to become a power that coordinates and cooperates multilateral initiatives in global affairs.

Implications for the West

China has changed so profoundly that it is superficial, misleading, and even counterproductive to label the country as "communist." That label still has some limited meaning in the context of politics. Nowhere is the transformation of China from "communist" to a market economy more evident than in the rise of the PRC's middle class. The trend towards a growing, more vocal, and increasingly influential middle class is irreversible: China's modernization, prosperity, and even political governance cannot fare well without this new social force.

Although it is somewhat immature and its numbers not fully adequate, in about ten years the middle class will set the pace of China's economic development. At the same time, this group can peacefully transform China's current centralized political system. Above all, as China enters the world, the middle class is an indispensable bridge and messenger.

With twenty years of business experience in China, multinationals should all have learned the importance of personal ties, or *guanxi*, in the Chinese working relationships. This business style could continue to exist to some extent after China's entry into the WTO. But it may likely decline as new generations of managers and employees adopt Western corporate culture and as a business legal system genuinely guides China's enterprise performance. Just as the Soviet-educated technocrats heavily influenced China from the 1950s to the 1970s, the Western-educated and exposed middle class will leave a deep imprint on China in the early twenty-first century.

Finally, it is a welcome fact that both the Chinese government and the middle class have maintained a generally positive attitude towards MNCs. With a gradual opening-up to the West, China is largely prepared for fair competition in the world market and under conditions whereby global rules prevails. Nevertheless, there will be economic and political friction and conflict. Just as is true in Western countries with large middle class populations, the Chinese middle class does not wish to lose its national identity as it embraces globalization.

Korea at a Crossroads

Joseph Winder

For the better part of the last half of the twentieth century, two aspects of the political and economic landscape of Korea (I use the terms "Korea" and "South Korea" interchangeably) seemed immutable. The first: that the economy would be very strong. The second: that relations with North Korea would be characterized by unremitting enmity and hostility. Recently, Korea experienced tectonic shifts on both fronts. First, it was struck by an unparalleled economic crisis; then the North-South "Cold War" began to thaw.

These shifts in the landscape provide a new context for Korea. For three decades Korea epitomized the Asian economic miracle. Per capita income rose from $100 to over $10,000. Then in 1997–98 Korea was infected by the East Asian financial crisis with devastating results. Stock market values declined by more than fifty percent, unemployment quadrupled to nine percent and GDP shrank to minus 6.7 percent in 1998 from the previous year. Koreans were in a state of shock.

They threw out the old government, elected an opposition candidate president, tightened their belts, and made some wrenching adjustments in their economy. The results were spectacular. Korea's growth rate bounced back in 1999 to 10.9 percent. Unemployment fell to less than four percent, and the stock market regained much lost ground.

The crisis revealed flaws in the structure of Korea's economy. Productivity growth was actually negative in certain sectors—finance, insurance and business services, and wholesale and retail trade. According to the Swiss-based Institute of Management Development, Korea fell from twenty-sixth in competitiveness in 1995 to thirty-eighth ranking four years later.

President Kim Dae Jung saw the need to strengthen Korea's ability to create and use new technology. He recognized Korea was increasingly being squeezed between the Information-Age economies and low-cost producers of labor-intensive manufactured goods.

An Economic and High-Tech Paradigm

The new administration moved quickly to implement a wide-ranging program to strengthen the banking sector, open the country to foreign investment, and implement other reforms. The social safety net was given priority. The Finance Ministry released an Information Technology (IT) plan that—among other things—expands investment in R&D and human capital and boosts the development of a high-speed communications network infrastructure. Korea's potential in R&D compares well with that of many OECD countries, and IT already accounts for more than ten percent of GDP.

Korea still faces many daunting challenges in making the shift to this new paradigm. The reform process in the financial, corporate, and labor sectors is only partially complete, and the economy has begun to weaken in part due to weaker growth in the United States and Japan. Political resistance could derail—or seriously delay—completion of necessary reforms. Korea also needs changes in its education system and must re-orient its approach to innovation to accommodate a knowledge-based economy.

At a Crossroads with North Korea

Immediately after taking office, President Kim Dae Jung enunciated a new policy toward North Korea. President Kim took a gamble that with proper incentives, Pyongyang would respond favorably to engagement. Dubbed the "Sunshine Policy," President Kim's initiatives are designed to stimulate more open, constructive interchange, increased contacts at all levels, and expand investment in the North.

An early result of the Sunshine Policy was Hyundai's decision to invest in tourism development at the base of Mount Kumgang, a site just north of the demilitarized zone and one known for its pristine beauty. Hyundai spent hundreds of millions of dollars to install deep-water docks, pave roads, and build infrastructure. Several hundred thousand tourists from South Korea have visited this site over the past three years.

The North-South Summit

On June 13–15 last year, President Kim Dae Jung met with his counter-part, Kim Jong Il in Pyongyang. This was the first meeting between the heads of North and South Korea since the country was divided at the end of World War II. The two leaders agreed to a number of concrete steps to begin the process of reconciliation. One dramatic step was agree-ment to reconstruct two rail lines connecting North and South which had been severed at the time of the Korean War. The two sides also agreed to establish an inter-Korean committee tasked with establishing the framework for economic cooperation between the two Koreas.

Is Unification in the Offing?

Both sides recognize that prospects for unification in the short-term are not high—and that it is not in anyone's immediate interest to push too hard for early reunification. In North Korea, the number one priority is regime survival, and early unification would undoubtedly undermine the current regime. For its part the South faces the specter of an enor-mous transfer of wealth to the impoverished, famine-stricken North if it were to occur any time soon. Living standards in the South would inevi-tably decline. Estimates of the cost of unification vary widely; Goldman Sachs calculated that unification would cost South Korea between US$770 billion and $3.6 trillion over a ten-year period.

Economic cooperation offers the least risk politically for reconcilia-tion on the Korean Peninsula. "Win-win" deals—not just the one-way transferance of goods and services to the North—are possible, but the North's decrepit "Social Overhead Capital" (SOC; basic physical infra-structure and energy systems) is only one obstacle.

The issue of rebuilding SOC raises questions of international com-munity support. South Korea would welcome North Korea's member-ship in the International Financial Institutions (IFIs; IMF, World Bank, and the Asian Development Bank). The United States and Japan, as the largest contributors, would need to approve IFI support for North Ko-rea, but there are both political and economic concerns that need to be addressed first. American legislation prohibits funding from the IFIs for North Korea as long as Pyongyang remains on the list of those governments sponsoring terrorism. And the North needs to meet certain economic conditions to qualify for IFI membership.

The North is plagued by its lack of familiarity with the outside world and by the norms of international trade and investment.

Conclusion

The process of reconciliation and eventual reunification on the Korean Peninsula is inextricably linked with structural reform in the economies of both countries. The South needs structural reform in order to be in a position to mobilize the resources necessary to assist the North Korean economy. The North needs to unleash and channel the energies of its people toward productive activities. A reduction in military expenditures—particularly in the North—can provide a "peace dividend."

The direction of changes unleashed by President Kim Dae Jung's "Sunshine Policy" and South Korea's economic reforms is clear. The pace of these changes, and reaction to the inevitable "rocks in the road" will determine much of the outcome.

Taiwan Dependence: Trade and Investment Dimensions of Cross-Strait Politics

John Tkacik

When Taiwan's Democratic Progressive Party (DPP) leader Chen Shui-bian announced he was running for the presidency in June 1999, Washington policy-makers were alarmed. The prospect of moving toward "Taiwan Independence"—a long-held DPP goal—was a nightmare that Pentagon planners often war-gamed in scenarios. They needn't lose sleep. Since his March 18, 2000, election, Chen has stepped back from "independence." No wonder—Taiwan is too dependent on China to be independent. Despite profound sympathies for a formal "non-Chinese" homeland, President Chen, his financial backers, and most DPP supporters are aware of Taiwan's economic predicament: its export manufacturing sector relies on mainland Chinese labor and factories. And it's not just "sunset industries" that are offshore, but cutting-edge computer industries as well. Into the twenty-first century, Taiwan's drift toward political "independence" will have halted, and increasing economic symbiosis with China will bind the island to the Mainland.

Turning Point

The atmosphere in Taipei's *Academia Sinica* auditorium was electrifying on the afternoon of March 10, 2000. With seven days left before

Taiwan's historic presidential election, reporters, TV cameramen and others jammed into the auditorium to witness the psychological turning point of a "hot" presidential campaign. On the dais, a lanky and owlish scholar stood up and moved next to former Taipei Mayor Chen Shui-bian. The two men had just completed a one-hour private meeting and were ready to face the cameras.

Nervously, *Academia Sinica* President Lee Yuan-tseh, Taiwan's most respected scholar and a Nobel Prize winner, cleared his throat and spoke into the microphones. Calling Chen a "proper national leader," Dr. Lee pledged to help Chen govern Taiwan as the island's first non-Kuomintang (KMT or "Nationalist") leader. "I admire Chen for his determination to carry out . . . reforms and to eradicate the 'black gold' politics of corruption," Lee said. The unprepossessing academic explained that his support for the former Taipei mayor was spurred by "members of organized crime groups stumping for other candidates." Flashbulbs snapped, motor-drive cameras whirred. Dr. Lee's endorsement sealed Chen's victory.

There were concerns regarding Chen's commitment to "Taiwan Independence," the defining plank of the DPP. Opinion polls showed the vast majority of Taiwanese, nervous about China's reaction, favored "maintaining the status quo indefinitely." Mr. Chen was backing away gingerly from full-separation from China. While China and Taiwan are two separate and independent countries, Chen would explain to his constituents and fellow partisans (as well as to uneasy Americans), this requires no change in Taiwan's political status. Taiwan, after all, had been sovereign and independent of Mainland China since 1949, and Chen promised to "maintain the status quo." Dr. Lee Yuan-tseh's words gave voters additional reassurance.

Another message to the electorate was clear. Taiwan's top tycoons were supporting Chen: a vote for him was a vote for prosperity. Because all these business leaders had extensive investments on the other side of the Taiwan Strait, a vote for Chen was a vote for stable China relations.

There was panic 1,000 miles away in Beijing, however. On March 15, with the election only three days away, Chinese Premier Zhu Rongji told foreign reporters: "Let me advise all these people in Taiwan," he warned, "do not just act on impulse at this juncture which will decide the future course that China and Taiwan will follow. Otherwise, I'm afraid you won't get another opportunity to regret." Premier Zhu vowed that Chinese were ready to "shed blood" to prevent Taiwan breaking away.

Chen won with 39.6 percent of the vote in a hard-fought three-way race. And the following week, Chen invited top corporate advisors to help choose a new cabinet.

Beijing Pressures Pro-Chen Businesses

An official Chinese newspaper targeted Chen corporate backers such as Chi-Mei Enterprises' Chairman Hsu Wen-lung. The paper said Hsu's operations in Taiwan ship over a million tons of raw petrochemicals to the People's Republic of China (PRC) each year, accounting for forty percent of China's petrochemical imports. Chi-Mei also has a 300,000 ton/year polystyrene plant in Zhenhai as well as a 125,000 ton/year joint venture acrylonitrile-butadine-styrene (ABS) plant under construction. Next on the list was Chang Jung-fa, chairman of Taiwan's Evergreen Group—operator of one of the world's largest merchant fleets, scores of container ports, international freight forwarding businesses, and EVA Airways. (Evergreen has fourteen offices in China and cooperates with PRC shipping lines running cargo across the Taiwan Strait via third ports.) The newspaper *Financial and Economic Times* recalled that Stan Chen-jung Shih's Acer Computers is China's top computer seller and plans to invest in 200 separate Internet portals in the PRC, investing US$3 billion in the China market during the next five years.

The article noted Beijing would not "sit idly by" and "watch Taiwan businesses make money in China to support Taiwan Independence back home." That week, the planned opening of Evergreen's Shanghai office was delayed, and Chi-Mei's shippers and factories along the China coast were all subject to incessant inspections of Chinese bureaucrats—tax collectors, safety inspectors, and customs agents. After other intrusions, Chi Mei now threatens to freeze future investments.

Yet, most Taiwanese entrepreneurs hope to remain in Beijing's good graces. Acer's Stan Shih was so worried about his appearance in the *Financial and Economic Times* that he flew to Beijing to emphasize he did not support Taiwan independence.

Taiwan Dependence on China

President Chen's fears for Taiwan's "sunset" sectors reflect his concerns that most of the island's light-industrial firms will have to move offshore—to the PRC—in order to remain competitive. This leaves the advanced information sector as the engine of future growth. As indicated in Brian Kuang-Ming Cheng's chapter, Taiwan is becoming a supplier of advanced-technology components to China's labor-intensive assembly lines. Taipei's economic planners are concerned by this out-migration and the "hollowing-out" of manufacturing. They have tried to control the problem, discouraging businesses from moving to the Chinese mainland while encouraging them to consider Southeast Asia (as an alternative to China). A large-scale move to Vietnam (where labor is truly cheap), new investments in China continued to increase at an annual rate of thirteen to thirty percent.

After his inauguration President Chen launched initiatives to encourage cross-Strait trade provided China doesn't levy "one China" preconditions. Taiwan businesses view Chen as sympathetic to cross-Strait trade; Taiwan investment flows into China ballooned in the first six months of Chen's administration. By September 2000 US$1.6 billion in new investments were approved. A cumulative $28 billion has been invested on the Mainland since 1986. The PRC estimates the amount is $50–60 billion.

The situation is disturbing: there are national security implications of close economic dependence on a politically hostile power. There appears to be no other option: China has labor, land, and markets. Taiwan has capital, expertise, and entrepreneurship. Entire production lines have been closed in Taiwan and reopened in the PRC. No wonder Chen held out the olive branch at his inauguration address, reassuring Beijing "the leaders on both sides possess enough wisdom and creativity to jointly deal with the question of a future 'one China.'"

How Dependent Is Taiwan?

Much early Taiwan investment in China—toys, textiles, electrical appliances, and footwear factories in Fujian and Guangdong—were older production lines with obsolescent equipment. No more. Last year an astonishing seventy-three percent of the total (US$26 billion) production value of China's information technology (IT) hardware sector was manufactured by Taiwan-owned production lines. China's $25 billion IT industry is now slightly bigger than Taiwan's own IT industry. Only one-half of all "Made in Taiwan" IT ($48.1 billion) is actually manufactured in Taiwan. Some $19 billion of the total is assembled on the Mainland. As of October 2000 desktop personal computer (PC) manufacturers moved forty-two percent of their production lines to China. Mitac International, Acer Inc., Tatung, and First International Computer Inc. are all in Guangdong and Shenzhen, the Chinese industrial and export heartland.

Engineering and technical staff salaries are one-third to one-fifth Taiwan's levels, and assembly labor is one-tenth the cost. Acer Display Technology, Taiwan's largest domestic notebook display manufacturer is setting up a new liquid crystal module (LCM) assembly line at a complex in Suzhou, Jiangsu (near Shanghai). Costs forced Lite-On Electronics to relocate its entire Taiwan opto-electronic production line to Tianjin (near Beijing) where three production lines will cover 750,000 square feet of floor space, employing 2,000 workers.

Similar trends affect other sectors. Taiwan's top electric wire and cable producers expanded Chinese output to meet ever-rising demand (in the PRC) for cable and wire. The petrochemical sector has also been drawn to Mainland. Formosa Plastics Group (FPG) seeks Taipei's approval for a $100 million PVC refinery in Ningbo and plans additional ones elsewhere in the PRC. The Taiwan media reported FPG plans to invest $13 billion in a vast 4,000–hectare petrochemical complex at the Ningbo site.

These are just a few examples of the major Taiwan investment initiatives in China during the two mid quarters of 2000. They are a snapshot of the migration of Taiwan's mid- and high-tech manufacturing to the mainland. But they also underscore the growing importance of China's market for high-tech products.

Taiwan's largest light industrial sector players, including foodstuffs giant Uni-President, are familiar features on China's landscape.

Patterns of Trade

These investments are the engine behind Taiwan's massive trade across the Strait. And China is the engine of Taiwan's export sector. Taiwan's trade with China is continuing at record levels. Exports to the mainland surged a year-on-year forty-two percent in July to $2.5 billion, while imports were $566 million (up 55.4 percent from the same month in 1999). Taiwan's trade with China grew to $18.5 billion in the first seven months of last year, accounting for eleven percent of the island's external trade.

This trade is mostly components shipped to Chinese factories, assembled into products for export beyond China. The Taiwan Ministry of Economic Affairs notes twenty-six percent of all Taiwan export orders (received by Taiwanese companies) are shipped from Taiwan-run factories in the PRC. Many of these goods are re-assembled, sent back to Taiwan and then exported from Taiwan as finished products. Half are shipped directly from China without showing up on Taiwan's export statistics. The implications are dramatic—over one-fourth of all Taiwan exports, directly or indirectly rely on China.

This explains why Beijing is not excited about foreign direct investment. Some estimates show that only one-third of every dollar of exported goods from a foreign venture stays within China. The rest goes to countries supplying components and entrepreneurship. Taiwan's dramatic reliance on China to fuel its own exports is far more important to the island than to China. This may now be understood in Beijing, where policies sought to insulate Taiwan economically.

Leading Taipei corporate brass certainly wield enough influence over President Chen to restrain overt moves towards independence. It's probably safe to assume he would not seek to precipitate an economic collapse should China force Taiwan companies to shut down Mainland operations.

Beware of Radical Labor

If Taiwan's "new economy" firms see the PRC as boosting growth and competitiveness, "old economy" manufacturers see China as a key to survival. One threat to the political status quo in the Taiwan Strait is that Taiwan's income gap is widening. Chen's DPP has traditionally put its ethnic-Taiwanese platform before its populism, but with independence on the back burner, the party has been focusing on its social and environmental agenda. (Hence the Chen Administration's controversial decision to abandon plans to build a nuclear power plant.) DPP Party literature terms Taiwan's income gap "alarming," noting the richest twenty percent of the population earn 5.5 times as much as the poorest twenty percent.

Ironically, that disparity is probably narrower than its "Communist" neighbor—but with thousands of jobs moving off the island (onto the Mainland) monthly, it's not getting narrower. Unemployment was a high (for Taiwan) 2.7 percent in May 2000, and reached 3.1 percent in October. In November a coalition of Taiwan labor groups flew to Hong Kong to demonstrate outside the (official PRC) Xinhua News Agency building to protest Taiwan jobs' exodus across the Strait. A pro-independence platform resurfacing under a protectionist, pro-labor guise is certainly plausible.

Conclusion

There is a large Taiwanese constituency for labor relief and for efforts to halt outflows of manufacturing jobs. Yet there is little sentiment for a challenge to the status quo that calls Taiwan the "Republic of China." If present trends continue, Taiwan's political leadership will be circumspect in dealing with "independence." Of course, there's no need to. Taiwan's formal position is that it's already independent and sovereign, and that's the status quo that has existed since 1949. The island has neither need nor desire to change the status quo.

China, on the other hand, has declared that "if the Taiwan authorities refuse . . . the peaceful settlement of cross-Straits reunification through negotiations, then the Chinese government will . . . adopt all drastic measures possible, including the use of force, to safeguard China's sovereignty and territorial integrity and . . . reunification." Strong words. They indicate that if any country would risk changing the status quo in the Taiwan Strait, it's the People's Republic of China. But that's another story.

Islam, Politics, and Regime Change in Wahid's Indonesia

Greg Barton

Indonesia is by any measure a large and complex nation, and never more so than at present as it struggles to complete its transition to democracy after four decades of authoritarian rule. The world's fourth most populous nation, the largest Muslim society in the world and now its third-largest democracy, Indonesia's complexity comes from both its geography and history. It is a nation made up of 13,000 islands with more than 300 ethnic and linguistic groups, a new nation finding its way, an amalgam of disparate elements brought together by the expedient logic of colonialism.

Islam will be a key factor in shaping Indonesian political developments. And although Indonesian Islam has long been recognized as being generally liberal and tolerant in nature, the potential for Islam to be a negative element cannot be dismissed. Ongoing communal violence in Eastern Indonesia, the push for separatism in Aceh, and the emergence of nationalist paranoia amongst the Indonesian legislators demands that we examine radical Islamism (that rigid linking of simplistic belief and narrow political agenda) if only to understand why it's not quite the threat that it first appears to be.

Underlying Indonesian complexity is the fact that the country began its transition to democracy long before it had a middle class—and a civil society of sufficient maturity—to support this transition with ease. As a result, sectarianism, nationalist paranoia, and natural anxiety (as severe economic depression in 1997–2000 followed decades of sustained growth) emerged. A frightened elite threatens to derail the fledgling democracy.

Abdurrahman Wahid is a reform-minded Muslim intellectual. As Indonesia's first democratically elected president, he had a clear vision of where he wanted to take Indonesia. Unfortunately, he had insufficient political capital to take charge of a newly belligerent legislature keen to contest the authority of the executive. He underestimated the extent to which the powerful clique of legislators associated with the Soeharto regime, most of whom remain enormously wealthy and powerful, were determined to subvert the workings of parliament for their own ends. In July 2001 he paid the price for this and suffered the indignity of being sacked by a parliament controlled by seasoned operators desperate to reign in reform before they became its victims.

Islamic Drama

Wahid wrestled with an opposition that drew heavily on Islamist imagery and rhetoric to undermine his authority. In Indonesia, an important divide exists between the so-called *santri,* or committed, Muslims—orthodox in their religious practice—and non-*santri* Muslims, often described as nominal Muslims. This distinction has blurred: Only a decade ago strong commitment to Islam was seen as provincialism, especially among urban middle-class professionals—but this is no longer true.

While probably around eighty-five percent of Indonesia's 220 million citizens are Muslims, no more than one in three are *santri.* Until the recent revival of interest in Islam, that ratio was even slimmer. Non-*santri* Muslims are syncretic and fluid, and they often embrace pre-Islamic beliefs and practices.

Modernist and Traditionalist Movements

Modernism arrived in Indonesia at the turn of the century and proved popular among urban traders and professionals. It was anchored by a rational application of Islamic teachings to modern life, and it challenged pre-Islamic superstitions. Modernism found fertile ground in Indonesia's burgeoning cities. In 1912 the socio-educational organization Muhammadiyah was established to promote modernist ideas and to do "good works": building schools, orphanages, health clinics, and constructing hospitals. By the end of the century it boasted twenty-eight million members and was probably the world's most successful modernist mass organization.

In post-Soeharto Indonesia, modernists cover a broad spectrum of convictions. The National Mandate Party (PAN), a "progressive" party, sought to harness modernist support. But with just seven percent of the national vote attained in the June 1999 democratic elections, it was clear that PAN failed. Many modernists voted, as they had for years, with the United Development Party (PPP), one of the two opposition parties allowed during the Soeharto era. Others voted for the long-entrenched Golkar, the political vehicle of the Soeharto regime. More liberal modernists no doubt voted for the Democratic Party of Indonesia of Struggle (PDI-P) led by Megawati Soekarnoputri.

Islamist parties generally appealed to the right wing of the modernist community. More conversative Islamists—such as the Defenders of Islam Front and Laskar Jihad (who have become infamous because of alleged vigilante activities in Maluku) were represented through parties such as the Crescent Moon and Star Party (PBB) and the Justice Party (JP). PBB and the Communist Party of Indonesia (PKI) gained only two and one percent of the vote, respectively, and the others but a fraction of that. Nevertheless, the Islamist parties wisely elected to pool their votes and gained a not insignificant bloc of seats in parliament. They were then able to further magnify their influence by joining forces with PPP and with PAN.

Traditionalism, as the name suggests, represents a continuation of Indonesia's centuries-old expression of acculturated, rural-based, and mysticism-bound beliefs. They are represented by Nahdlatul Ulama (NU), considered tolerant and with a claimed membership of thirty to forty million. For fifteen years the NU was led by Abdurrahman Wahid. Its support base is the rural poor and Javanese, both within Java and in regions where they moved as a result of government transmigration programs.

Under Wahid's leadership (1984–99) NU experienced a profound cultural transformation. Although no great manager, Wahid was successful in encouraging younger members of NU to investigate new religious thought and its application to society. Emphasis was given to programs in community development, along with addressing women's rights, social justice, and "church-state relations." Wahid defended minority communities such as the Christians and the Chinese.

By harnessing support from Islamic parties, Wahid emerged as

Indonesia's first democratically elected president in the October 1999 National Consultative Assembly (MPR) meeting. Key backers of Wahid were associated with the Indonesian Association of Muslim Intellectuals (ICMI). Established in December 1990, ICMI was carefully cultivated by Soeharto, via his trusted research and technology minister B.J. Habibie, as part of his strategy of winning over modernist *santri* support.

Political Shadow Plays

Wahid outmaneuvered both interim President B.J. Habibie and Megawati Soekarnoputri, the popular daughter of the first president: conservative Muslims and Islamists feared Megawati. At the same time Megawati seemed blithely indifferent to the need to forge a credible coalition, evidently believing that the one-third share of the national vote gained by her secular nationalist party was sufficient to assure her presidency. Meanwhile, Habibie's promotion of the referendum in East Timor— and his involvement in a US$80 million campaign finance scandal—led to his censorship by the MPR and exit from the presidential contest.

Wahid began his presidency laboring under the unwieldy "national unity" his cabinet foisted upon him; yet he intended to promote liberal ideals. It was not very long before this saw him at odds with conservative Muslims, and one of their leaders, Amien Rais, again became his most vocal critic. Initially the president deftly outflanked moves to impeach him—or limit his authority—and Wahid gambled all on consolidating his power in the cabinet.

It would be wrong to assume that Islamism and conservative Islam were Wahid's greatest problems. Few Indonesians are committed to supporting an Islamist political platform. Nevertheless, repeated demonstrations and protests by conservative Muslims and Islamists and—more worryingly—violence, continue in Aceh, Maluku, and central Sulawesi, where what began as conflict between locals and immigrants is now sectarian violence. Vigilante groups such as Laskar Jihad have heightened inter-communal tensions. Meanwhile, in Jakarta and Surabaya and in the other big cities, groups such as the Islamic Defenders Front have been vocal in their anti-government attacks.

This turmoil is no barometer of rising Islamist influence. The struggle in Aceh, for example, has to do with years of neglect and abuse at the hands of the authoritarian military-backed Soeharto regime. The Acehenese seek justice and equitable treatment. The fact that Islam is an important part of their ethnic identity is incidental to the primary issues. Similarly, there is no evidence to suggest that the violence in Ambon and North Maluku started because of religious issues. Groups such as the Defenders of Islam Front have relatively few members.

Many such Islamist groups are creatures of their patrons in the old political elite. The greater Jakarta metropolitan region, for example, is home to twenty million people, the majority of whom are unemployed or under-employed. It is significant that radical groups have not enjoyed greater support. Under current circumstances demonstrations of several thousand young men in central Jakarta are not remarkable, especially when many are being paid to demonstrate.

The government of President Abdurrahman Wahid was a transitional government in the early stages of regime change. It met serious but often subtle and insidious resistance from both civilian and military elements opposed to reform. Prominent individuals from Golkar and the military were active in opposing Wahid's government. It is clear that figures such as these had a vested interest in either intimidating the government into backing down from the prosecution of cases against corruption and past abuses. Such so-called status-quo forces do not hesitate to use their considerable financial resources to influence the media and fund radical Islamist groups. Ironically, the very same religious and political conservatives who blocked Soekarnoputri's ascension to the presidency in 1999 used her to topple Wahid in 2001. They hope that they will find her to be much more compliant and much less reformist than the subborn and indefatigable Wahid proved to be.

The Outlook

Given the difficult nature of any regime change, what grounds are there for hoping Indonesia can successfully negotiate this difficult terrain— and ensure that a democratic, tolerant society is established? One of the main grounds for hope is the underlying cultural orientation of many Indonesians to support cooperation between liberal modernists, traditionalists, non-*santri* Muslims and non-Muslims. In practice, this means cooperation between PKB and PDI-P together with liberal modernists within PAN (although not with those close to Amien Rais in PAN's right wing).

The tragedy of Wahid's sacking was not just that this bumbling but well-intentioned reformer did not get a chance to complete what he had started, it was also that the reform movement was split in two. Wahid's opponents utilized the schism that had developed between the president and his vice-president to stop PKB and PDI-P from consolidating their loose alliance. Despite the bitterness that has been produced by this rift, many within both parties hope that the partnership between tolerant traditionalists and secular nationalists can eventually be restored. Certainly, once her honeymoon in office is over, and she finds herself hemmed in by military hard-liners and Golkar conservatives on one side and Islamists on the other, Megawati Soekarnoputri will find herself in need of true friends—especially in the runup to the 2004 elections.

Bibliography

Barton, Greg. "The Impact of Islamic Neo-Modernism on Indonesian Islamic Thought: The Emergence of a New Pluralism." In *Indonesian Democracy: 1950s and 1990s,* ed. David Bourchier and John Legge. Clayton: Monash University, 1994. See especially pp. 143–150.

——. "The Origins of Islamic Liberalism in Indonesia and Its Contribution to Democratisation." *Democracy in Asia.* New York: St Martins Press, 1997.

——. "Indonesia's Nurcholish Madjid and Abdurrahman Wahid As Intellectual *Ulama*: The Meeting of Islamic Traditionalism and Modernism in Neo-Modernist Thought." *Islam and Christian-Muslim Relations* 8, no. 3 (October 1997): 323–50.

——. "The Liberal, Progressive Roots of Abdurrahmen Wahid's Thought." In Nahdlatul Ulama, *Traditional Islam and Modernity in Indonesia,* ed. Greg Barton and Greg Fealy. Clayton: Monash Asia Institute, 1996, pp. 190–226.

Bhaskara, Harry (ed.). *Questioning Gus Dur.* The Jakarta Post, 2000.

Hefner, Robert W., and Patricia Horvatich (eds). *Islam in an Era of Nation States: Politics and Religious Revival in Muslim Southeast Asia.* Honolulu: University of Hawaii Press, 1997.

Nakamura, Mitsuo. *The Crescent Arises over the Banyan Tree: A Study of the Muhammadiyah Movement in a Central Javanese Town.* Yogyakarta: Gadjah Mada University Press, 1983.

Rahman, Fazlur. *Islam and Modernity: Transformation of an Intellectual Tradition.* Chicago: University of Chicago Press, 1982.

Ramage, Douglas E. *Politics in Indonesia: Democracy, Islam and the Ideology of Tolerance.* London: Routledge, 1995.

Schwarz, Adam. *A Nation in Waiting: Indonesia's Search for Stability.* Sydney: Allen & Unwin, 1999.

Woodward, Mark R. (ed). *Toward a New Paradigm.* Tucson: University of Arizona Press, 1996.

Contributors

Fred S. Armentrout has lived in Hong Kong for twenty-four years, and has, for fifteen of them, been the publisher and chief editor of a monthly business magazine (and books) for the American Chamber of Commerce in Hong Kong. Prior to moving to Hong Kong he was Executive Editor of *Petroleum News Southeast Asia.* Mr. Armentrout was a research director on environmental issues for the Council on Economic Priorities (CEP) in New York City and co-author, with James Cannon, of a 1977 study, *Environmental Steel: Pollution in the Iron and Steel Industry.*

Dennis T. Avery is Director of the Center for Global Food Issues of the Hudson Institute, a not-for-profit public policy "think-tank" headquartered in Indianapolis, Indiana. He served as the senior agricultural analyst of the United States Department of State, where he won the National Intelligence Medal of Achievement in 1983. He is the author of *Saving the Planet with Pesticides and Plastics,* the second edition of which has just been published by the Hudson Institute.

Junji Ban is General Manager, Asian Planning Office, Asian Headquarters of the Global Corporate Banking Business Unit at the Bank of Tokyo-Mitsubishi. He joined the Bank of Tokyo, Ltd. in 1975, and five years later he was in the bank's Australian Industry Development Corporation. He held other positions before serving as Group Leader in the

Jakarta office. In 1994 he became Senior Vice President & Group Manager at the Bank of Tokyo Trust Company and two years later was appointed Senior Vice President & Group Manager of the Bank of Tokyo-Mitsubishi Trust Company. From 1997 to 2000 he was Chief Representative of the Bank of Tokyo-Mitsubishi in Washington, D.C.

Greg Barton is a senior lecturer in the School of Social Inquiry at Melbourne's Deakin University and an internationally respected scholar and author. He was an adviser to former Indonesian President Wahid and has established a reputation as an authority on Islam as applied to the world's largest Islamic country, Indonesia. He has contributed to numerous books and publications on this and related topics.

Peter Brookes is Principal Advisor for Asian Affairs at the House International Relations Committee, reporting directly to the committee chairman, Congressman Ben Gilman (Republican from New York State). He lectures widely on defense and security issues and has traveled extensively throughout East and Southeast Asia. A graduate of the U.S. Naval Academy at Annapolis, Mr. Brookes served the U.S. Department of State and other government organizations on assignments overseas.

Deborah A. Cai is an associate professor in the Department of Communication at the University of Maryland. She specializes in intercultural communication, persuasion, and conflict management. She has examined the effects of culture on cognitive processes related to decision making and perceptions of conflict. Her research has been presented at national and international conferences and has been featured in journals such as *Communication Yearbook, Human Communication Research,* and in the *Asian Journal of Communication.*

Dean Cheng is a specialist in Chinese national security strategies at the Center on Naval Analysis in Washington, D.C. He completed one of the first translations of the Chinese book *Unrestricted Warfare.* His articles have appeared in books and journals. He has lectured before the CIA, at the National Defense University, and at other organizations focusing on security as well as on defense industrial planning. Prior to joining Science Applications International Corporation (SAIC), Mr. Cheng was Morris K. Udall Fellow at the U.S. Congress Office of Technology

Assessment, where he authored studies on civil-military integration in the United States, the PRC, and Japan. All views expressed in this chapter are those of the author and are not associated with SAIC or its affiliates.

Takashi Chiba served as Director for Hitachi and President of the Japan Commerce Association in Washington, D.C. He is now President of Chiba International, LLC, a Northern Virginia–based consulting firm advising American companies on ways of doing business in, and with, Japan. He held numerous executive positions for Hitachi. Mr. Chiba has been active in civic affairs and serves on the boards of various foundations and other institutions.

Brian Kuang-ming Cheng is a widely respected journalist. He received his M.A. Degrees in Philosophy from the University of Chicago in 1998 and National Taiwan University in 1994. He is a staff writer at the *Taipei Journal* and a lecturer at National Open University in Taiwan.

David Dodwell is an executive director of Golin/Harris Forrest and was a director of the Jardine Fleming Group, responsible for corporate communications and public affairs. His private consulting clients included the Hong Kong Trade Development Council. He spent eighteen years with the *Financial Times*. A graduate (with honors) of the University of East Anglia, Mr. Dodwell co-authored (with Professor Michael Enright) *The Hong Kong Advantage,* published by the Oxford University Press. He serves on several government advisory committees and lectures outside the region.

Seth Dunn is a Research Associate at the Worldwatch Institute. He focuses on energy and climate change issues. He writes regularly for the Institute's acclaimed *State of the World* and contributes to publications such as *The Journal of International Affairs*, and *U.S.-China Business Review.* Mr. Dunn's studies have been cited in *The Economist, International Herald Tribune*, and in *Xinhua News Agency* reports.

Mr. Dunn participated in rounds of UN climate change negotiations and in expert meetings of the Intergovernmental Panel on Climate Change. Prior to joining Worldwatch, he was a consultant with the Natural Resources Defense Council and a research assistant at the Yale (University)

Center for Environmental Law and Policy. He holds a B.A. with majors in History and Environmental Studies from Yale University.

Elizabeth Economy is Senior Fellow for China and Deputy Director of Asia Studies at the Council on Foreign Relations, and directs projects on China, the environment, and U.S.-China relations. Her most recent publications include a volume edited with Michel Oksenberg, *China Joins the World: Progress and Prospects* (1999). She is active in academic programs sponsored by leading institutions on both sides of the Pacific. Dr. Economy was a research fellow at Princeton University's Center for Energy and Environmental Studies and earned a Ph.D. in Political Science from the University of Michigan.

Mark T. Fung is Assistant Director and Research Fellow of China Studies at the Nixon Center. As a doctoral candidate at the Johns Hopkins University School of Advanced International Studies (SAIS), he received the Loe Fellowship for Excellence in China Studies. Mr. Fung graduated from the politics honors program at New York University with a second major in East Asian studies and a minor in philosophy. He was elected a member of the *Journal of Law and Policy* at the Brooklyn Law School, where he received a J.D. The author is indebted to Prof. Fouad Ajami for enlarging the dimensions of philosophical consciousness with the predicaments of modern political thought and practice.

Gerard Henderson is Executive Director of the Sydney Institute. He is a regular contributor to publications such as *The Sydney Morning Herald* and *The Age* (Melbourne) and is heard weekly on the Australian Broadcasting Corporation. He was Senior Adviser to John Howard for the period 1984–86, during which time Howard served as leader of the Liberal Party. Henderson is the author of several books, including *A Howard Government? Inside the Coalition* (1995). The Sydney Institute is a high-profile, privately funded policy forum that enjoys good relations with both sides of mainstream Australian politics.

Richard Katz is Senior Editor of *The Oriental Economist Report*, a monthly newsletter on Japan. He is the author of *Japan: The System That Soured—The Rise and Fall of the Japanese Economic Miracle* (1998). He is a visiting lecturer at the State University of New York

(SUNY) at Stony Brook, and was a member of the Task Force on the Japanese Economy established by the New York Council on Foreign Relations in the year 2000.

Peter H. Koehn is Professor of Political Science at the University of Montana—Missoula, where he served as the founding Director of International Programs from 1987 to 1996. He taught as an exchange professor at Shanghai International Studies University (1996–1997) and held a Fulbright Senior Scholar position at the Chinese University of Hong Kong (1997–1998). Dr. Koehn is the author of *Refugees from Revolution: U.S. Policy and Third-World Migration* (1991) and co-editor, with Joseph Y.S. Cheng, of *The Outlook for U.S.-China Relations Following the 1997–1998 Summits: Chinese and American Perspectives on Security, Trade, and Cultural Exchange* (1999).

Kog Yue Choong is President of East-West Engineering Consultants and the immediate past president of the Association of Consulting Engineers in Singapore. He holds a Ph.D. in Civil Engineering and was an adjunct professor at the Civil Engineering Department, National University of Singapore, from 1992 to 2000.

Alexei T. Kral was Program Associate for Japan at the Woodrow Wilson Center's Asia Program. He earned his M.A. in Social Science at the University of Chicago and his B.S.F.S. (Bachelor of Science in Foreign Service) in Asian Studies at Georgetown University. At Georgetown, he was elected to Phi Beta Kappa and Phi Alpha Theta (International Honors Society in History). He grew up in Romania, Afghanistan, the Philippines, and Thailand, and lived in Japan for four years. He studied at Tokyo's Sophia University, lived for one year in a mountain village of Gifu prefecture while teaching, and spent two years in a suburb of Nagoya working for a city hall and writing material for a cable television series on cultural differences. In June 1994, he served as a White House interpreter for Japanese guests at the Emperor's State Visit.

At the Woodrow Wilson Center, Washington, D.C., Kral focuses on contemporary Japanese society and American-Asian relations. Alexei Kral lives in Maryland with his wife, Kaori. His *haiku* poems have been published in the *Chunichi Shimbun*.

Michael Kurtz is an analyst at Bears Sterns (Hong Kong). He holds an MBA, with honors, in International Business/Finance and an M.A. in International Relations from George Washington University. Mr. Kurtz has also studied at universities in both Taiwan and the People's Republic of China and speaks Mandarin.

Tion Kwa is editorial page editor of the Hong Kong-based *Far Eastern Economic Review*. He is a former Kuala Lumpur bureau chief for *Bridge News*, and was previously editor of the law journal of the New York City bar association. The views expressed in his chapter are his own.

C. H. Kwan is a senior economist at the Tokyo-based Nomura Research Institute. He studied at the Chinese University of Hong Kong and received a Ph.D. in Economics from Tokyo University. Dr. Kwan is the author of *Economic Interdependence in the Asia-Pacific Region* (1994) and *Yen Bloc: Toward Economic Integration in Asia* (2001). Dr. Kwan has served on various Japanese government committees, including the Economic Council (advising the prime minister) and the Council on Foreign Exchange and Other Transactions (advising the minister of finance).

Larry H.P. Lang is Chair Professor of Finance at the Chinese University of Hong Kong (CUHK). He earned his Ph.D. in Finance at the Wharton School, University of Pennsylvania, and has taught at leading institutions. He is an expert in corporate governance. Mr. Lang's works in project financing, direct investments, corporate restructuring, mergers & acquisitions, and bankruptcy have been cited in *The Economist* and *Business Week*. He has served as a consultant for The World Bank and the Asian Development Bank Institute.

Franklin L. Lavin is U.S. Ambassator to Singapore. He served on the Reagan White House senior staff and the National Security Council Staff. In the administration of President George Bush (1989–93), he was responsible for Asia-Pacific activity at the U.S. Department of Commerce. After spending several years with major U.S.-based banks in Hong Kong and Singapore, he currently runs an Internet incubator in Hong Kong. Mr. Lavin holds degrees from the School of Foreign Service at Georgetown University, the School of Advanced International Studies at the Johns Hopkins University, and the Wharton School at the University of Pennsylvania.

Ooi Giok Ling earned her Ph.D. from the Australian National University in Canberra. She is Senior Research Fellow at the Institute of Policy Studies and, concurrently, an associate professor (adjunct) at the National University of Singapore. She was Director of Research in the Ministry of Home Affairs. Giok Ling holds leadership positions in organizations including a Malay self-help organization, an environmental NGO, and a youth group. She has been consultant to international agencies such as UNESCAP and UNCTAD.

Robert A. Manning is Senior fellow and Director of Asian Studies at the Council on Foreign Relations. He is author of *The Asian Energy Factor: Myths and Dilemmas on Energy, Security and the Pacific Future* (2000). He was a senior fellow at the Progressive Policy Institute. He has also written numerous monographs on Korea, Japan and Asian security.

From 1989 to 1993 Manning was Advisor for Policy to the Assistant Secretary for East Asian and Pacific Affairs at the U.S. State Department. He has been widely published in leading magazines and newspapers on both sides of the Pacific. Other recent books include *Asian Policy: The New Soviet Challenge in the Pacific* (1988). He was diplomatic correspondent for *U.S. News and World Report* and was a correspondent for the *Far Eastern Economic Review* from 1979 to 1985.

Richard Martin is Senior Editor for Technology at San Francisco-based *The Industry Standard*—considered one of the premier publications covering e-commerce. Previously he was the technology producer at ABCNEWS.com. His work has appeared in *The Asian Wall Street Journal*, the *Far Eastern Economic Review*, on MSNBC, and other outlets. In 1993-94, Martin was a visiting scholar at the University of Hong Kong. He is the recipient of the White Award for Investigative Reporting, a Rotary Journalism Fellowship, and an "Excellence in Journalism" award from the Society of Professional Journalists.

Edward Neilan's career in Asia and in the media spanned nearly five decades. As a correspondent in the 1950s for *The Christian Science Monitor*—based in Hong Kong and Tokyo—he witnessed the region's rise. He was a Tokyo-based syndicated columnist, Senior Fellow at The Heritage Foundation, and Media Fellow at the Hoover Institution (at Stanford University). In 1996 he was Visiting Professor of Journalism at Taiwan's National Chengchi University, and was a visiting scholar at Shanghai's Fudan University.

Roland Rich is Director of the Centre for Democratic Institutions at the Australian National University (ANU). He holds Arts and Law degrees from the University of Sydney and the degree of Master of International Law from the ANU. He served for more than twenty years as an Australian Foreign Service officer and held the position of Legal Adviser to the Australian Department of Foreign Affairs and Trade. He served in various places, including Paris, Rangoon, Manila and most recently as Australia's Ambassador to Laos.

Ricardo Saludo is Assistant Managing Editor for *Asiaweek*. He was Managing Editor of *The Makati Business Club Economic Papers* and joined Hong Kong-based *Asiaweek* in 1984. He has covered business, regional politics, and social affairs while launching special reports and other innovative editorial coverage for *Asiaweek*.

Adam Schwarz is Public Sector Specialist at McKinsey & Co. in Jakarta, Indonesia. From 1997 to 2000 he was President of Nusantara Consultants, a leading political and economic risk consulting firm. He is a widely respected analyst on Southeast Asian security and economic issues. Mr. Schwarz has authored and edited several books on contemporary Indonesian politics and economics, including the highly acclaimed *A Nation in Waiting: Indonesia's Search for Stability* (1994, 1999) and *The Politics of Post-Suharto Indonesia* (1999). He has written for scholarly journals such as *Foreign Affairs* as well as for in-house publications of the Council on Foreign Relations and the World Economic Forum. He is also a regular contributor to *the International Herald Tribune,* the *Wall Street Journal* and the *Washington Post* and testified before U.S. Senate and House (of Representatives) committees on Southeast Asia.

H.E. Rodolofo C. Severino, Jr., held numerous positions in the Philippine government and was Special Assistant to the Undersecretary of Foreign Affairs (in Manila) from 1967 to 1974. He was Ambassador to Malaysia and from 1992 to 1997 served as Undersecretary of Foreign Affairs. He graduated from Ateneo de Manila University in his native Philippines and in 1970 received his M.A. in International Relations from the Johns Hopkins University School of Advanced International Studies (SAIS) in Washington, D.C. He became ASEAN Secretary-General three years ago.

A. Gary Shilling is President of A. Gary Shilling & Co., Inc. In addition to his forecasting record, his portfolio management, and his column for *Forbes*, which he has written since 1983, he is also known for his well-received books—*Is Inflation Ending? Are You Ready?* (1983); *The World Has Definitely Changed: New Economic Forces and Their Implications for the Next Decade* (1986); *After the Crash: Recession or Depression? Investment and Business Strategies for a Deflationary World* (1988)—concerning economic themes and investment strategies, and for his numerous articles on the business outlook and techniques of economic analysis and forecasting. He is a member of *The Nihon Keizai Shimbun* (Japan Economic Journal) Board of Economists and appears frequently on radio and television business shows.

Daljit Singh was educated at Balliol College, Oxford University, studying politics, philosophy and economics. He spent many years in public service in Singapore before joining the Institute of Southeast Asian Studies (ISEAS) in Singapore in 1991.

His research interest at the Institute focuses on regional security and on ASEAN-related issues. His most recent articles include "Southeast Asia in 1999: A False Dawn?" in *Southeast Asian Affairs 2000* (2000) and "The Evolution of Asia-Pacific Security Dialogue," in *Southeast Asian Perspectives on Security*, edited by Derek Da Cunha (2000).

Paul J. Smith is a research fellow with the U.S. Department of Defense, Asia-Pacific Center for Security Studies, Honolulu, Hawaii. His research focuses on transnational security issues, with particular reference to international migration and refugee issues. He is editor of *Human Smuggling: Chinese Migrant Trafficking and the Challenge to America's Immigration Tradition* (1997). He also contributed a chapter on international migration for the book *Fires Across the Water* (1998) and has published numerous articles on international migration topics. Mr. Smith earned his B.A. from Washington and Lee University, his M.A. from the University of London, and his J.D. from the University of Hawaii.

Dr. Tan Chi Chiu, a practicing gastroenterologist and physician, became Executive Director of the Singapore International Foundation (SIF) in October 1999 and is in charge of SIF's voluntary Third World development and international networking programs. He has participated in overseas humanitarian relief and earned several international awards.

Dr. Tan sits on numerous national councils and committees dealing with the practice of medicine, youth development, family values and the growth of civil society. He is widely published and speaks regularly at major conferences and seminars.

Simon S.C. Tay, LL.B. Hons. (National University of Singapore, or NUS), LL.M. (Harvard), teaches international and constitutional law at the Faculty of Law at NUS. He is a publicly nominated member of the Singapore Parliament and is Chairman of the Singapore Institute of International Affairs. His research focuses on the environment, human rights and civil society in Asia. A Fulbright scholar, Mr. Tay is a winner of the Laylin Prize at Harvard Law School. He is also a prize-winning fiction writer. In January 2000, the World Economic Forum at Davos listed him as a "Global Leader of Tomorrow."

John Tkacik is President of China Business Intelligence, an Alexandria, Virginia, firm providing information to American companies doing business with China and Taiwan. He was a career foreign service officer with more than twenty years' experience related to Taiwan and China. Mr. Tkacik was Chief of China Analysis at the U.S. State Department's Bureau of Intelligence and Research and received the Department's Superior Honor Award. He was Asia-Pacific Vice President for External Affairs at R.J. Reynolds Tobacco International. His op-ed articles have appeared in the *Washington Post* and in other well-known outlets. Mr. Tkacik graduated from Georgetown University in 1971 and holds an advanced degree from Harvard University.

Julian Weiss is a Senior Fellow and a specialist in futures studies research at the Institute of Chinese Global Affairs (at the University of Maryland). A regular traveler to East and Southeast Asia for two decades, he contributed to leading publications such as *The Economist*, *Asian Wall Street Journal*, the *Asian Reader's Digest*, and the *Christian Science Monitor*. He was *Asiaweek* Washington correspondent from 1981 to 1991. He gained a reputation for "calling the shots" on Japan's protracted economic decline and on other events. Weiss specializes in economic development and high-tech. He authored four books including *The Asian Century* (2000), and was Senior Fellow at the Georgetown University Center on International Business. Mr. Weiss is enrolled at the Johns Hopkins University School for Advanced International Studies.

Joseph A.B. Winder is President of the Korea Economic Institute of America (KEI). Prior to joining KEI as vice president in February 1996, Mr. Winder had a thirty-year career in the United States Foreign Service. He retired with the rank of Minister-Counselor in September 1995. During his career he had assignments as economic officer in American embassies in Bonn, Santiago and Tokyo. He was Deputy Chief of Mission at the American Embassy in Bangkok.

Mr. Winder was the recipient of the State Department's Superior Honor Award in 1989, 1993, and 1995. He won the Treasury Secretary's Award in 1980. He earned a B.A. in Political Science from the University of Michigan in 1964 and an MBA from the same school one year later. He served as director of the Office of Economic Analysis at the U.S. Department of State from 1993 to 1995. From 1985 to 1986 he was Deputy Director of the State Department's Policy Planning Staff.

Chris Yeung is an associate editor and political editor of the *South China Morning Post* in Hong Kong. Yeung joined the *Post* in 1984. He writes on a wide range of political and social issues. Yeung recently completed research at the Center for Northeast Asian Policy Studies at the Brookings Institution (in Washington, D.C.), where he was a visiting fellow.

Leslie Young is Chair Professor of Finance, and Executive Director of the Asia-Pacific Institute of Business at Chinese University of Hong Kong. He holds a D. Phil. in Mathematics from Oxford University. He taught economics at Oxford, M.I.T. and at other campuses. Professor Young has published widely and serves on the editorial board of the *American Economic Review.*

Ming Zhang is affiliated with the Asia Research Institute/IHS International, based in Oakton, Virginia. Previously, he was a research analyst at the Library of Congress and was Visiting Fellow at the Institute for National Strategic Studies of the National Defense University. He has been a consultant with the Carnegie Endowment for International Peace in Washington, D.C. Dr. Zhang studied at the Johns Hopkins University Center in Nanjing, China, and received his Ph.D. in Political Science from Purdue University in 1994.

Zhang's expertise includes Asian government systems, politics, economics, technology, and military security; infrastructure assessment; international trade; and data analysis. Dr. Zhang is the author of *Major Powers at a Crossroads: Economic Interdependence and an Asia Pacific Security Community* (1995) and *China's Changing Nuclear Posture: Reactions to the South Asian Nuclear Tests* (1999), and is co-author of *A Triad of Another Kind: The United States, China, and Japan* (1999). His articles have appeared in leading American and Asia-Pacific quarterlies.

D. R. Zhou is co-founder of the Center For American Studies at Fudan University, Shanghai. He has achieved international recognition for research on China's economic reform and the U.S. Congress. He is widely published and a frequent traveler to conferences in the United States, the EU, and Asia.

Index